D1017458

Beyond Reason and Tolerance

BEYOND REASON AND TOLERANCE

The Purpose and Practice of Higher Education

Robert J. Thompson, Jr.

OXFORD
UNIVERSITY PRESS

OXFORD
UNIVERSITY PRESS

Oxford University Press is a department of the University of
Oxford. It furthers the University's objective of excellence in research,
scholarship, and education by publishing worldwide.

Oxford   New York
Auckland   Cape Town   Dar es Salaam   Hong Kong   Karachi
Kuala Lumpur   Madrid   Melbourne   Mexico City   Nairobi
New Delhi   Shanghai   Taipei   Toronto

With offices in
Argentina   Austria   Brazil   Chile   Czech Republic   France   Greece
Guatemala   Hungary   Italy   Japan   Poland   Portugal   Singapore
South Korea   Switzerland   Thailand   Turkey   Ukraine   Vietnam

Oxford is a registered trademark of Oxford University Press
in the UK and certain other countries.

Published in the United States of America by
Oxford University Press
198 Madison Avenue, New York, NY 10016

© Oxford University Press 2014

All rights reserved. No part of this publication may be reproduced, stored in
a retrieval system, or transmitted, in any form or by any means, without the prior
permission in writing of Oxford University Press, or as expressly permitted by law,
by license, or under terms agreed with the appropriate reproduction rights organization.
Inquiries concerning reproduction outside the scope of the above should be sent to the
Rights Department, Oxford University Press, at the address above.

You must not circulate this work in any other form
and you must impose this same condition on any acquirer.

Library of Congress Cataloging-in-Publication Data
Thompson, Robert J. (Robert Joseph), 1945–
Beyond reason and tolerance: the purpose and practice of higher education /
Robert J. Thompson.
    pages cm
Summary: "Beyond Reason and Tolerance argues that to prepare students to engage political, ethnic,
and religious differences, higher education must adopt a developmental model for a formative and
liberal undergraduate education as a process of growth involving empathy as well as reasoning, values
as well as knowledge, and identity as well as competencies"—Provided by publisher.
ISBN 978–0–19–996978–4 (hardback)
1. Education, Higher—Philosophy.   2. Education, Humanistic—United States.
3. Education, Higher—Aims and objectives—United States. 4. Education,
Higher—Social aspects—United States. 5. Educational psychology—United States. I. Title.
LB2322.2.T46 2014
378—dc23
2013028664

9 8 7 6 5 4 3 2 1
Printed in the United States of America
on acid-free paper

To Ralph Kolstoe for teaching me how to think as a psychologist and fostering the integration of empiricism and humanism; to George McAdoo for being a model of the scientist-practitioner; and to William Chafe for providing the opportunity to formulate and implement a developmental model of undergraduate education.

CONTENTS

PREFACE

Throughout my professional life I have been fortunate to have the privilege of serving as a psychologist and educator in university settings. In the process, I have come to view higher education as both a transformative experience and a moral enterprise. Higher education is not just a gateway to success. It is also a pathway to improving society. I am particularly passionate about the power of a liberal education to transform lives and make a difference in society. I find inspiration in William Cronon's (1998) eloquently expressed purpose of a liberal education: "To nurture the growth of human talent in the service of human freedom" (p. 74) and nurture "human freedom in the service of human community" (p. 80).

As dean of Trinity College of Arts and Sciences and vice provost for undergraduate education at Duke University, I was engaged for more than a decade with the challenge of enhancing undergraduate education in a research university. This process involved generating curricular and cocurricular experiences, developing academic support and advising services, and building a diverse and inclusive academic community that affirms and empowers difference. These experiences lead me to understand and appreciate more deeply the social contract that is fundamental to the role of higher education in the United States. Simply stated, colleges and universities are afforded a high degree of autonomy in both the belief and expectation that they will operate in the service of society. This contract requires that higher education be responsive to societal needs through doing what colleges and universities are uniquely structured to do: generate knowledge and provide an educational experience that prepares students to meet societal needs and realize a meaningful and rewarding life.

The beginning of the twenty-first century is a time of major transformations in our society, and higher education now has the challenge of preparing students for lifelong learning, leadership, and service in our knowledge-based economy and pluralistic, globally, interconnected world. The major challenge is to improve the quality of undergraduate education so that students are prepared to meet society's twenty-first-century needs for civic-minded individuals who have the intellectual and personal capabilities to work effectively and live together with many different kinds of people in a more global society.

More specifically, the forces of globalization not only increase engagement of countries and markets but also result in greater interdependency and heighten the potential for conflict among diverse groups and cultures, along multiple dimensions of difference, around numerous issues. In particular, society has a pressing need for higher education to prepare individuals who have the intellectual and personal capabilities to go beyond tolerance and constructively engage political, ethnic, and religious differences.

To be responsive to this societal need and prepare students to constructively engage difference, higher education must adapt by transforming both its educational goals and practices. Furthermore, this transformation must be guided by advances in our understanding of human development and learning. Developing the skills of reasoning, critical thinking, problem solving, and effective oral and written communication have been long-standing goals of higher education. These goals are no less important in the twenty-first century. In fact, students will need to develop the higher-order intellectual skills necessary to discern among competing claims, construct meaning from complex information, and generate and apply knowledge to address complex problems. While necessary, however, these traditional goals are not sufficient. From my perspective as a psychologist, the ability to constructively engage difference also requires the development of an interrelated set of intellectual and personal capabilities: a personal epistemology that reflects a sophisticated understanding of knowledge, beliefs, and ways of thinking; empathy and the capacity to understand the mental states of others; and an integrated identity that includes values, commitments, and a sense of agency for civic and social responsibility. To foster the development of these capabilities, colleges and universities must recommit to the goal of providing a formative education that is both liberal and practical and adopt a developmental model of undergraduate education as a process of intellectual and personal growth, involving empathy as well as reasoning, values as well as knowledge, and identity as well as competencies.

The transformation of higher education must also be guided by advances in understanding of human development and learning, which have direct implications for both the purposes and practices of undergraduate education. Major advances include the understanding that cognitive and emotional development are interrelated and continue beyond adolescence, and the recognition of "emerging adulthood" as an especially dynamic time of reorganization and development of the brain. Of particular importance is the continued development of the prefrontal cortex, which supports key higher-order functions including evaluative judgments, the integration of cognition and affect, and self-regulation. The undergraduate experience typically occurs during this period of emerging adulthood and is not only impacted by developmental processes, but also influences cognitive and personal development. It is worth the effort, therefore, to formulate and implement educational experiences to promote this dynamic developmental reorganization and integration.

The purpose of this book is to provide a developmental science basis to inform the transformations in undergraduate educational goals and practices that are necessary to empower students to act globally and constructively engage difference. The approach taken is to synthesize current scholarship on the nature and development of the core capacities of personal epistemology, empathy, and identity and consider how these capacities can be enhanced by educational practices. The research literature regarding these three core capacities is quite extensive and multidisciplinary, and the aim of this book is not to provide an exhaustive review of the numerous theories and empirical studies in each area. Rather, the aim is to provide a synthesis of our current understandings of these three interrelated capacities specifically with regard to their essential role in empowering students to engage difference and as salient targets, therefore, of a formative undergraduate education. Thus, this synthesis is selective and purposive. This book has two intended audiences: faculty, and academic and student affairs administrators in higher education concerned with preparing students to meet twenty-first century societal needs; and faculty, graduate students, and undergraduate students in psychology, human development, and education who have an interest in intergroup relations and cognitive and social development during the period of emerging adulthood. The specific focus is on the ways in which the undergraduate experience can promote the development of personal epistemology/evaluativist thinking, empathy, and identity.

The first chapter begins by engaging Derek Bok's call in his book, *Our Underachieving Colleges*, for a reconsideration of the purposes of higher education. In response to this call, it is argued that responsiveness to societal needs is one source of guidance for formulating an institution's purposes and that the societal needs of the twenty-first century require a transformation in the purposes and practices of higher education. The current need for a transformation in educational goals and practices is situated in the context of previous transformations in higher education, including secularization, postsecularization, the move to general education, and recent efforts to reform undergraduate education, particularly at research universities.

Chapter 2 focuses on the developmental and neurocognitive changes occurring in late adolescence and emerging adulthood, particularly with regard to the integration of cognitive and affective processes. These developmental changes provide the basis for arguing that higher education should renew its commitment to the goal of providing a formative liberal education and adopt a developmental model of undergraduate education that focuses on personal as well as intellectual development to guide these efforts. In addition to developing students' capacity for reasoning, it is argued that colleges and universities must foster the development of three capacities in particular that are necessary to move beyond tolerance and constructively engage difference: personal epistemology (that is, understanding of knowledge and ways of thinking); empathy; and an integrated sense of identity that includes commitment to social responsibility and civic engagement.

The next three chapters provide integrative reviews of the nature and development of the three core capacities that contribute to the ability to constructively engage difference. Chapter 3 addresses ways of knowing, the justification of knowledge, the epistemology of academic disciplines, and the role of educational practices in enabling students to develop evaluative thinking and a sophisticated personal epistemology. Chapter 4 considers how we are able to understand the mental states of others and more specifically, the nature of empathy and its development, the relation of empathy with pro-social behavior, and the role of educational practices in enhancing empathy. Chapter 5 considers the construct of identity, both personal and collective, in terms of its functions, the determinants of identity development, and the role of narrative in the process of self-authorship.

The next two chapters address the role of higher education in fostering the development of the core capacities necessary to constructively engage differences. Chapter 6 examines the role of campus culture, particularly with regard to the impact of diversity, on reducing intergroup bias and promoting intergroup relations. The multicultural and social identity perspectives are considered as sources of guidance to issues such as self-segregation and promoting intergroup dialogue.

Chapter 7 considers how the core academic components of undergraduate experiences can be reshaped and aligned to provide a formative liberal education. The role of curricular and cocurricular experiences, pedagogical approaches, and academic advising are addressed, with a focus on the evidence regarding the role of high-impact practices in promoting student engagement and personal development. The chapter concludes with a consideration of the transformation in assessment practices that are needed not only to be responsive to recent societal calls for increased accountability, transparency, and evidence regarding student learning on the part of higher education, but to inform a continuous process of adaptation to improve student learning and development. This transformation involves two interrelated components: reframing assessment as a process of inquiry for the purpose of improving educational practices and student learning rather than for external accountability, and establishing a culture of experimentation and evidence with regard to the efficacy of educational practices.

The motivation to undertake this book was enhanced along the way by separate conversations with colleagues, one a physicist and the other a neurobiologist, who had inquired about my projects after serving as dean. I indicated that I intended to address what higher education could do to promote the development of empathy and identity. I had anticipated that they might express the objection that personal development was not the purview of universities. The response of both colleagues was nearly identical, although not what I had anticipated. They expressed surprise about my choice of project, because they believed that the capacity for empathy and identity were already established by the time students entered college.

These responses reminded me that beliefs matter, and highlight the need to better disseminate knowledge about learning and development, even among those who daily engage in undergraduate and professional education. If certain capacities are viewed as fixed, then there is little chance that educators will create the context and engage in practices intended to foster the development of these capacities or support such efforts by the university. Similarly, if faculty believe that students' ways of thinking and constructing meaning are already fully formed, then little attention will be paid to the impact of individual differences in epistemic beliefs on learning, the generation and application of knowledge, and engaging difference.

In contrast, my experiences as a psychologist have served to affirm a belief in the continuing potential for growth and development. Assisting others with ways of thinking and constructing meaning, enhancing the capacity for empathy, and fostering identity development are central to the functioning and training process not only for psychologists but also for physicians, educators, and other service providers. Moreover, the understanding of emerging adulthood as an active period of biopsychosocial development and reshaping of the brain serves to enhance the motivation to determine ways in which undergraduate educational experiences can make a difference in the formative development of our students. Thus, I believe that colleges and universities have a particular opportunity to be responsive to the societal needs of the twenty-first century by adapting our goals and practices to foster the development and integration of the cognitive and affective dimensions of human functioning necessary to empower civic-minded individuals to constructively engage political, ethnic, and religious differences.

Beyond Reason and Tolerance

CHAPTER 1

American Higher Education in the Twenty-First Century

It is the various civic purposes served by colleges and universities that provide the foundation for their social legitimacy (Shapiro, 1997, p. 66).

In the United States, higher education evokes strong emotions, both high regard and high dissatisfaction. We take national pride in our system of higher education and have enduring personal commitments to specific colleges and universities, and at the same time higher education is the focus of continuous debates, criticisms, and calls for reform and improvement. Alarms are sounded almost daily about ideological perspectives, declining standards, the deficiencies of the graduates, and the ever-increasing costs. These critiques come from those inside the academy as well as from society at large. These critiques, however, have had little impact on changing the nature of undergraduate education.

In *Our Underachieving Colleges*, Derek Bok (2006) argues that one reason for the lack of impact is that these critiques have diverted attention from a more fundamental consideration of the purposes of higher education. Bok contends that the lack of careful formulation of the purposes a college or university education ought to serve has resulted in neglect of important issues, such as moral reasoning and civic education, and the absence of a framework to guide decisions about the curriculum and cocurricular experiences. Bok also advocates that efforts to appraise strengths and weaknesses and improve the performance of our colleges and universities must begin with "a careful look at the purposes to be achieved" (p. 57). Any careful consideration of the purposes of higher education must engage what Bok terms the threshold problem: whether there should be only one dominant purpose, promoting the development of intellectual skills, or whether the ends should also include nurturing the development of other qualities, such as values, moral reasoning, and civic engagement. Bok does not advocate an exclusive focus on intellectual development, or a single overriding aim, but rather encourages a variety of purposes.

Focusing the efforts to improve undergraduate education on an appraisal of the purposes or ends it seeks to achieve makes sense. Careful formulation of the fundamental purposes of higher education would provide the necessary basis for colleges and universities to evaluate the effectiveness of their curricular, cocurricular, and pedagogical practices in achieving these aims. What, however, should guide the formulation of purposes and practices?

The premise of this book is that responsiveness to societal needs is one source of guidance for formulating higher education's purposes and practices. It is further argued that one of the major challenges of the knowledge-based, globally interconnected, and increasingly conflicted world of the twenty-first century is to prepare students to constructively engage ethnic, religious, and political differences. Meeting this challenge requires a transformation in the purposes and practices of higher education. More specifically, higher education must recommit to providing a formative undergraduate liberal education and adopt a developmental model to guide educational practices in going beyond a focus on enhancing students' capacities for reasoning and tolerance to include fostering their capacities for evaluative thinking, empathy, and an integrated identity that includes a commitment to civic and social responsibility. However, in being adaptive and responsive to societal needs, it is also essential to understand and maintain the special nature and role of the university as a place of inquiry and critique:

> It is the academic's job in a free society to serve the public culture by asking questions that the public doesn't want to ask, investigating subjects it cannot or will not investigate, and accommodating voices it fails or refuses to accommodate (Menand, 2010, p. 158).

ADAPTATION TO SOCIETAL NEEDS

Within the overall mission of knowledge generation, education, and public service, the system of higher education in the United States is distinctive in both the number and diversity of institutions. Data provided by the National Center for Education Statistics indicate that in 2009 there were 4,474 institutions that awarded the associate's degree or higher, with a total enrollment of more than 20 million students. There are more than 2,800 four-year institutions of higher education that offer the baccalaureate degree. These institutions differ in size, mission, and scope, ranging from liberal arts colleges to research universities. For example, the Carnegie Foundation for the Advancement of Teaching 2010 classification of institutions that award the baccalaureate degree lists 662 baccalaureate colleges, of which 270 offer degrees in arts and sciences and 392 in diverse fields; 727 masters colleges and universities; and 297 doctorate-granting universities. Of the more than 11 million students enrolled in these institutions, 49% are enrolled at doctorate-granting research universities, 39% at masters colleges and universities, and 12% at baccalaureate colleges. Along with the traditional mix of public and private institutions, there has been growth in recent years in the number of students attending for-profit institutions. Overall, about 76% of students are attending public institutions, 15% private nonprofit institutions, and 10% private for-profit institutions.

Although the number and diversity of institutions is distinctive, the distinguishing characteristic of American higher education is that it adapts in response to societal needs for knowledge, expertise, and leadership.

> American higher education—especially in its most formative moments—has been characterized by a sensitive recognition of its civic role. Higher education in America, whether public or private, has always drawn its most creative energy from the desire to meet its civic responsibilities (Shapiro, 1997, p. 75).

American higher education adapts to societal needs through changes in goals, structures, and practices. Most often, the adaptations evolve in a rather continuous fashion. At other times, however, societal needs and expectations require that the adaptations be more transformative. We are in such a transformative moment for higher education now at the beginning of the twenty-first century.

Higher education in the United States is facing increased demands for accountability in a time of fiscal constraints. Calls for greater accountability for student learning, in particular, were prompted by the 2006 report of the Spellings' Commission on the Future of Higher Education (US Department of Education, 2006). These demands for accountability, however, mask that colleges and universities are not just being asked to perform their traditional functions better and more efficiently, but also to be responsive to a new set of societal needs reflecting the challenges and opportunities of our knowledge-based economy and pluralistic, globally interconnected world of the twenty-first century.

The importance and power of knowledge in modern life is well recognized. "The pursuit, production, dissemination, application, and preservation of knowledge" have been identified as "the central activities of a civilization" and the "ability to create knowledge and put it to use is *the* adaptive characteristic of humans" (Menand, 2010, p. 13). This view of knowledge as a form of human capital, along with the recognition that it is unevenly distributed and affords advantages to those who have knowledge or access to it over those who have less, is the basis for other defining characteristics of American higher education.

> As a society, Americans are committed to the principle that the production of knowledge should be uninhibited and access to it should be universal. This is a democratic ideal (Menand, 2010, p. 14).

We also have a fundamental commitment to the value of individual differences and the need for, and power of, bringing diverse perspectives to bear on our tasks of increasing knowledge and understanding and problem solving.

The challenges to higher education go beyond increasing access, retention, and graduation rates. These are necessary but insufficient goals. Leadership and effective citizenship will increasingly require higher levels of intellectual and personal capabilities and social responsibility. The major challenge is to improve the quality of undergraduate education so that students are prepared to meet society's twenty-first century needs for civic-minded individuals who have the personal skills, dispositions, and intellectual capabilities to work effectively and live together in a more global society with many different kinds of people with tolerance, understanding, and mutual respect. More specifically, the forces of globalization not only result in increasing engagement of countries, cultures, and markets but also result in interdependency, and heighten the potential for conflict among diverse groups and cultures, along multiple dimensions of difference, around numerous issues. In particular, society has a pressing need for higher education to prepare individuals who have the capabilities to go beyond tolerance and constructively engage political, ethnic, and religious differences.

If one of the purposes of higher education is to prepare students to constructively engage differences, several questions need to be addressed:

- What foundation of knowledge, skills, and dispositions will students need?
- How can these capacities be developed?
- What corresponding changes are needed in educational practices to foster the development of these capacities?

The responses to these questions must be informed by recognition of the changing nature of intellectual work and advances in our knowledge about learning and human development.

With regard to the capacities needed to engage difference, certainly the intellectual abilities to think and reason critically, construct meaning from complex information, and generate knowledge to address societal problems are essential. However, while necessary, these intellectual skills are not sufficient. In addition, three core capabilities are needed and also are appropriate aims for undergraduate education: understanding of knowledge and ways of thinking; empathy and the ability to understand the mental states of others; and an integrated sense of identity that includes values, commitments, and agency for civic and social responsibility.

With regard to the changing nature of intellectual work, knowledge production, transmission, and application are undergoing fundamental changes that drive scholarship and the efforts to reshape undergraduate education. Information is increasingly available in multiple formats, electronically mediated, and generated through human interaction and collaboration across the boundaries of traditional disciplines. Both knowledge generation and application have become highly interdisciplinary. Furthermore, knowledge generation is moving away from an emphasis on reductionistic approaches, which have characterized the twentieth century, to more integrated perspectives in which functioning of the system as a whole is emergent and cannot be predicted from the functioning of parts in isolation. Intellectual work now requires integrative systems perspectives, and students must have opportunities to develop the requisite higher-order skills of integration and collaboration and become self-motivated and self-regulated lifelong learners.

Higher education must also adapt to advances in understanding about learning and human development. For example, we know that learning is most effective when it is active, problem based, and collaborative, and that people construct new knowledge based on their preexisting knowledge and beliefs (Bransford et al., 2000). One of the most powerful educational experiences we can provide for our students is to engage them directly, inside and outside the classroom, in the experiences of generating, integrating, and applying knowledge. We also know that the brain continues to develop and be reshaped by experiences well into the adult years. This understanding has given rise to the recognition of *emerging adulthood* as a distinct period characterized by: specific psychosocial issues; the development and integration of higher-order cognitive, social, and self-regulatory abilities; and readiness for experiences that enhance these neurocognitive functions. Since many emerging adults will be engaged in higher education, colleges and universities need to determine how to foster the development of these higher-order capabilities.

These changes in knowledge generation and application place a premium on integrative modes of education and pedagogies of engagement that include experiential, inquiry-based, and problem-based learning both inside and outside the classroom. Increasingly, what is taught must go beyond theory and content to include the higher-order skills of information processing; that is, analysis and synthesis of information, and application of knowledge to address societal problems. In addition, students must acquire the metacognitive skills, knowledge about their own thinking processes, which are necessary to monitor and regulate their learning. Correspondingly, there is a need to facilitate collaborative discovery and learning processes and provide the necessary social context to enable students to make meaning of complex information.

Educational practices also must be informed by what is known about the need to foster readiness to learn new information and ways of thinking, about how prior beliefs and views regarding knowledge and its justification affect learning, and about how to employ pedagogies of engagement to develop the essential capacities for perspective taking, empathy, and commitment. The focus on integration, however, cannot be limited to intellectual and interpersonal skills, but must also include fostering an integrated sense of identity—that is, a coherent sense of oneself that includes affective and cognitive functioning; beliefs, values, and a sense of meaning and purpose; and commitments to personal and social responsibility.

The adaptation required of higher education to respond to current societal needs argues for restoring formative education of the whole person as the primary purpose. More specifically, it is the premise of this book that colleges and universities must adopt a developmental model of undergraduate education in which education is viewed as a process of intellectual and personal growth and integration involving multiple dimensions of human functioning, including empathy as well as reasoning, values as well as knowledge, and identity as well as competencies.

In undertaking this transformation to a developmental model of undergraduate education, it is informative to briefly consider the previous transformations in American higher education. This historical narrative is well known, and our purpose is to call attention to the dynamic processes of challenge and adaptation that have shaped the current state of higher education and set the stage for the next phase. Of particular relevance to the focus of this book are the changes that have occurred with regard to the role of religion and moral education, the commitment to providing a formative liberal education, and the efforts to reform undergraduate education in research universities. We will then consider the advances in our knowledge of human development, and corresponding changes in societal expectations that have given rise to the recognition of emerging adulthood as a new developmental period for many youth in our society. Thus, the specific focus of our consideration is on the traditional, four-year undergraduate experience, which typically occurs during this developmental period. We will conclude this chapter with a consideration of the characteristics of a formative liberal education for the twenty-first century.

TRANSFORMATIONS IN HIGHER EDUCATION

There have been several transformations in higher education in the United States that have been well chronicled (Anderson, 1993; Marsden, 1992; Reuben, 1996). These transitions reflect emerging conceptualizations of the nature and purposes of higher education. Originally, higher education in colonial America took the form of colleges supported by various religious faiths. The classical curriculum of colonial colleges was inherited from the English Renaissance and Reformation (Turner, 1992). This humanistic curriculum "placed little emphasis on speculative critical philosophy, preferred rhetoric over logic, and focused on the aesthetic qualities of the text and a particular sense of virtue, the good citizen, and moral philosophy (i.e., moral control, obedience, and deference to authority)" (Shapiro, 1997, p. 73). Colleges typically functioned as the intellectual arm of American Protestantism up to the Civil War period, when the first major transition occurred in higher education (Roberts & Turner, 2000).

From Colleges to Universities

The modern American arts and sciences university emerged in the decades between the Civil War and WWI (Wilson, 2000). The 49-year period between 1870 and 1919 has been categorized as the "big bang" of American higher education (Menand, 2010). Charles Eliot contributed to the transformation in American higher education through reforms undertaken at Harvard during his 40-year term (1869–1909) as president. These reforms included requiring a bachelor's degree as a prerequisite for admission into professional school, establishing curricular and graduation requirements for the professional schools, and professionalization of the professoriate by requiring that college teachers hold a doctoral degree (Menand, 2010). Undergraduate education was understood as liberal, in the sense of nonvocational, with knowledge being pursued disinterestedly, "that is, without regard to political, economic, or practical benefit" (Menand, 2010, p. 55), and as a gateway to graduate professional education, which was specialized and utilitarian.

The transformation in the configuration of higher education from colleges to universities was driven by three factors: expansion of public state universities through the Morrill Act of 1862, adoption of the German research university model, and the commitment to the scientific approach to knowledge (Wilson, 2000). In particular, the founding of land grant universities demonstrated the changing expectations of society for higher education. The Morrill Act of 1862, also known as the Land Grant College Act, sought to enable the United States to respond to the knowledge and manpower needs of the industrial revolution. The purpose of this legislation was to establish institutions in each state that would

> without excluding other scientific and classical studies and including military tactics, to teach such branches of learning as are related to agriculture and the mechanic arts, in such manner as the legislatures of the States may respectively

prescribe, in order to promote the liberal and practical education of the industrial classes in the several pursuits and professions in life (United States Code: Title 7, Chapter 13, Subchapter 1, Section 304).

The influence of the German research university model was reflected not only in the establishment of graduate degree programs and the association of professional schools with the university, but also in conceiving the arts and sciences as subjects of inquiry sustained by research and scholarship (Wilson, 2000). The process of inquiry, characteristic of the natural sciences, was extended to human nature. The sciences studied natural phenomenon and human affairs, and the humanities studied cultural products and the inner life of human consciousness and sensibility.

Research Universities and Mass Education

A second transition in higher education occurred during the post-WWII period with the commitment of the United States government to finance research and mass higher education (Fallis, 2007). This commitment spawned the emergence of the research university, sometimes referred to as "multiversities," to provide advanced research and undergraduate, graduate, and professional education in response to postindustrial society's need for knowledge as the source of innovations and policy (Fallis, 2007).

The period from 1945 to 1975 is referred to as the Golden Age of American education that was marked by a tremendous expansion in students, both undergraduate and graduate, and faculty. This expansion reflected the confluence of three factors: the baby boom, high economic growth, and the Cold War (Menand, 2010). One outcome was a commitment to mass education. For example, the GI Bill of Rights of 1944 prompted a great influx of veterans into higher education as a gateway to social and economic mobility, and similar to the Morrill Act in the nineteenth century, had a profound effect on shaping higher education. With the commitment to mass higher education, Fallis (2007) notes that "the university becomes connected to democracy" (p. 61) and the role of universities changes: "The university system becomes the institutional embodiment of the political commitment to equality of opportunity," and "the university becomes an institution for social justice, for changing the class structure of a nation, for including the previously excluded" (p. 61).

Federal support was also provided for scientific research as knowledge, and, more specifically, the relationship between theory and application was recognized as the most important factor for economic prosperity and social progress (Fallis, 2007). Across the sciences and the humanities, there was increasing specialization and the emergence of new disciplines. In particular, the National Defense Education Act of 1958, in response to the Cold War in general and the launch of Sputnik in particular, resulted in the federal government directly subsidizing higher education through civilian agencies including the National Science Foundation, the National Institutes of Health, and the National Aeronautics and Space Administration (Menand, 2010). Part of the national security rationale was the need for an educated citizenry as a strategic resource. Higher education's response to these needs for scientific and technical knowledge and expertise changed the relationship of higher education to society:

> Universities became important in American life, as earlier colleges had not been, because they served the technological economy, training experts and its supporting professionals, and conducting much of its research (Marsden, 1992, p. 20).

The periods after the Civil War and WWII are clear examples of major transformations in higher education. These were periods of growing faith in the primacy of reason and cognition and the realization that enhancing students capacities to learn, to develop new knowledge, and to innovate were practical goals through which colleges and universities could benefit society (Shapiro, 1997). Furthermore, Eliot's reforms at Harvard "helped put universities in the exclusive business of credentialing professionals" (Menand, 2010, p. 47). Across these transitions there was a shift in undergraduate education from the collegiate tradition of the antebellum period, with its emphasis on moral philosophy and teaching, to the research university, with its emphasis on inquiry and generation of knowledge (Roberts & Turner, 2000).

These changes in the conceptualizations of the nature and purposes of higher education were accompanied by changes in the characteristics of the educational experiences provided. Three changes in particular warrant consideration: secularization, the marginalization of morality, and the movement of liberal education to general education.

Secularization

By the end of the nineteenth century, the term *secularization* was used to "describe a generalized process of replacing religious with lay values in the character and direction of morality, education, and culture" (Keddie, 2003, pp. 15–16). The process of secularization in higher education—that is, the transition from an era in which religion and Protestant ideals of Christianity in particular had a major role in higher education to an era in which it had almost none—has itself become a topic of study. In his historical study of this process of secularization, George Marsden (1992) addressed two interrelated questions: why universities were constructed as a secular enterprise, and why the Protestant Christian enterprise of higher education was seemingly voluntarily abandoned. In response to the question of why universities were constructed as a secular enterprise, Marsden (1992) identified the demand for more practical and scientific subjects in the curriculum, which fueled the rise of graduate education and specialization, as one force that contributed to the decline of clerically controlled classical education. To fully embrace the scientific approach and compete in the modern world colleges needed to be freed from clerical control, and they embraced methodological secularism and the philosophy of *naturalism*, which held that nature is all that exists and observable events are fully explainable by natural causes without reference to the supernatural. During the rise of universities after the Civil War, "academics saw the disestablishment of religion in higher education as simply a liberation and hence a step toward the laudable triumph of science, free inquiry, and liberalism" (Marsden, 1992, p. 6).

In response to the question of why the Protestant Christian enterprise of higher education was seemingly voluntarily abandoned, Marsden (1992) offered two explanations. In the service of achieving the liberal Christian goal of advancing civilization, Protestant Christianity embraced methodological secularism and religious beliefs were suspended to obtain greater scientific objectivity: "The sacred status of scientific knowledge and free inquiry was thus confirmed and to a large extent institutionalized" (p. 19). Another contributing factor was that Liberal Protestantism embraced the increasing pluralism of American society and promoted the melting-pot ideal of assimilation, good character, and democratic principles as common American values. Protestant institutions of higher education saw themselves as serving the general public as well as their church and made equity a preeminent concern: "The combination of the pressures of cultural pluralism and Christian ethical principles made it awkward if not impossible to take any decisive stand against the secularizing trend" (p. 28). Thus, disestablishment of religious control of higher education seemed the right thing to do.

In this process of secularization, civilization itself, rather than religion, became the source of values, and the humanities, rather than the moral philosophy of the pre-Civil War period, were seen as providing coherence to the curriculum. In large part, the universities became "religion free zones" (Wilson, 2000). Western civilization was to be the functional replacement for religion, and the net effect was the "marginalization of morality" in the secular university (Sommerville, 2006).

Marginalization of Morality

Julie Reuben (2010), who has written about the marginalization of morality in the modern university, notes that there are two "seemingly contradictory features of morality in American higher education—the long-term attenuation of moral purposes and the constancy of this aspiration" (p. 28). Concurrent with the process of secularization, there has been a continuous debate about whether higher education in America should include moral well as academic purposes.

The attenuation of moral education has been associated with the adoption of science and research as the guiding paradigms of scholarship and education, which placed an emphasis on "objectivity" and "value-free" scholarship and the distinction between knowledge and morality (Reuben, 1996). In particular, there was increasing opposition to the idea that higher education was in the business of character education, viewed as promoting indoctrination of a particular set of values of the right, the good, and the norm as being in conflict with the need to foster open inquiry and critical evaluation of all authoritative claims. For a time, there was a shift to the humanities as a source of moral guidance and then to the notion that "the moral education of students would be achieved outside of the classroom" (Reuben, 1996, p. 265). Through the cultural changes of the twentieth century resulting in increasing diversity and pluralism on college and university campuses, the feasibility and appropriateness of moral education became increasingly questioned outside of colleges serving a subpopulation typically defined by religious identity. Universities with a commitment to research and service to diverse constituents have struggled to maintain a modest commitment to moral education, while some colleges defined by religious identity have struggled to establish their legitimacy as educational institutions (Reuben, 2010).

> Depending on one's perspective, American higher education has either regressed from a clearly defined, religiously based, moral education to a relativistic, unmoored, amoral education; or it has progressed from an authoritarian, church-controlled, narrow education to an open, inclusive, inquiry-based education (Reuben, 2010, p. 28).

Closely related to moral education is the concept of civic education, which has also been debated as the proper purview for higher education. At some level, however, there has been continuing recognition of the need to prepare students to participate in democratic citizenship, but there have been differences with regard to content and methods. Beginning in the latter half of the twentieth century, there has been increasing interests in fostering the civic engagement of students. For example, *Campus Compact* was created in 1983 by prominent university presidents to promote service learning and community service, and has grown to more than 900 college and university members.

The notion of value-free scholarship and whether the purposes of higher education include moral development and civic engagement continued to be both advocated and challenged. Reuben (2010) argues that "since it has proven to be impossible to separate fact and value, we should begin to explore ways to reintegrate them" (p. 269). In addressing the challenges going forward, Reuben (2010, p. 52) has articulated the essential questions:

How to emphasize moral formation and still respect diversity?
How to reconcile freedom of thought and expression with a strong moral education?
How to deal with the intersection of morality politics and morality and religion?
How to reconcile individual and institutions self-interests with moral demands?
How to balance the multiple missions of higher education?

Liberal Education to General Education

In his 1873 seminal work *The Idea of a University*, Cardinal Newman advocated the mission of a university as providing a liberal education. The term "liberal" connotes freedom from ignorance, tradition, and dogma, and since the time of the Enlightenment, the chief instrument for fostering freedom has been the cultivation of the power of reasoning. Newman did not, however, limit liberal education to enhancing reasoning alone. He viewed liberal education as cultivating the intellect and expanding its capacities to both reason and empathize. The cultivation of the intellect is in the service of both the growth of the individual and the betterment of the community. In describing the education he was advocating, Newman (1976) remarked:

It shows him how to accommodate himself to others, how to throw himself into their state of mind, how to bring before them his own, how to influence them, how to come to an understanding with them, how to bear with them (pp. 154–155).

Liberal education also connoted freedom from practical demands for immediate relevance of knowledge and focused on general knowledge and broad understanding of different ways of thinking. Developing specific competencies was viewed as the purview of graduate and professional education, and not undergraduate education. Newman did, however, view university education in terms of its obligation to society: "If then a practical end must be assigned to a University course, I say it is that of training good members of society" (p. 154). Among the aims of liberal education, he included "raising the intellectual tone of society" and "cultivating the public mind" (p. 154). Consistent with the *artes liberals* ideas of classical thought, Newman's viewed the college years as a time of both learning and character formation (Fallis, 2007). Thus, from the beginning, one of the goals of liberal education was an informed citizenry, and included the prescription of values and standards for character and conduct (Kimball, 1995).

Over time, the idea of liberal education has embodied two conflicting traditions. The philosophical tradition emphasizes the pursuit of knowledge as the highest good. The oratorical tradition emphasizes the public expression of what is known and education as the moral enterprise of imparting the truth, cultivating values and character, and fostering community (Kimball, 1995). The dynamic tension between these two traditions has been played out with regard to the proper role of the university and its mission, curriculum, and pedagogical practices. In particular, there has been an

> ongoing struggle between an intellectual vision that is secular and that focuses on the development of both the independent individual and new knowledge and an alternative intellectual vision that is less secular, emphasizes common cultural commitments, and focuses on traditional values (Shapiro, 1997, p. 64).

In the nineteenth century, higher education was liberal education in the sense of focusing on general knowledge provided through a required common or core curriculum. In the twentieth century, however, the secularization of higher education, the movement away from an inclusion of character education as part of the university mission, and the transformation to mass undergraduate education were accompanied by an increasing emphasis on disciplinary education and the major. Liberal education became synonymous with *general education*, which was often relegated to a loose distribution requirement across the humanities, natural sciences, social science, and the arts. Furthermore, there were changes in the locus of undergraduate education. Whereas undergraduate enrollments historically had been predominately in the arts and sciences, the percentage of undergraduates in the professions increased from 38% in 1969 to 58% in 1976 (Fallis, 2007). The extent to which this dispersion of undergraduate students continues at the beginning of the twenty-first century is reflected in the *Chronicle of Higher Education Almanac* data for 2009–2010 regarding the percentages of enrolled students with a declared major in fields of study: business 18.8%; humanities 17.7%; science, engineering, and math 17.6%; and health professions 16.7%.

The focus on general learning that emerged early in the twentieth century can be seen as an effort to preserve elements of a liberal education in response to the increasing specialization in universities and the corresponding decline in required courses, increase in elective courses, and fragmentation of knowledge. General learning referred to learning that was not dependent on specific content knowledge but rather broad knowledge of history, culture, and modes of thinking. Within universities general education became the vehicle through which to achieve some common set of learning objectives and experiences for undergraduate students across an increasing array of departments and schools. Moreover, general education served as the "public face" of liberal education, "where colleges connect what professors do with who their students are and what they will become after they graduate—where colleges actually think about the outcome of the experience they provide" (Menand, 2010, pp. 31–32).

The prominence of general education at the end of the century was reflected in the findings of a survey conducted by the Association of American Colleges and Universities which indicated that the average general education requirement constituted 37.6% of the baccalaureate degree (Ratcliff et al., 2001). The way to achieve a general education, however, has always prompted debate. For some, general education meant a focus on common experiences for undergraduates, often around a core set of courses or great books, reflecting a desire to reaffirm a common heritage or shared culture. For others, general education meant acquiring a set of skills essential to all fields, including writing, critical thinking, and quantitative reasoning and a commitment to ethical behavior, civic responsibility, and lifelong learning. Thus, there was little consensus on the meaning or content of general education other than in contrast with specialization (Lucas, 1998). The sharp distinction between general education as "breadth" in contrast to education in the major as "depth" began to blur with the recognition that general and integrative skills could be developed through engagement with the specific areas of disciplinary inquiry. Derek Bok (2006) expressed the view that it was time to get over our "fixation on general education," and others have argued that "if we improve learning in the disciplines, we will have improved general education" (Beyer et al., 2007, p. 363).

It has been argued that the reduction of liberal education to general education has resulted in a loss of some of the distinctive aspects (Harward, 2012). More specifically, liberal education is viewed as comprising three interrelated dimensions: epistemic, psychological, and civic. The epistemological dimension involves propositional knowledge (knowing that), procedural knowledge (knowing how to), and the relation of knowledge to action (judgment). The psychosocial or eudemonic dimension focuses on the integration of learning with the full development of the learner. The learning "positively affects the flourishing, the sense of identity, the persistence and resiliency, and the self-realization of the learner" (Harward, 2012, p. 11). The third dimension is civic, and focuses on knowing and learning as ethical acts connected to the awareness of responsibilities to others and to the community. The challenge going forward is to provide an undergraduate education that comprises these essential dimensions.

With the beginning of the twenty-first century we are experiencing another period of transformation in higher education. This period of transformation is being driven in part externally by societal expectations for accountability and involves concerns about the purposes of higher education, but also about the quality. The transformation is also being driven internally by changes in the nature of intellectual work and our understanding of the nature and process of learning and effective teaching practices.

THE TWENTY-FIRST CENTURY: REFORM OF UNDERGRADUATE EDUCATION

The Golden Age of American education came to a halt around 1975 (Menand, 2010). The years since have been characterized by a dramatic increase in diversity of the undergraduate student body and faculty, debates about the curriculum (sometimes referred to as "culture wars"), a movement away from value-free inquiry, and the emergence of new fields of study, such as ethnic studies and women's studies. By the end of the twentieth century, however, there was increasing dissatisfaction with the way in which colleges and universities were fulfilling their responsibilities for undergraduate education.

Quality and Purpose

Much of this dissatisfaction focused on concerns that students were not acquiring the intellectual skills—particularly critical thinking, quantitative reasoning, problem solving, and communication skills—necessary to function in the knowledge-based economy, and the dispositions and skills necessary for civic engagement. There was particular concern about undergraduate education in research universities. For example, the Boyer Commission report, *Reinventing Undergraduate Education: A Blueprint for America's Research Universities* (1998), identified a number of deficiencies in undergraduate education at research universities including little contact with world-famous professors, little engagement with genuine research, little broad intellectual engagement, little coherence of knowledge, and little understanding of how information is related.

Concerns about the quality of undergraduate education and student engagement continue to persist. For example, in their recent book *Academically Adrift: Limited Learning on College Campuses*, Richard Arum and Josipa Roksa (2011) report on their study of a large sample of students enrolled in a diverse range of 24 four-year liberal arts colleges and research universities. Their findings reveal that gains in student performance during the first two years of their college experience are disturbingly low. Arum and Roksa (2011) view their findings about limited student learning as the consequences of a lack of rigor in higher education, in terms of both faculty expectations and student effort. To address the problem and improve learning students need to spend more time studying, which can be brought about through increased academic requirements and more rigorous grading.

Concerns have also been expressed about higher education's neglect of purpose. For example, it has been argued that the notion "the academy exists to research and disseminate knowledge and skills as tools for economic development and the upward mobility of individuals" has resulted in a focus on individualism that has left "the larger questions of social, political, and moral purpose out of explicit consideration" (Sullivan, 2000, p. 21). Similarly, the claim has been made that by allowing higher education to be framed as a commodity and students as customers, "we have reinforced the popular understanding of higher education as a private gain" (Harward, 2012, p. 6). It has also been argued that "colleges and universities ought to make moral, civic, and political development central goals of undergraduate education" (Colby, 2008, p. 391). The dynamic tensions about the purposes of an undergraduate education continue to play out, as some argue that moral and civic education are not appropriate or feasible goals of undergraduate education (Fish, 2003). Also, there is uncertainty about the locus of responsibility within the university: "Moral growth does not fit neatly into traditional disciplines" (Colby, 2008, p. 306). Thus, moral and civic development have been, for the most part, an implicit goal of the general education component of undergraduate education.

Replacing the emphasis on individualism with a more socially responsive view of the purposes of higher education would require moving away from a socially detached positivist epistemology—that is, conception of knowledge and its purposes—to one that emphasizes the interconnection of means and ends (Sullivan, 2000). An expanded purpose would also necessitate a focus on fostering the development of a set of interrelated capabilities and values seen as critical to effective citizenship. This set would include an understanding of ethical and democratic principles, such as impartiality, equity, distributive and procedural justice, and welfare; the commitment to act on moral and civic understandings; and the ability to work effectively with others very different from oneself (Colby, 2008).

The focus on reform of undergraduate education has been fostered by higher education professional associations. For example the Association of American Colleges and Universities (AAC&U) maintained a several-decade-long focus on promoting the role of higher education in fostering social responsibility and civic engagement (Schneider, 2000) and *practical liberal education* as the most empowering form of learning for the twenty-first century. Practical liberal education reflects the intentional integration of the traditional liberal education focus on developing intellectual and personal skills with the traditional professional and technical focus on solving complex problems.

AAC&U also has sustained a multiyear dialogue among colleges and universities and employers to improve the quality of undergraduate education through formulating learning outcome objectives, identifying and implementing high-impact practices, and adopting an approach to accountability in which assessment is designed to improve learning. These efforts have amounted to a "reinvention" of liberal education for the twenty-first century that is characterized by three formative themes: cultivating inquiry skills and intellectual judgment, social responsibility and civic engagement, and integrative learning

(Schneider, 2009). These themes yield four key liberal educational outcome objectives considered as essential for all students:

- Knowledge of human cultures and the physical and natural world.
- Intellectual and practical skills including critical and creative thinking, written and oral communication, quantitative literacy, and teamwork and problem solving.
- Personal and social responsibility, including civic and intercultural knowledge, ethical reasoning and action, and the foundations and skills for lifelong learning.
- Integrative and applied learning, including synthesis of knowledge across general and specialized studies and application of knowledge to new settings and complex problems.

Achieving these learning objectives requires a high level of student engagement, and research has identified a number of high-impact educational practices, such as service learning, study abroad, undergraduate research, and culminating capstone experiences, that promote student engagement and result in gains in learning and personal development (Kuh, 2008).

The Postsecular University

Another driver of change in higher education is the increasing dissatisfaction with the secular university's ability to meet societal needs in the postmodern world that it helped to create. From the 1960s until the end of the twentieth century, liberal Enlightenment ideas, and not just Christian ideals, have been under attack (Marsden, 1992). One of the foundations of the secular university was the fact/value dichotomy: One should not derive a value from a fact, or an "ought" from an "is." Under the influence of positivist approaches, inquiry was to be value free: "Values were assumed to be subjective and personal or merely traditional, and not a fruitful subject for discussion" (Sommerville, 2006, p. 45). Now, however, the need to engage values is increasingly clear. Furthermore, some scholars see the secular university as increasingly marginal to American society because "questions that might be central to the university's mission are too religious for it to deal with" (Sommerville, 2006, p. 4).

Universities are being criticized for not engaging our deepest interests and most pressing concerns, and for not addressing the "big questions" that involve ultimate values and standards. One purported reason is that the humanities did not, as expected, replace the more religious core of earlier colleges as a source of values and coherency, in part because the liberal arts have changed: "They've turned into technical specialties. They're often addressing questions nobody is asking, and giving answers nobody can understand"

(Sommerville, 2006, p. 8). In contrast, religion is viewed by some as reflecting "humanity's ongoing search for meaning, purpose, and comfort" (Jacobsen & Jacobsen, 2008a, p. 12).

While recognizing that a return to Christianity as a basis for moral consensus is neither feasible nor advocated, some academics are seeking to reconstruct a place for religious perspectives in higher education. One motivation is that religion engages one's ultimate concerns and is embedded in our thinking:

> We can't even discuss the concepts of wealth, justice, sanity, truth, the human, and the humane without finding their irreducibly religious dimensions. For all of these involve the question of what human life is all about, of what would be optimal for humanity. Naturalism is silent on these subjects. A century ago it seemed reasonable to restrict the university to questions we could answer definitively, to everyone's satisfaction. We are now finding that this leaves out too much (Sommerville, 2006, p. 21).

Beyond the desire to engage the questions of meaning and purpose, another reason offered for readmitting religion into higher education is the role that religion plays in world politics, and more specifically, as a source of radical discord as different religious traditions encounter the truth claims of others (Carroll, 2003). It is argued that there will be no peace among nations without peace among religions, which requires dialogue and examination of their foundations:

> Democratic values, ideological openness, freedom of conscience, positive regard for those who are different (also known as pluralism), as well as the capacity to tolerate even those who remain intolerant: these pillars of the post-Enlightenment social order will not stand unless exactly equivalent pillars are erected to reform—and thus secure—the institutions of traditional religion (Carroll, 2003, p. 12).

We need to be clear about what the postsecular conversation about religion and higher education promises. First, moral questions abound, and "the moral domain is not limited to religious contexts" (Brandenberger, 2005, p. 306). Second, the aim is "not to help religion regain its lost power" (Jacobsen & Jacobsen, 2008b, p. 227), nor to open the door to proselytism. Andrew Delbanco (2012) clearly articulates the issue: " All colleges, whatever their past or present religious orientation, now exist in a context of secular pluralism that properly puts inculcation at odds with education" (p. 16). Understanding, not conversion, is the goal of the university. More specifically, the aim is to foster understanding of religion as part of the human condition and reality in the world that universities explore and evaluate. Engaging religious beliefs and insights has the potential to enrich the intellectual climate and conversation by addressing societal issues and questions that otherwise might be ignored. More specifically, in terms of the focus of this book, religion shapes identity and behavior throughout the world, and engaging religious perspectives and differences has the potential to foster intergroup understanding and relations. Engaging religious perspectives, however, also has the potential for creating discord rather than understanding. In addition to the critical analysis of beliefs and respect for differing perspectives that are essential to academic discourse, achieving a constructive dialogue "requires self-conscious honesty about who we are and our own predispositions" (Jacobsen & Jacobsen, 2008b, p. 230). Engaging religious perspectives offers the opportunity to develop those capacities necessary for constructive dialogue between people who are religious and those who are not and among those from different faith traditions. Those capacities that are necessary for constructive religious dialogue are also prerequisites for effective civic and political life (Jacobsen & Jacobsen, 2008b). Therefore, developing those capacities needs to be included among the purposes of higher education in the twenty-first century.

Engagement of religious beliefs will intensify the consideration of epistemology—that is, our views about the nature and justification of knowledge. The academy, although embracing multiple perspectives and ways of knowing, is committed to the provisional nature of knowledge and the process of inquiry, reasoned argument, and evidence as the methods for discerning among competing claims: "If you commit yourself to intellectual openness and scientific inquiry, you must give up dogma" (Wolfe, 2006, p. 11). In particular, in the process of developing an integrated identity, it will be a challenge for some students to reconcile matters of faith—which frequently entails belief in the supernatural, the certainty of knowledge, and revealed truth—with a commitment to an evaluativist approach to the construction and justification of knowledge, which we will consider more fully in Chapter 3.

Scholarship on Teaching and Learning

Changes in the purposes of higher education are not the only adaptations that are occurring. Pedagogical and curricular innovations are also occurring throughout higher education, with the increased recognition that change needs to be informed by research about learning and teaching (Bransford et al., 2000). Mayer (1992) describes the paradigm shift in the view of learning that occurred in education over the course of the twentieth century as having gone through three phases with corresponding implications for instructional practices. Early in the century learning was viewed as response acquisition, a relatively automatic strengthening or weakening of responses through environmental feedback, and instructional practices involved creating situations to elicit responses from learners, such as drill and practice exercises, and providing appropriate reinforcement. By mid-century, learning was viewed as knowledge acquisition: The learner is the processor of information, who places new information in long-term memory, and the teacher is the dispenser of information. Information is a commodity that can be transferred from the teacher to the learner, and instructional practices involved a curriculum-centered approach. By the end of the century learning was viewed as knowledge construction, involving the processes of "selecting relevant information and interpreting it though one's existing knowledge" (Mayer, 1992, p. 407). The focus of instructional practices changed from the curriculum to developing the learner's metacognitive skills, such as monitoring and evaluating one's comprehension, and learning strategies, including elaboration and integrating new information with prior information, appropriate for various subject domains.

At the beginning of the twenty-first century, learning is understood as best accomplished through discovery guided by mentoring rather than passive receipt of transmitted knowledge, and instruction is increasingly characterized by an emphasis on active, student-centered, experiential learning. The curriculum is beginning to be recognized not as just a list of courses, but rather as the hallmark of the university reflecting the values of the faculty, the capabilities of the students, and the aspirations of the institution. Major trends in curricular revision include fostering coherency as well as depth and breadth, promoting interdisciplinarity and fluency across the domains of knowledge, and enhancing civic responsibility.

Universities are also continuing to adapt to the changing nature of intellectual work. Knowledge production, transmission, and application are undergoing fundamental changes. Inquiry and discovery increasingly occur at the boundaries of disciplinary knowledge. Correspondingly, there is currently a shift from disciplinary-based learning to problem-based learning, with an emphasis on interdisciplinary and transdisciplinary education (Keller, 2008). Now colleges and universities must continue to nurture the generation and application of new knowledge and methods within disciplines while also promoting interdisciplinary scholarship and education across departments and schools.

Globalization, Commercialization, and Technology

Beyond adapting to advances in our understanding of learning and the changing nature of intellectual work, higher education is having to adapt to unprecedented demographic, technological, and budgetary trends that are challenging the very nature of higher education. One form of adaption, for example, is the rise of for-profit institutions. However, traditional colleges and universities are challenged with adapting without losing their distinctive characteristics.

Derek Bok, president emeritus of Harvard University, has called attention to the influence of commercialization in higher education, by which he means "the efforts within the university to make a profit from teaching, research, and other campus activities" (2003, p. 3), including athletics. Commercialization has multiple causes, but Bok argues that the main driver is that an increasingly technologically sophisticated and knowledge-based economy provided money-making opportunities. Bok argues that the appropriate response of universities to the dilemmas of commercialization is to "promote the purposes and protect the values of the institution" (p. 32). One of these values is generosity:

> Academic communities work well only when professors voluntarily choose to give generously of their time to help their institution, colleagues, and students. It is this willingness to do more for others than the job officially requires that is at particular risk in an age when able scientist and scholars have so many opportunities to seek fame and fortune in the outside world (Bok, 2003, pp. 114–115).

James Duderstadt, president emeritus of the University of Michigan, has called attention to the implications of other trends on the future of higher education and public research universities in particular (Duderstadt et al., 2002; Duderstadt, 2000; 2012). The forces of globalization and the rapid advances in information technologies add whole new dimensions to the current challenges of accessibility, affordability, and accountability, and go to the heart of higher education's societal contract. The need and demand for quality higher education is growing, and responding to the issues of what it is, who will get it, and how it will be paid for are major adaptive challenges for the twenty-first century. These challenges are interrelated, as is evident by a consideration of the increasing costs of higher education in the United States. We are experiencing a decline in funding, particularly at the regional and state level, at the same time that more is being expected of colleges and universities and their faculties. One contributing factor is that higher education "is being increasing perceived as a benefit rather than a public good" (Darden 2009, p. 3). When the investment in higher education is perceived as a benefit to the individual rather than to society, funding drops lower on the public's priority list, which puts addition upward pressure on tuition as a source of funding.

While the regional ties are lessening, universities in particular are moving in the direction of defining themselves in global terms. Students and faculty are increasingly recruited from around the world. Furthermore, the decreasing half-life of knowledge means that people will need to be lifelong learners, and thus have access to higher education throughout their life course. One consequence will be an increase in adult learners, not just in the United States but around the world, who also will be maintaining jobs while they learn new skills. Not only will this change the demographics of the college population, but it will also change the presence of students on campus; said another way, it will increase the need for open online access.

One way to increase access that already is underway is to make courses available online, which is evident with the advent of massive online open courses (MOOCs) being developed and offered by some of our nation's most highly regarded universities. In turn, these advances in the provision of and access to information are prompting the development of new structures for organizing and paying for education, new pedagogical approaches and ways of learning, and methods of fostering the capacities and motivation for lifelong learning. Advances in information technology enable teaching to be not only less focused on the provision of knowledge content, but also more focused on the meaning-making process. In addition, developments such as social media enable the establishments of networks that foster dialogue and engagement with information in multiple formats. In adapting to these technological advances, it is important to be reminded that the university engages in the production of knowledge and understanding as a social institution (Duderstadt et al., 2002), and new types of learning communities must also emerge to enable the types of experiences and social interactions essential for the construction of knowledge and understanding. With these forces that are reshaping higher education so pressing, the commitment to providing a liberal undergraduate education—all along the continuum of colleges to universities, to multiversi-ties, to open universities—needs to be reaffirmed in light of the current and future needs of society. The reality of lifelong learning as the new norm makes all the more compelling the need for undergraduate education to be formative.

In *College: What It Was, Is, and Should Be,* Andrew Delbanco (2012) engages the basic questions about the purpose and possibilities of a college education. Delbanco argues that at its core, a college should "be a place where young people find help for navigating the territory between adolescence and adulthood," and "help them develop certain qualities of mind and heart requisite for reflective citizenship" (p. 3). These qualities are not commodities that can be purchased by students, and they "make themselves known not in grades or examinations but in the way we live our lives" (p. 3). Delbanco further argues that beyond the economic purposes of preparing students to enhance their individual and our national competiveness, and preparation for inclusive democratic citizenship, colleges should maintain the commitment to provide a liberal education:

> A college should not be a haven from worldly contention, but a place where young people fight out among and within themselves contending ideas of the meaningful life, and where they discover that self-interest need not be at odds with concern for one another (p. 177).

The consideration of the purposes of undergraduate education and a recom-mitment to providing a liberal education is part of the self-correcting process through which higher education is responsive to societal needs. Continuing efforts to transform undergraduate education must also respond to the ongo-ing advances in knowledge about human development, and particularly with regard to emerging adulthood, the period that typically comprises the under-graduate years, which is the focus of the next chapter.

CHAPTER 2

Emerging Adulthood

A Developmental Science Perspective

It is the age of identity explorations; it is the age of instability; it is the most self-focused age of life; it is the age of feeling in-between; and it is the age of possibilities (Arnett, 2006, p. 7).

The study of human development has evolved from reductionist nature or nurture approaches to an integrated biopsychosocial approach, and in the process a new interdisciplinary field of developmental science has emerged. The field of developmental science is characterized by a systems approach that emphasizes relations among levels of organization, from the biological to the sociocultural and historical, and the integration of both nature and nurture conceptions of human development, and basic and applied scholarship (Lerner, 2006). Development is now understood as a dynamic process that occurs as a function of the transactions of the individual with her or his social environment. This developmental systems perspective has particular implications for undergraduate education. It calls attention to the marked changes in the development and integration of higher-order capacities that characterize the transition from childhood to adulthood, and the role of the transactions between the person and his or her environment in promoting these changes.

EMERGING ADULTHOOD

One of the characteristics of the transition from childhood to adulthood in our postindustrial society is its increasing length. This recognition has led to a proposed new phase of development, *emerging adulthood,* spanning the period from adolescence to young adulthood, or roughly the ages from 18 to

25 (Arnett, 2000). Occurring after the dependency of childhood and adolescence but before the responsibilities of adulthood, emerging adulthood is the period of life that offers the most opportunities for explorations of possible life directions and commitments in the areas of love, education, work, and worldview. The exploratory quality of this period is reflected in the relative lack of demographic markers compared to adolescence and young adulthood (Arnett, 2000). The adolescence years of 12–17 are marked by more than 95% being unmarried, living at home with one or both parents, and enrollment in school, whereas by age 30, 75% are married, have become parents, and fewer than 10% are enrolled in school (Arnett, 2000).

Emerging adults subjectively experience this phase of life as distinct. They no longer see themselves as adolescents, but do not yet see themselves as adults. Their subjective sense of ambiguity does not, however, arise from the demographic characteristics cited above. Emerging adults rank these demographic characteristics and transitions at the bottom of criteria considered necessary for the attainment of adulthood and rank at the top of the list indicators of *self-sufficiency*, including accepting responsibility for one's self, making independent decisions, and becoming financially independent (Arnett, 2000). Furthermore, having a sense of being an adult is related to a having a sense of coherency, being employed, and making commitments (Luyckx et al., 2008).

Neurocognitive Development

Emerging adulthood is not only a subjective state. It is also a period marked by changes in physical, cognitive, and emotional development and self-consciousness. Furthermore, it has become increasingly clear that neurocognitive development continues through adolescence into this period of emerging adulthood as the brain goes through a remodeling process (Choudhury et al., 2006). Two main changes in the brain before and after puberty have been identified in fMRI studies: a linear increase in white matter and a simultaneous nonlinear reduction in grey matter (Blakemore & Choudhury, 2006). In particular, the prefrontal cortex (PFC) undergoes the most pronounced structural development, while the superior temporal cortex, including the superior temporal sulcus (STS), undergoes the most protracted development (Blakemore et al., 2007). These changes in brain regions are paralleled by changes in the cognitive abilities that are supported by these regions, and in particular the development of cognitive skills involved in executive functions, social cognitions, and self-regulation.

Executive functions refers to a number of capacities involved in control and coordination of thoughts and behaviors, including selective attention, decision making, working memory, and voluntary response inhibition (Blakemore & Choudhury, 2006). In accordance with the changes occurring in the prefrontal cortex, behavioral studies demonstrate that the performance of tasks involving these functions continues to improve during adolescence (Blakemore & Choudhury, 2006). Some aspects of developmental changes in executive functioning in adolescence reflect aspects of brain development associated with pubertal change, more specifically the effects that emotional factors exert on cognition, and some are independent and reflect the effect of age and experience.

Social cognition involves a number of processes that are supported by the prefrontal cortex, including self-awareness and perspective taking—that is, the ability to understand others minds and infer mental states such as intentions, beliefs, and desires. It has been proposed that the changes in the social thinking and behavior of adolescents and the changes in neural circuitry could be mutually influencing (Blakemore & Choudhury, 2006). For example, peer relationships become increasingly important during adolescence and could provide experiences that impact the synaptic reorganization process and social cognition.

Self-regulation is the ability to control one's attention, emotions, and behavior. It is an adaptive system that is central to the development of competence and effective functioning throughout the life course, and is shaped by a person's experiences as well as disposition (Masten & Coatsworth, 1998). Self-regulation is an example of an adaptive system that includes both cognitive and affective components and their underlying neurocortical interconnections. For example, self-regulation relies on executive functions, such as reasoning and problem solving, in the face of strong emotions such as anger and fear. At the neurocortical level there are links between the prefrontal cortex, which is responsible for executive functions, and the limbic system, which is responsible for emotional processes (Blair, 2002).

Another advance in knowledge about human development is the increasing awareness of the extent to which cognitive and affective components are mutually influencing and work together, particularly with regard to self-regulation:

> The behavioral and emotional control necessary to attain adult social competence brings together components of behavior previous labeled as either "cognitive" or "affective" (Nelson et al., 2002, p. 515).

The proliferation of projections of white matter tracts across different brain regions, which continues well into late adolescence, results in an increase in the connections among cortical areas involved in the processing of emotional and social information and cognitive control, which is especially important for emotion regulation. Furthermore, there is increasing recognition of the degree to which the self-regulation adaptive system is modifiable by experience, and in particular the role of experience in stimulating the development of the underlying neurocortical structures (Blair, 2002).

In addition to changes in neurocortical regions that support higher-order cognitive processes, there are changes in the dopaminergic system that plays an important role in the brain's reward circuitry (Steinberg, 2008). There is first a proliferation and then reduction and redistribution of dopamine receptors in paralimbic and prefrontal cortical regions. Dopaminergic activity in the prefrontal cortex increases significantly, and is higher during early adolescence than at any other point in development. Thus, systems involved in reward processing mature early in adolescence, but there is only a gradual development and strengthening of brain systems involving self-regulation and the coordination of emotion and cognition over the course of adolescence and early adulthood. This combination of an easily aroused reward system and a still immature self-regulatory system in middle adolescence has been likened to "starting an engine without yet having a skilled driver" (Steinberg et al., 2006, p. 721).

The recognition of emerging adulthood as a distinct developmental period, subjectively and socioculturally, during which the brain is undergoing remodeling of the neurobiological underpinnings for higher-order cognitive functions, has prompted a consideration of the implications for undergraduate educational practices. For example, it has been speculated that as a consequence of synaptic reorganization, "the brain might be more sensitive to experiential input at this period of time in the realm of executive function and social cognition" (Blakemore & Choudhury, 2006, p. 307). This speculation leads to a more specific research question: What educational practices and opportunities should be provided to promote neurocortical development on which these higher-order cognitive functions are dependent? In addressing this question, we need to be clear about our current understanding regarding the mechanisms that link neurocortical development, cognitive development, and experiences.

Brain Development, Cognitive Functioning, and Experience

Seven major processes of brain development have been delineated and these are operative at different periods of development (Brynes, 2001). Beginning in the prenatal period, the processes of *proliferation, migration,* and *differentiation* produce the right number and types of brain cells in the right location across the six layers of the cortex. Cells grow in size and send projections to other cells, and through the process of *synaptogenesis*, cells form a synapse with some of the cells to which they connect. A correlation of activity patterns in neurons that are close to each other promotes the formation of synapses. Initially there is an overabundance of synapses, which is reduced through the processes of *synaptic pruning* that occurs in part as a result of disuse. In addition to growing in size, neurons also sprout new dendrites through the process of *aborization*, and some neurons acquire a myelin sheath along their axons through the process of *myelination*, which speeds up their firing (Brynes, 2001). Cortical development and the processes of synaptogenesis, myelination, and dendritic arborization proceed regionally and hierarchically, with construction in some regions dependent on the prior development of others, from primary motor and sensory areas to higher association areas in the temporal, parietal, and frontal lobes. The prefrontal cortex is the latest structure to mature and undergoes the greatest postnatal development.

The protracted postnatal period of development of the human brain creates the opportunity for experiences to influence both the structure and function of some cortical regions. Brain development involves two types of neural plasticity. *Experience-expectant* plasticity relies on the regularities in the environment to shape the development of neural circuits, and the mechanism of change involves overproduction of synapses followed by pruning. *Experience-dependent* plasticity involves the creation of new synapses or reorganization of synapses in response to experiences with unique features of the environment (Brynes, 2001), primarily through a process of progressive elaborations in cortical structure. Environmental stimulation can have different effects on brain structure and functioning, depending on the neurodevelopmental process operative at the time. The effects can be negative as well as positive. For example, viral infections such as meningitis can have a pronounced deleterious effect during the early neonatal period when the process of proliferation, migration, and differentiation are going on at the same time (Brynes, 2001).

Brain growth, cognitive development, and learning all occur in cyclical growth spurts, and cognitive development and brain development go together (Fisher, 2008). That is, there is a link between a cortical growth spurt and the emergence of new levels of skills and functioning that arise through a cyclical process of rewiring and retuning of neural networks (Fisher, 2008). Neurons that fire together, wire together—that is, form synapses with each other—and experience strengthens these synaptic connections and the functions they support. Differences in neural networks arise from differential experiences that shape the brain to more efficiently support specific functions. Thus, learning can be understood as an extended cyclical process of repeatedly building and rebuilding performance through synaptic reorganization.

Caution is needed in extrapolating from findings regarding brain development to the implications for teaching and learning, particularly with regard to viewing periods of brain development as time-limited "critical periods" for the impact of specific types of educational experiences. The neural correlates of cognitive processes have been identified, and links have been established between cognitive processes and educational practices: "However, the current state of knowledge does not allow direct extrapolation from brain growth cycles to educational practices" (Fisher, 2008, p. 146). The links from educational practice to learning and neurocognitive processes have not yet been established (Bruer, 2008). The linking of specific instructional methods to particular patterns of synapse generation as a way to enhance both brain growth and functional performance is as yet unwarranted. It is reasonable to view periods of neurocortical development as times of sensitivity to stimulation that fosters the development of the neurocortical circuits that in turn support cognitive functions. The beneficial effects of specific practices, however, must be demonstrated empirically and not just assumed. Furthermore, the brain is not just the passive recipient of environmental stimulation. The person actively shapes his or her environment and intentionally pursues some experiences and not others.

While the claims of a narrow critical time period in which specific instructional must occur are unwarranted, we know that optimal functioning requires both the readiness of the system to respond to input and the appropriate input (Brynes, 2001). The reshaping of the brain occurring during the period of emerging adulthood provides the necessary context of readiness to engage in experiences that promote the development of the capacities necessary to accomplish the cognitive and psychosocial tasks associated with the transition from childhood to adulthood. We turn now to a consideration of those developmental tasks.

Developmental Tasks: Psychosocial

Neurocognitive development is not the only change going on during the period of emerging adulthood. This period is also characterized by changing societal expectations with regard to the nature and level of functioning. Within a developmental systems perspective, the biologically based drive toward growth combined with the expectations, constraints, and opportunities provided by the social environment give rise to the concept of *developmental tasks* that need to be mastered throughout the life course. Developmental tasks arise from three sources: physical maturation, such as learning to walk; societal expectations, such as learning to read; and personal desires and values, such as career aspirations (Havighurst, 1972). Successful achievement of each developmental task is viewed as necessary for success with later tasks. It is appropriate to consider the role of higher education in promoting the accomplishment of the developmental tasks that characterize the period of emerging adulthood.

Foremost among the developmental tasks in the adolescent and emerging adulthood periods is the process of identity formation. This is essentially a process of self-authorship: coming to know who you are, what you believe in and value, to whom and to what you want to commit, and what you want to accomplish and get out of life. One must come to terms with new potentialities for thinking, feeling, and acting and rearrange one's self-image accordingly.

A second task is to continue the process of developing competencies. This is crucial to self-definition. This is not just a matter of acquiring knowledge and developing cognitive, interpersonal, and technical skills, but also the capacity for independent thought. We know that competence is fostered by the combination of optimal challenges, feedback that the person is efficacious, and freedom from demeaning evaluations (Ryan & Deci, 2000).

A third task is to develop autonomy, not just in terms of independence, but also in terms of the capacities for self-motivation and self-regulation. Mature autonomy is manifested through openness to change and to growth and a willingness to push oneself—not frenetically but purposefully, to develop intellectually and personally. Mature autonomy is also manifested in the motivation to seek new knowledge based on the belief about the value of knowledge and in the ability to commit to a point of view. We know that autonomy is fostered by contexts that the person perceives as affording choices and freedom from external pressure toward behaving or thinking in a certain way (Ryan & Deci, 2000).

A fourth task is to develop the capacity for intimacy, which refers to experiencing mutual openness, responsiveness, and a sense of closeness in friendships and relationships (Collins & Steinberg, 2006). Intimacy complements autonomy in terms of being able "to experience others' needs and concerns as equally important as one's own" (Colarusso, 1995, p. 2498). This capacity for intimacy is essential for success with the challenges of marriage and parenthood that, along with establishing a career, are among the major markers of adulthood in our society.

The challenge for higher education is to foster students' accomplishment of these developmental tasks. To be responsive to the advances in our understanding of human development in general, and emerging adulthood in particular, colleges and universities must intentionally promote their students' development of higher-order cognitive skills and nurture the process of self-authorship so that students integrate their intellectual skills into a sense of identity that includes beliefs, values, and commitments. In short, a more formative and integrative developmental approach to education is required.

Developmental Tasks: Higher-Order Mental Capacities

One way to understand the developmental changes associated with emerging adulthood is with regard to the increasing expectations and demands of modern culture on a person's mental capacities (Kegan, 1994). We have come to recognize the qualitative changes in mental capacities that occur with the development of the brain across childhood, adolescence, and adulthood. The mental demands that the social environment and culture make as the person develops go beyond the mastery of knowledge and the acquisition of specific skills, and include qualitatively different ways of knowing and making meaning. These considerations lead to a focus on assessing the fit between societal expectations at any point in development and the person's mental capabilities. More specifically, we can consider the mental demands of society and of higher education.

Qualitative changes and differences in mental capacities can be understood with regard to the growth in how a person constructs meaning (Kegan, 1994). From a constructivist perspective, people do not passively absorb reality but rather actively shape and give meaning and coherence to their experiences. There is a hierarchical order of complexity involved in constructing and organizing meaning in which basic principles are subsumed by more complex, higher-order principles.

In his seminal book *In Over Our Heads*, Robert Kegan (1994) characterizes this hierarchical order of complexity in terms of "order of consciousness" levels which progress from the concrete to the abstract. The first order involves prelogical sensations; the second order involves forming concrete durable categories such as objects, emotions, needs, roles, and self-concept; the third order involves abstracting cross-categorical relationships among these durable categories; the fourth order involves establishing relationships between the relationships; and the fifth order involves critical analysis of the system.

Kegan (1994) uses this analytic framework to clarify the levels of mental capabilities with regard to ways of knowing and constructing meaning, which are expected in higher education. Adolescents typically manifest the third order of mental complexity reflected in their abilities to self-reflect, form abstract generalizations, make inferences, and generate hypotheses. Higher education, however, expects adolescents and young adults to function at least at the fourth level of mental capabilities, as evidenced by the commonly espoused expectations for students to be self-directed and engaged learners.

These expectations encompass an array of complex skills. We expect students to be self-initiating; to set their own goals and standards; to take responsibility for their learning; to engage in self-evaluation and self-correction; and to exercise skills in critical analysis, time management, information gathering, and use of educational resources. These are not just skills to be taught and learned. Rather, what is required is for the student to develop a level of mental complexity that enables *self-direction*, a view of oneself as a cocreator of the environments that shape us; and *self-evaluation*, or distinguishing between what one knows, feels, values, or does from what one *should* know, feel, value, or do. Thus, in the process of higher education, students are asked to transform the ways in which they understand themselves, the world, and the relation between the two (Kegan, 1994). Often these changes in understanding involve issues of identity across domains such as ethnicity, religion, and social class, and with regard to commitments to goals and values. These transformations in understanding link the development of higher-order mental capabilities with the formation of an integrated identity, which is the central developmental task of adolescence and emerging adulthood.

Beyond self-direction, higher education also expects students to be intellectually engaged learners in general, but also particularly, with regard to a major or field of study. More specifically, students are expected to engage their learning with "the cognitive sophistication necessary to master the knowledge-generating and knowledge-validating processes of an intellectual field or discipline" (Kegan, 1994, p. 285). Intellectual disciplines are more than repositories of facts and principles; they are systematic, public procedures for generating and evaluating ideas, opinion, and hypotheses. Whereas third-order thinking is sufficient for a student to participate in a disciplinary community, fourth-order thinking is needed to subject inferences and opinions to systematic evaluation and to synthesize new formulations. The fifth order of mental complexity is required for evaluation of the formulations of the fourth order and critical analysis of the discipline itself (Kegan, 1994).

As educators we do not just teach skills. We must also create environments that promote transformations in mental capabilities and ways of thinking, knowing, and understanding. This aim is one of the distinctions between training and education. A training model focuses on providing information—that is, *changing what people know*—but does not necessarily aim to change the form of thinking. Education aims to be transformational, and focuses on changing the form of thinking—in other words, *transforming how people know*. Education involves providing coaching, modeling, and scaffolding for the gradual growth of mental capabilities from the level of concrete fact of the second order, to the level of abstraction and inferences of the third order, to the level of cross-categorical, evaluative, and formative relationships of the fourth order, to the level of critical, evaluative, stance of the fifth order. Neither too much support for the existing mental capacities nor too much challenge to think at a new level of mental complexity promotes development in ways of thinking. Rather, a balance of support and challenge is necessary to foster engagement and promote development (Kegan, 1994).

The magnitude of the challenge for higher education is reflected in the contention that only half the adult population is functioning at the fourth level of mental complexity (Kegan, 1994). The good news is that transformations in ways of thinking are demonstrated by some students. We would like to believe that this transformation is, at least in part, a function of the educational experience provided. To make such transformations a normative expectation for college and university graduates, however, we first need to determine the mechanisms of effect with regard to how specific educational practices evoke transformations in thinking.

Developmental tasks, whether considered from a psychosocial perspective or in terms of mental capacities, are intertwined such that in the process of moving from a novice to an expert, ways of thinking and reasoning are enhanced, specific skills are learned, self-knowledge is gained, and commitment to a point of view and choice of beliefs are manifested. The academic community, in particular, constitutes a special environment with characteristics that foster the accomplishments of these developmental tasks.

THE ACADEMIC COMMUNITY AS DEVELOPMENTAL CONTEXT

As an academic community, colleges and universities embrace values and principles that promote human development. The academic community is characterized by its commitment to freedom of inquiry and expression, respect for individual differences, civility of discourse, and competition of ideas and values as the best method to successive approximations to the truth. The common bond that unites all members of the academic community is the pursuit of increased knowledge and understanding.

Several distinguishing principles guide the interaction of members of the academic community. The first is academic integrity. It is essential for the work of the community that there is no deceit and no misrepresentation. Second, force and coercion have no place in an academic community. We rely on reason, evidence, and dialogue. Third, knowledge and understanding are considered provisional, subject to revision upon new evidence. The aim is to replace good ideas with better ideas. Fourth, competition of ideas and values is the method for attaining successive approximations to the truth, and is facilitated by multiple perspectives achieved not only through an array of disciplinary lenses, but also through the diversity of experiences and perspectives of faculty, staff, and students. Fifth, education is not a spectator sport or a commodity purchased at university concession stands. We are all learners and learn from each other, and undergraduates are expected to be active participants in the community of learners. Sixth, each member of the academic community holds oneself and each other accountable for functioning in accordance with these core values and principles. As with all community memberships, it is essential that these values and principles be made explicit to students who have been accepted into the academic community, so that they understand and embrace the expectations and responsibilities of membership.

DEVELOPMENTAL MODEL OF EDUCATION

Colleges and universities need to go beyond articulating and practicing these basic principles and values to intentionally employ their resources to promote the accomplishment of the essential developmental tasks of emerging adulthood. One of the transformations that higher education needs to make in response to advances in our understanding of human development is to adopt a developmental model of undergraduate education to inform considerations about the purpose of higher education and to guide choices about educational outcomes and practices.

There is no single developmental model, but rather a way of thinking about education that draws on various theories and empirical evidence regarding progressive changes in cognitive and psychosocial dimensions of development that characterize the late adolescent and emerging adulthood periods in our culture. More specifically, adopting a developmental model focuses attention on the mutual influence of development and education, and provides a framework for considering both the role of educational practices in fostering cognitive and psychosocial development and the implications that the development of these capabilities have for educational practices.

Adopting a developmental model of education provides a basis for integrating academic and student life dimensions of the undergraduate experience around the common task of promoting development of the whole person. Experiential pedagogies in particular, such as service-learning courses that combine community service with classroom experience, "have strong potentials to unite elements too long separated in the academy: thinking and feeling, reflection and action, theory and practice" (Brandenberger, 2005, p. 319).

A developmental model can also serve to guide the intentional sequencing of experiences that promote readiness for successive challenges across the undergraduate years. For example, the first year can be conceived as a period of transition into the academic community during which students are acculturated to its main values and develop the competencies they need to be active participants. These competencies include learning how to join an intellectual conversation, formulate and support an argument, and make claims in public space. This is a time of developing one's voice as a member of the community and having the experience of being taken seriously for the quality of one's thoughts and ideas.

The sophomore and junior years are a time of building intellectual, personal, and leadership competencies that involve acquiring a depth of knowledge and understandings through a major or interdisciplinary course of study and through multiple opportunities for engaged experiences such as study abroad, service learning, research, and internships. These competencies also include moving beyond tolerance of differences to respect for traditions and identities different than one's own and to an affirmation of the value of diversity as a way of enriching one's life. This is a time for deepening civic engagement through developing active agency for community change as a component of one's identity, learning how to link inquiry to the social good, and developing the capacities for discernment and commitment. The senior year is both a culminating and a transitional period: culminating in the sense of refining and integrating intellectual and personal skills and the capacities for autonomy and self-regulation; transitional in the sense of fostering engagement with the next phase of development that will continue in the larger world beyond the university.

With the beginning of the twenty-first century, we now see converging trends in the changes that are occurring along the continuum of higher education from colleges through research universities to professional schools. Colleges and universities, adopting practices that have characterized professional education, are enhancing undergraduate education by directly engaging students in the inquiry and discovery processes and application of knowledge to societal problems through experiential and service-learning programs. Professional education, with its emphasis on developing the competencies, commitments, and sense of responsibility for clients, is now striving to incorporate humanistic learning objectives of enhanced capacities for empathy and insight into the human condition that characterize the liberal education. This convergence of liberal and practical goals and approaches in conjunction with the specific societal needs of the twenty-first century sets the stage for a reformulation of the purposes of an undergraduate education. This reformulation involves a reaffirmation of the value of a formative liberal education committed to fostering the development of the whole person as not only practical, but necessary to prepare students to confront the challenges of our globally interconnected, and increasingly conflicted, world.

This focus on developing the whole person does not suggest a diminution of focus on intellectual development. On the contrary, enhanced critical analyses skills are essential, and educational goals must include developing students' capacities to evaluate perspectives, ideas, and diverse bodies of knowledge. Students must develop their capacities for appraisal, discernment of excellence and error, and self-correction. The role of higher education is not just to pass on traditions, but more importantly, to model and teach students how to interpret and find meaning in traditions and evaluate what intellectual positions are worthy of transmission. Furthermore, with knowledge now recognized as the most important factor in economic and social progress, universities must not only produce knowledge in the service of society but also foster the critical analysis of the implications of trends in knowledge production and application.

Students in turn must learn to resist clichés, dogma, doctrine, and received ideas and accept responsibility for reasoning to a coherent conclusion and judgment, or, as James White (2004) remarked, learn "to think oneself to the point where one actually has something valuable to say or do" (p. 119).

Along with developing their analytic reasoning skills, students must also acquire an appreciation of the higher purposes for which these skills are needed and formulate a sense of identity that includes utilizing their skills and capabilities to improve society. William Cronon (1998) has eloquently expressed the higher purpose of a liberal education "to nurture the growth of human talent in the service of human freedom" (p. 74) and nurture "human freedom in the service of human community" (p. 80).

While a commitment to community and civic engagement is an integral part of a liberal education, the application of a constructively critical perspective is also needed in a liberal democracy. Thus, a liberal education

> would encourage both an empathetic understanding and a critical assessment of the different social arrangements and cultural experiences designed to give meaning to our individual and community lives (Shapiro, 1997, p. 90).

It is also clear that the growth in human talent that is needed is not limited to enhanced reasoning ability, but includes other dimensions of human development as well. William Cronon (1998) provides a comprehensive rendering of the outcomes that are the aim of a liberal education through his delineation of the characteristics of liberally educated people:

> They have the intellectual range and emotional generosity to step outside their own experiences and prejudices, thereby opening themselves to perspectives different from their own (pp. 77–78).
> They work hard to hear what other people say. They can follow an argument, track logical reasoning, detect illogic, hear the emotions that lie behind both the logic and the illogic, and ultimately empathize with the person who is feeling those emotions (p. 76).
> They nurture and empower the people around them (p. 78).
> [They] understand that they belong to a community whose prosperity and well-being are crucial to their own, and they help that community flourish by making the success of others possible (p. 78).
> They understand that knowledge serves values, and they strive to put these two-knowledge and values-into constant dialogue with each other (p. 77).

BEYOND REASON

American higher education adapts in response to societal needs for knowledge, expertise, and leadership. The knowledge-based, globally interconnected world of the twenty-first century requires lifelong learners who are civic-minded and have the intellectual capabilities, personal skills, and dispositions to constructively engage political, ethnic, and religious differences. It is the premise of this book that meeting these societal needs requires that higher education adapt by transforming its purpose and practices. More specifically, it is argued that colleges and universities must restore the goal of providing a formative liberal education of the whole person and adopt a developmental model of education to guide its practices.

In addition to developing students' capacity for reasoning, it is further argued that colleges and universities must foster the development of three capacities in particular that are necessary to move beyond tolerance and constructively engage difference: personal epistemology, empathy, and an integrated sense of identity that includes commitment to social responsibility and civic engagement. Subsequent chapters present a review, through a developmental science perspective, of our understanding about the nature of these dimensions of functioning and how undergraduate experiences both inside and outside of the classroom can promote the development of these essential capacities.

To return to Derek Bok's (2006) call to address the purposes of higher education, this book argues that the purpose is to provide a formative liberal education that empowers students for a life of meaning and purpose through developing the whole person. The aim is for students to discover that they have developed their own unique personal style; that they have something to say in their own way; that they are responsible for what they say and do; that they are worthy of self-respect and the respect of others; and ultimately to realize their own humanity as a creative, empathetic, and committed person.

CHAPTER 3
Personal Epistemology

Individuals who can weigh competing truth claims, evaluate sources of evidence, and understand how knowledge evolves in a field are essential to the effective functioning of democratic societies (Hofer & Sinatra, 2010, p. 118).

One of the goals of a formative liberal education is to transform students' ways of thinking, knowing, and understanding. The aim is to assure that students function at the evaluativist level of thinking with regard to themselves as well as the larger world within which they live and work. Evaluativist level thinking is reflected in the capacities to construct meaning, evaluate different perspectives, discern among competing claims, and constructively engage differences.

This goal to transform students' way of thinking and knowing, however, is rarely made explicit. All colleges and universities emphasize the development of critical thinking but typically do not identify the underlying cognitive processes, intentionally foster the developmental progression involved, or determine the types of educational experiences that promote transformations in ways of thinking. Moreover, it is not evident that faculty give much consideration to the level of thinking of their students or to the level required to accomplish the objectives of their courses. Faculty appear to assume that all students arrive on campus functioning at the evaluativist level of thinking. Therefore, ensuring that students develop this level of thinking is not recognized as part of their teaching mission. The evidence, however, indicates that many students graduate from college not having achieved an evaluative level of thinking (Kuhn et al., 2000).

This chapter addresses ways of thinking and knowing and has two objectives. The first objective is to review our current understanding of the nature and development of beliefs about knowledge, ways of knowing, evaluative thinking, and the formation of an integrated personal epistemology. The second objective is to increase student and faculty awareness about the goals of undergraduate education with regard to ways of thinking and knowing. If students have a more sophisticated understanding of the aims and basis of the undergraduate experience and how it is structured, they then can intentionally engage the experience in ways to optimize their intellectual and personal development and learning. Similarly, if faculty see that part of their task is to transform students' ways of thinking and knowing, they can modify their teaching and mentoring practices to accomplish this task.

Research on students' beliefs about the nature of knowledge and the process of knowing was initiated with the work of William Perry (1970), who proposed that beliefs about knowledge spanned nine levels of development from the absolutist view that facts are handed-down by authority to the relativistic view that knowledge is tentative and derived from reason and empirical inquiry (Hofer & Pintrich, 1997). Subsequently, research has addressed the progression in the development of students' beliefs about knowledge and how these beliefs influence the processes of reasoning and learning (Hofer & Pintrich, 1997). However, before considering these findings and implications, we first need to review the philosophical foundations regarding the nature and justification of knowledge.

PHILOSOPHICAL CONSIDERATIONS

Epistemology is the branch of philosophy that is concerned with the nature and justification of human knowledge; that is, the "theory of knowledge." More specifically, epistemology focuses on propositional knowledge ("knowing that") and not performance knowledge ("knowing how"). *Knowledge* is generally understood to be a true belief that is appropriately justified (Rescher, 2003). Different philosophical views or positions exist about the criteria for justifying knowledge claims.

Foundationalist philosophies maintain that knowledge claims or beliefs require a secure noninferential foundation established either through reasoning (*rationalism*) or experience (*empiricism*). For rationalists, such as Descartes, the foundation is some form of clear and distinct idea, or synthetic a priori claim or theologically privileged claim. For the empiricists, such as Locke, the foundation is some form of direct experience. These foundationalist approaches have in common a knowledge claim and reasons or evidence that ground those claims (Southerland et al., 2001).

Positivism is a form of empiricism that emphasizes not only that knowledge originates in experiences, but also that knowledge claims must be justified or warranted in terms of competently gathered empirical evidence (observation, data) and accepted by the appropriate research community. Positivism also emphasizes defining concepts in terms of the operations or procedures used to measure the concept (Phillips & Burbules, 2000). One of the problems with positivism, however, is that no number of positive tests can prove, or negative tests disprove, a hypothesis because any finite set of data can be accounted for in more than one way. Furthermore, through inductive reasoning we extend our knowledge beyond the evidence available such that conclusions are not certain but can be more or less probable.

These problems with positivism have led to a nonfoundational, postpositivist, orientation to epistemology that recognizes that there are no ultimate sources of knowledge (Phillips & Burbules, 2000). Postpositivism embraces the *fallibilism* position that we can never know anything to be absolutely true. Knowledge is considered conjectural and therefore always open to reconsideration, and knowledge claims can be withdrawn or revised upon further investigation and evidence. Although certainty is not a condition of knowledge, comparisons can be made between competing theories or propositions and one can be judged better than another (Southerland et al., 2001).

Types and Sources of Knowledge

It is customary to distinguish several types of knowledge. For example, propositional or declarative knowledge refers to "what is," whereas procedural knowledge refers to "how to," and conditional knowledge refers to "when to." There also have been numerous theories and views about the source of knowledge and the process of knowing. Murphy et al. (2012) have reviewed and organized these theories in terms of the intersection of claims regarding two central issues: (1) The source of knowledge (horizontal axis), ranging from the view that knowledge is individually formed and solely the construction of one's mind to socially derived from the social, cultural, and physical world; and (2) the location of knowledge (vertical axis), ranging from "in the mind" of the knower (that is, knowledge entails acquiring or processing information that is stored in the mind) to the view that knowledge resides in the environment, is socially mediated and culturally embedded, and bound to some specific time or place (Murphy et al., 2012). Social constructivism is an example of a theory defined as Socially Derived and In the Mind, whereas postmodernism is an example of a theory defined as Socially Derived and In the Environment. Behaviorism is an example of a theory defined as Individually Formed and In the Environment, whereas foundationalism is an example of a theory defined as In the Mind and Individually Formed.

Multiple Ways of Knowing

There is no single way in which people come to know something. Individuals employ different cognitive and affective processes and different justification criteria. However, efforts have been undertaken to delineate and categorize specific ways of knowing as a means of understanding individual differences and also the basic epistemology of different academic disciplines and fields.

One example is Royce's (1978; 1983) proposal of three basic ways of knowing that rely primarily on different cognitive processes and employ different justification criteria:

- *Rationalism* involves the cognitive process of conceptualizing, and relies more on deductive than inductive reasoning. Claims are accepted as true if logically consistent and rejected as false if illogical.
- *Empiricism* involves the cognitive processes of perceiving and analysis of the meaning of experiences or data, and relies on inductive more than deductive reasoning. Claims are judged on the accuracy of perception and strength of evidence.
- *Metaphorism* involves the cognitive process of symbolizing; that is, the formation of representations of reality, and is more analogical than inductive or deductive. Claims depend on the degree to which symbolic representations lead to universal awareness.

Individuals employ all of these ways of knowing, but depending on their relative reliance on the underlying cognitive process of conceptualizing, perceiving, and symbolizing, their epistemic style can be characterized as typically rationalist, empiricist, or metaphoric (Royce, 1983). In making such a characterization it must be realized that ways of thinking are not a fixed, immutable trait, and individuals demonstrate different ways of thinking depending on the specific context (Hofer & Sinatra, 2010). Also, the underlying cognitive processes do not operate independently of each other (Royce, 1978).

In contrast to the view of knowing as rational and analytic and involving various cognitive processes, other ways of knowing also have been recognized. For example, *intuition* refers to the direct apprehension of the overall form or structure of the perception of the situation conveyed by the senses (Arnheim, 1985). *Aesthetics,* typically associated with the arts, is recognized as another mode of knowing that involves the making of forms "that give rise to feeling" (Eisner, 1985, p. 27): "Whether collective or individual, the common function of the aesthetic is to modulate form so as that it can, in turn, modulate our experiences" (Eisner, 1985, p. 25).

There is also an affective, phenomenological dimension to knowing that can be relatively unconscious. Experience is the base of both cognitive and affective knowing, but a phenomenological perspective positions experience as a verb, a felt encounter, rather than as a noun; that is, a resource that can be objectified and reflected on (Yorks & Kasal, 2002). The phenomenological perspective calls attention to expressive ways of knowing, or to forms of expression that engage the person's imagination and intuition (Davis-Manigaulte et al., 2006). One form of expressive knowing is through the process of empathy—knowing others by sharing or identifying with their emotional experiences. The nature, components, and development of empathy are the focus of our next chapter. For our purposes, it is useful to recognize that there are different ways of knowing that rely on different cognitive/analytic and affective/expressive process and justification criteria. The cognitive and affective processes are, however, interrelated.

Distinguishing Knowledge and Beliefs

Differentiating between the constructs of knowledge and beliefs has been a focus in both philosophy and psychology. Knowledge is commonly understood as a true belief that has been justified. Not all beliefs are true, some are inaccurate, and some are incompatible. The challenge is to provide a basis for distinguishing true beliefs from beliefs that are not true.

The dominant epistemological position has been that knowledge is verifiable in some objective way whereas beliefs are subjective and affect laden (Southerland et al., 2001). However, the notion of objectivity itself has been challenged. In particular, postmodern critiques reject the notion of an objective reality independent of human thought, deny that there is a distinction between knowledge and beliefs, view knowledge not as objective but as a social construction, and assert that there is no unfiltered access to the physical world but rather that knowledge claims reflect the influence of the knower and her or his culture.

Consistent with the understanding that the mind is active in the construction of knowledge by making connections, social constructivist epistemologies view humans as constructing knowledge rather than discovering an objective reality. People formulate concepts, models, and schemes "to make sense of experience" and "continually test and modify these constructions in the light of new experience," and do so against a sociocultural "backdrop of shared understandings and practices" (Schwandt, 2000, p. 197). One can accept the social construction of knowledge, however, and also hold that there is "truth to the matter" of interpretations and not subscribe to the view that "any interpretation is as good as another" (Schwandt, 2000).

In response to the postmodern critiques, the fallibilist position is that although knowledge is socially constructed and imperfect, and we can never know anything with absolute certainty, useful comparisons can be made between competing positions: "What is at issue here is the adequacy and nature of the justification of a proposition," and "there are very different epistemological warrants supporting knowledge propositions than support beliefs" (Southerland et al., 2001, p. 345). Truth is not a matter of strength of belief or the existence of reasons for the belief. People have reasons for their beliefs, but those reasons are not held to the same evidential criteria as knowledge. A belief is not a weak form of empiricism. Beliefs are a more subjective way of knowing that are not dependent on empirical evidence (Southerland et al., 2001). That is, beliefs are not held to the same epistemic criteria as knowledge. Beliefs are inherently subjective and based on "personal conviction, opinions, and degree of congruence with other belief systems" (Southerland & Sinatra, 2003, p. 319). This distinction between knowledge and beliefs based on the evaluation of evidence is made even clearer in some areas of science where it is customary to distinguish between "belief in" and "acceptance of" a theory or claim (Southerland & Sinatra, 2003). Indicating that one believes in a theory implies that the judgment of the validity of the claims is based on subjective criteria, whereas indicating that one accepts a theory implies that the recognition of the validity of the claims is based on systematic evaluation of the evidence rather than merely opinion.

As we engage a consideration of epistemic beliefs and personal epistemology, it is useful to sharpen our focus. We can consider human understanding along a continuum ranging from claims about the physical and social world based on the senses and consensually justified in terms of objective referents to claims about aesthetics, tastes, and opinions that are based on subjective, internal referents (Chandler & Proulx, 2010). While remaining open to new understandings, we can accept some claims as facts and others as personal preferences. It is the middle ground, often involving values and based on insights, theories, and propositional statements derived from our understanding of our physical and social worlds, that requires an evaluative epistemology to adjudicate. There are several compelling reasons for adopting a postpositive approach to epistemology.

The postpositive approach promotes a quest for knowledge that is self-corrective. It seeks to establish criteria and methods that can support truth claims that do not depend on subjective experience (Phillips & Burbules, 2000). The postpositive approach embraces a pluralism of methods. The methods appropriate for investigating phenomena at the micro level of the cell are not appropriate at other levels, such as the macro level of society. No matter the level of the phenomena, competent inquiry in all fields has similar characteristics and employs standards of truth and falsity that subject propositions or hypotheses to potential disconfirmation and revision (Phillips & Burbules, 2000).

PERSONAL EPISTEMOLOGY

With these philosophical considerations of epistemology as background, we can now consider the construct of *personal epistemology*, which "refers to what individuals think knowledge is and how they think that they and others know"

(Hofer & Bendixen, 2012, p. 227). Hofer and Pintrich (1997) proposed that personal epistemology encompasses two areas, an individual's beliefs about the nature of knowledge and the nature of knowing, with two dimensions in each area, each expressed on a continuum. With regard to the nature of knowledge, the two dimensions include the certainty of knowledge ranging from a view of knowledge as fixed and absolute to a position that knowledge is fluid, tentative, and evolving; and the simplicity of knowledge ranging from viewing knowledge as simple, discrete, knowable facts to complex, interrelated, contingent, and contextual ideas. With regard to the nature of knowing, the two dimensions include the source of knowledge that is completely outside of the knower and transmitted from authority or constructed by the knower in interaction with texts, experiences, experts, and others; and the justification for knowledge, or the ways in which individuals evaluate knowledge claims ranging from uncritical acceptance of facts and opinions to evaluating competing claims bases on reasoning and evidence, and the ability to support claims and coordinate theory with evidence (Hofer & Bendixen, 2012).

Conceptualizations of Epistemic Belief and Models of Personal Epistemology

Research has focused on how personal epistemology is conceptualized, how epistemic beliefs develop and change qualitatively as a function of maturation and experiences, and how epistemic beliefs are related to other dimensions of development, learning, and engagement. Several models of epistemic beliefs and personal epistemology have been formulated, including *The Reflective Judgment Model* (King & Kitchener, 2004), *The Epistemological Reflection Model* (Magolda, 2004), *The Embedded Systemic Model* (Schommer-Aikins, 2004), and the *Integrated Model* (Bendixen & Rule, 2004). These models build on each other and reflect the progression in conceptualizing the nature and development of personal epistemology. One way to synthesize our current understanding of the construct of personal epistemology is to address, across the models, the major paradigmatic issues regarding the conceptualization of epistemic beliefs and the mechanisms of change (Bendixen & Rule, 2004).

A major contribution of the *Epistemological Reflection Model* is the conceptualization of personal epistemology as socially constructed (Magolda, 2004). This model proposes that the individual's assumptions about knowledge and the process of knowing themselves and the world influence their construction, interpretation, and evaluation of information; that is, the process of making-meaning of their experiences (Magolda, 2004). Personal epistemology is interrelated with other dimensions of development including identity and social relationships and involves the intertwining of cognitive ("How do I know?"), intrapersonal ("Who am I?"), and intrapersonal ("What kind of relationships do I want?") dimensions (Kegan, 1994). An understanding of knowledge as socially constructed is essential to the complex ways of meaning-making associated with moving from dependence on authority to *self-authorship*. This sense of self-authorship involves taking responsibility for one's beliefs, identity, and relationships and provides both the foundation for deciding what to believe and the drive to integrate core beliefs into an internal belief system that guides one's life (Magolda, 2004). Self-authorship, personal meaning-making, and the engagement with others are central in the social construction of knowledge.

The Embedded Systemic Model also posits that personal epistemology is a system among other systems, including cognition, affect, and motivation. The particular contribution of this model is the inclusion of beliefs about the ability to learn (fixed at birth or improvable) and the speed of learning (quick or gradual) (Schommer-Aikins, 2004). A developmental progression is proposed from immature to more complex views that support higher-order thinking, but it is also recognized that development can be asynchronous; individuals can express different levels of epistemic sophistication across different situations and about different matters.

Beyond socially constructed beliefs about knowledge and the processes of knowing and learning, personal epistemology has also been conceptualized as a cognitive developmental process, as a system of beliefs, and as a metacognitive process (Hofer, 2004). Personal epistemology conceptualized as a cognitive developmental progression involves moving from a dualistic and absolutist view of knowledge through a relativistic perspective to regarding knowledge as continuously evolving and coordinated with justification. Personal epistemology conceptualized as a system of beliefs involves ways of knowing both at the domain-general and domain-specific levels. Individuals are seen as typically having both an overall generalized theory of knowledge and specific theories about knowledge in different domains or disciplines. Personal epistemology conceptualized as a metacognitive process involves "knowing about knowing"—that is, a set of interrelated beliefs about knowledge and the process of knowing.

These three conceptualizations of personal epistemology are not mutually exclusive, but do have different implications for educational approaches (Hofer, 2004). For example, cognitive developmental conceptualizations consider epistemological sophistication as the outcome against which different educational approaches can be evaluated. In contrast, belief system conceptualizations view epistemic beliefs as the predictors of educational outcomes, such as learning and academic achievement. Metacognitive conceptualizations of personal epistemology include both outcome and predictor dimensions, and enables a more interactive conception of educational outcome as the dynamic process of learning and knowledge construction that is influenced by epistemic beliefs that are malleable.

Although it is generally recognized that epistemic beliefs refer to assumptions about the nature of knowledge and the process of knowing, it is important to include a third dimension in personal epistemology: the purpose of knowledge. One of the contributions of the postpositive approach has been the recognition that beliefs about knowledge have an impact on how knowledge is generated and used. The positivist approach that characterized higher education and the pursuit of knowledge in the early twentieth century was a socially detached view of knowledge that sought to separate "fact" from "values." William Sullivan (2000) points out that these positivist views, along with the societal needs of post-WWII for technological advances and upward mobility of the middle class, lead to a neglect of the question of purpose and to a "default program of instrumental individualism" that "leaves larger questions of social, political, and moral purpose out of explicit consideration" (p. 21). The postpositive alternative to the socially detached, positivist conception of knowledge and learning "emphasizes the fusion of fact and value in practical experience, the interconnection of means and ends" (p. 29). From this perspective, knowledge is viewed as growing out of the social process of inquiry and must be evaluated in relation to its public purposes. Thus, it is important to recognize that one's personal epistemology includes beliefs about the purposes and uses of knowledge as well as the nature of knowledge and the process of knowing. We can now turn our attention to a fuller consideration of how epistemic thinking develops.

EPISTEMIC DEVELOPMENT

We have seen that there is a consensus across models that there is a developmental progression in the sophistication of epistemic thinking about knowledge from the absolute through the relative to the evaluative level. For example, *The Reflective Judgment Model* (King & Kitchener, 2004) proposes a seven stage developmental progression in the individual's underlying assumptions about knowledge, how knowledge is gained, and concepts of knowledge justification. Thinking is viewed as progressing from the level of prereflective thinking, in which knowledge is assumed to be certain and known by authorities and justification relies on restatement of beliefs; through quasi-reflective reasoning, in which it is recognized that knowledge is constructed and uncertain, there are multiple views, and evidence is a part of the knowing process; to reflective thinking, in which making a conclusion is firmly linked to evidence. These qualitative changes in thinking emerge through interactions with the environment that both challenge and support growth. Longitudinal studies provide support for this proposed developmental sequence and suggest that reflective thinking evolves slowly and steadily from adolescence through young adulthood (King & Kitchener, 2004). There are, however, differences across models and in research findings about the timing of the emergence of relativist and evaluativist thinking; when, and the extent to which, the individual's pattern becomes consistent; and the extent to which epistemic development is moderated or mediated by other dimensions of cognitive and social development.

In response to this diversity of findings, it has been argued that the most plausible explanation is that epistemic development is recursive and influenced by the transition in cognitive development from concrete to formal operational thinking (Chandler et al., 2002; Boyles & Chandler, 1992). More specifically, as children develop they progress through a sequence of epistemic levels: They first become aware that different people hold different beliefs about one and the same thing, then recognize that this diversity holds beyond a specific situation, and then understand that diversity of opinion and subjectivity are intrinsic to the knowing process. This progression requires the ability to generalize which in turn is dependent on having attained formal operational modes of thinking.

While there is a general consensus regarding a developmental progression in the sophistication of epistemic thinking about knowledge from the absolute through the relative to the evaluative level, the limitations of a stage model have been recognized. In particular, the multiple defining features of any stage make it difficult to identify both the essence of each stage and what drives the movement from one stage to another (Kuhn & Weinstock, 2002). In response, Kuhn and Weinstock (2002) argue that "the developmental task that underlies the achievement of mature epistemological understanding is the coordination of the objective and subjective ways of knowing" (p. 123). Thus, this coordination of the objective and the subjective serves as a developmental marker. The early epistemic levels are characterized by realist and absolutist thinking. The objective dimension is dominant and knowledge is viewed "as located in the external world and knowable with certainty" (p. 123). The next stage reflects a radical shift to multiplist thinking. The subjective dimension becomes dominant as the person becomes aware of conflicting assertions and "relocates the source of knowledge from the known object to the knowing subject" (p. 123). The highest level of epistemic thinking is characterized by evaluativist thinking. The objective dimension is reintegrated with the subjective by "acknowledging uncertainty without forsaking evaluation" (p. 123).

> Thus, two people can have legitimate positions—they both can be "right"— but one position can have more merit ("be more right") than the other to the extent that that position is better supported by argument and evidence (Kuhn & Weinstock, 2002, p. 123).

This integration of the objective and subjective dimensions drives the progression in qualitatively different ways of thinking about knowledge claims from facts to opinions to judgments, which is the essence of epistemological development (Kuhn & Weinstock, 2002).

In addition to the consensus about the developmental progression in sophistication of epistemic thinking, there is also a consensus that a sophisticated epistemological stance is characterized by viewing knowledge as tentative and evolving rather than certain and unchanging, as constructed rather than authoritative, as complex rather than simple, and as evaluative rather than relative/multiplist. However, just as it is recognized that individuals vary in the characteristics of their epistemic beliefs depending on the context, it has also been recognized that "a sophisticated epistemology does not consist of blanket generalizations that apply to all knowledge in all disciplines in all contexts; it incorporates contextual dependencies and judgments" (Elby & Hammer, 2001, p. 565).

Rather than considering it as more sophisticated to view all knowledge as tentative, it is more sophisticated to take in to consideration the discipline, the nature of the claim, and the intended use of the knowledge. For example, it would not be sophisticated to consider the claim that the heart pumps blood throughout the body to be tentative. The point to be made is that a sophisticated epistemology is nuanced and contextual and is employed in a discerning way. We would, however, expect an epistemologically sophisticated person to evaluate the competing claims based on an understanding of the assumptions about the source of knowledge and the justification for knowledge underlying those claims.

With this developmental progression in epistemic thinking, the awareness that knowledge is not absolute can lead to a loss of epistemic certainties and result in periods of *epistemic doubt*. This doubt can be unsettling and lead to periods of less sophisticated levels of thinking until new ways of responding to competing claims are formulated. Moreover, precisely because epistemic doubt is unsettling, it can motivate changes in epistemic thinking to resolve the doubt and alleviate the distress. Thus, we can understand the formation of personal epistemology as a recursive process and epistemic doubt as a catalyst for change. As we shall see in Chapter 5, epistemic doubt is also a catalyst for change in another recursive process, identity formation (Boyles & Chandler, 1992).

Mechanism of Change

If epistemic development is progressive and recursive and catalyzed by epistemic doubt, what are the mechanisms or processes by which changes in personal epistemology occur? Conceptualizations of personal epistemology as a developmental process adopt the Piagetian notion of *equilibration* as the mechanism or driving force by which the person progresses through the stages of cognitive development. Two processes are involved: assimilation, whereby new information is incorporated into one's existing beliefs; and accommodation, whereby new information cannot be assimilated and existing beliefs are reorganized or replaced to incorporate the new information.

The *integrated model* of personal epistemology focuses on accommodation as the mechanism of change with three interrelated components: epistemic doubt, epistemic volition, and resolution (Bendixen & Rule, 2004). The conditions for change or accommodation are personal relevance; that is, the individual has a personal stake in the matter, and dissonance (when the experience does not match expectations), which sets the stage for doubt. Doubting one's epistemic beliefs involves the recognition of a discrepancy between one's beliefs and new information, weighing the relevant evidence, and discerning the truthfulness of those beliefs. If this discernment results in evidence that seems credible, one can take action and change or reshape their beliefs if they have sufficient volition and motivation. Volition refers to the metacognitive awareness of the dissonance one is experiencing and intentionally accepting responsibility to take action to resolve it. Social expectations and relationships can encourage and facilitate or constrain change in epistemological beliefs. For example, peer relationships have been found to have an important role in initiating and resolving doubt. Beyond doubt and volition to resolve it, methods of resolution are also needed. Methods to resolve doubt include reflection, the process of reviewing experiences and analyzing the implications of beliefs, and social interaction, more specifically argumentation. Consistent with the notions of self-authorship and reshaping of beliefs emphasized by constructivist's approaches, the model allows for regression and recursive thinking as a part of the growth process (Bendixen & Rule, 2004). Causation is reciprocal: The person influences his or her environment and the environment influences the person's epistemic thinking.

With this understanding of the nature of the construct of personal epistemology and the developmental progression in ways of thinking and sophistication of epistemic beliefs, we can undertake a consideration of the implications for undergraduate education. We will examine the epistemological foundations of academic disciplines and then consider how the undergraduate experiences can foster the development of epistemic thinking and the formulation of a personal epistemology. But first, we must consider further the generation and interpretation of knowledge in contemporary society.

THE DISTRIBUTED NATURE OF KNOWLEDGE

The constructivist perspective views the individual as responsible for constructing knowledge and its justification and for bringing meaning to information. A sophisticated personal epistemology is considered to be characterized by a rejection of the view of knowledge as absolute and external authority as the source. Rather than receiving knowledge from authoritative sources, the person is responsible for constructing their own knowledge, in interaction with others.

In modern life, however, much of our knowledge is derived from other's experiences, expertise, and analysis not from our own. Data collection often amounts to gathering and assessing the knowledge claims made by experts. Furthermore, through the impact of modern information technologies, specialized information, even in professional fields such as science, medicine, law, and economics, is readily available. This information, however, is at various levels of vetting. Some information has been carefully prepared for general public consumption, but some information is intended for discourse among experts, is preliminary and contradictory, and has not yet been evaluated by other experts. Thus, individuals are increasingly confronted with the responsibility for evaluating the evidence in support of complex knowledge claims. Hypermedia technologies in particular bring challenges but also opportunities with regard to fostering personal epistemology (Hofer & Bendixen, 2012). Studies indicate that searching the Internet activates epistemic beliefs about knowledge and its justification, and that epistemic beliefs influence search approaches and evaluation of information (Hofer & Bendixen, 2012).

Returning to the issue of epistemological sophistication, a conceptual distinction can be made between first-hand and second-hand evaluation of knowledge claims (Bromme et al, 2010a). First-hand evaluation involves the person determining the veracity of knowledge claims directly through their own critical thinking about the consistency of claims with other pieces of knowledge. Second-hand evaluation transforms this direct evaluation of what is true to which source of knowledge is credible and relevant (Bromme et al., 2010a).

First-hand evaluations about the relevance and veracity of knowledge claims requires considerable domain-specific knowledge and expertise. Given the uneven distribution of specialized knowledge and expertise, "everyone is a layperson with regard to most knowledge domains" (Bromme et al., 2010a, p. 171) and must employ second-hand evaluations. Sophisticated second-hand evaluations requires knowledge about the division of cognitive labor and distribution of knowledge—that is, who is responsible for which topic, and how to discern among competing claims.

The evaluativist level of epistemological judgment can now be understood as reflecting a balance of first-hand evaluation ("Does this fit with my experiences?") and second-hand evaluation ("Is the source and argument/evidence credible?") (Bromme et al., 2010a) as well as the integration of the subjective and objective views of knowledge argued by Kuhn & Weinstock (2002). Improving epistemological judgments requires "improvement of a person's capacity to understand how specialized knowledge is distributed (who knows what) and to evaluate expert sources (whom to believe)" (Bromme et al., 2010a, p. 163). This level of sophisticated personal epistemology is the basis for critical thinking skills that all institutions of higher education seek to develop. Students need to develop an understanding of the distribution of knowledge and the conceptual differences and knowledge structures of disciplines; how the professional, academic, and institutional structures are organized in our society; and how to assess the relevance and veracity of knowledge claims (Bromme et al., 2010a). The implication for educational practice is that colleges and universities must intentionally promote the development of a sophisticated personal epistemology through curricular and pedagogical approaches that specifically target evaluative thinking as a leaning objective.

THE EPISTEMOLOGY OF ACADEMIC DISCIPLINES

Inherent to a liberal education is the commitment to a diversity of perspectives as reflected in the array of academic disciplines that differ in subject matter and methods. Just as we typically fail to make the transformative goal of a liberal education explicit, we also typically fail to make explicit how academic disciplines differ in their epistemological foundations. It seems that we assume that students will figure this out by themselves. Understanding of these foundations is necessary not only to appropriately evaluate claims, but also contributes to student's intellectual growth. One of the primary ways in which students develop sophisticated intellectual capacities is through their choice of a major or area of concentration. It is primarily through being enculturated into the discourse of an academic discipline or field that students move from novice to expert and in the process develop sophisticated ways of thinking and knowing and formulate their own personal epistemology. For these reasons, it is important to briefly consider the epistemology of academic disciplines as one component of the undergraduate context that influences personal epistemic development.

Differences in Subject Matter, Methods, and Truth Criteria

Disciplines differ in subject matter, the methods and cognitive processes involved in the construction of knowledge, and the truth criteria employed for the justification of claims. These differences are evident at the broadest level in the humanities and sciences. The humanities focus on human thought and action as text and rely on the method of *hermeneutics*, or the interpretation of meaning. For interpretations to be judged as valid, the interpreter must have some competently gathered evidence supporting the interpretation that meets the criteria of internal consistency and universality. The sciences focus on the natural and social world and rely on objective evidence that is publicly available for inspection and replicable by the relevant professional community (Phillips & Burbules, 2000).

One basis for distinguishing among academic disciplines is the extent to which the discipline has a clearly delineated *paradigm*, a framework of theory accepted by members of the field that specifies the problems for study and the appropriate methods to be used. Paradigms are considered more or less "hard" depending on adherence within the field to a specific content and methodology. For example, the physical and biological sciences are considered more paradigmatic or "hard," whereas the humanities are considered less paradigmatic or "soft," with the social sciences considered somewhere in between. While the choice of the descriptive terms "hard" and "soft" has proven unfortunate in suggesting relative strength, disciplines do differ with regard to the nature of the questions or subjects studied and methods employed. Academic domains also differ according to how concerned they are with the practical applications of knowledge. Those disciplines or subfield within a discipline that focus on theoretical development are referred to as "pure," whereas "applied" disciplines focus on using knowledge in practical ways. An analysis of scholars' judgments about the similarities of the subject matter of different academic areas (Biglan, 1973) indicated that academic disciplines could be organized in terms of three dimensions according to the extent of their concern with a single paradigm (hard vs. soft), application of knowledge (pure vs. applied), and systems of study (life system vs. nonlife system). It is useful to recognize the relative placement of different disciplines along these dimensions but it is also essential to recognize that these dimension are not mutually exclusive in that, for example, some disciplines have both pure and applied subareas and new disciplines emerge at the interface of existing disciplines as approaches and methods evolve to address new problems, questions, and understandings.

Differences in Ways of Knowing

As we have discussed above, it is generally recognized that there are three basic ways of knowing with different criteria for the justification of claims: rationalism, empiricism, and metaphorism (Royce, 1978; 1973). These different ways of knowing are evident across the array of academic disciplines that comprise the humanities, natural sciences, and social sciences, and disciplines can be characterized by an epistemic profile reflecting different weightings given to these three epistemologies (Muis et al., 2006). For example, a theoretical natural science such as physics gives primary weight to rational epistemology, little emphasize on empiricism, and very little or no weight to metaphorism; the empirical social sciences give emphasis to empiricism, whereas the interpretive social science emphasize metaphorism; the humanities give weight to metaphorism and rationalism; and the arts give primary weight to metaphorism.

Although there has been an enduring focus in higher education on developing critical thinking and reasoning as a general skill across academic disciplines, research is increasingly providing support for the view that reasoning is situation or domain-specific (Beyer et al., 2007). The evidence about whether personal epistemic beliefs are general or domain-specific, however, has been mixed. For example, a review of the findings from 19 studies that evaluated students' epistemic beliefs across a number of different academic disciplines found support for both domain specificity and domain generality in student's epistemic beliefs (Muis et al., 2006). Early in their academic experience students demonstrated a relatively consistent developmental level of epistemic beliefs across domains and their epistemic beliefs became more specific with increasing levels of exposure to a field. That is, students exhibited the epistemic beliefs appropriate to their academic field of study. Thus, the generality-specificity of epistemic beliefs is not an either–or issue.

The constructivist perspective acknowledges the importance of social context in the development of personal epistemology. One important context for undergraduates is the academic environment. Development of epistemic beliefs occurs as a function of interactions with one's context and is spiral-like rather than linear (Bendixen & Rule, 2004). There is, however, a general progression, such that "as individuals progress through higher levels of education, general epistemic beliefs are less dominant and domain-specific epistemic beliefs become more influential" (Muis et al., 2006, p. 31). Thus, personal epistemic beliefs are shaped by educational experiences through a process of enculturation, such that student's epistemic beliefs reflect their academic major as they learn to view knowledge and its justification from the same perspective as the academic community with which they associate and identify.

EPISTEMIC BELIEFS MATTER

Beliefs affect the ways in which individuals interpret and give meaning to their experiences, which in turn affects their processing of information and behavior. For example, some individuals view fundamental personal attributes such as intelligence or personality as relatively fixed, whereas other view these attributes as incremental and able to be modified (Molden & Dweck, 2006). Those holding a fixed view tend to interpret failure and setbacks as indicative of inability and threatening to their self-esteem and respond by employing avoidance strategies. Since competency is fixed, it can only be demonstrated, not improved (Rhodewalt & Tragakis, 2002). In contrast, those holding an incremental view tend to interpret failure as reflecting lack of effort or the need for improvement and engage in efforts at mastery (Molden & Dweck, 2006). The impact of beliefs on social information processing is particularly evident with regard to stereotypes. In contrast to those holding an incremental view regarding personal attributes, those holding a fixed view have been found to more readily endorse and apply social stereotypes and resist stereotype-inconsistent information (Molden & Dweck, 2006).

Beliefs also affect a person's response to new information. Once formed, beliefs tend to self-perpetuate and persevere even against contradictions. In fact, people tend to value more positively information that is consistent with their beliefs and distort contradictory information to make it consistent with their-preexisting beliefs and attitudes (Kardash & Scholes, 1996). Some beliefs are more resistant to change than others, and, as might be expected given the tendency for perpetuation, beliefs formed early are more difficult to alter than those formed later (Pajares, 1992). Furthermore, an individual's core beliefs that coincide with the views of groups to which they belong are even more resistant to change because they are consensually validated by the members (Eidelson & Eidelson, 2003).

Evidence is accumulating that epistemic beliefs also matter (Hofer & Bendixen, 2012). In particular, epistemic beliefs affect the interpretation of knowledge (Kardash & Scholes, 1996). The focus of research has been on establishing relationships between a student's epistemic beliefs and various dimensions of academic motivation, learning, and achievement (Muis et al., 2006). Epistemic beliefs have been shown to be significantly related to academic performance, conceptual change, text comprehension, moral reasoning, social relationships, and strategy use (Bendixen & Rule, 2004). For example, students with more complex epistemic beliefs have been found to have higher academic achievement (Bendixen & Rule, 2004; Schommer-Aikins, 2004).

A comprehensive review of this research literature through the perspective of the previously discussed embedded systems model of personal epistemology (Schommer-Aikins, 2004) provides an integrated summary of the evidence regarding the association of specific components of epistemic beliefs regarding the certainty and structure or complexity of knowledge and beliefs about learning with students' academic performance and self-regulated learning. Belief in the certainty of knowledge was found to be associated with misinterpreting and the drawing of absolute conclusions from tentative information (Kardash & Scholes, 1996; Schommer, 1990). Belief regarding the structure of knowledge as simple was associated with poor comprehension of text and less use of integrative study strategies (Schommer, Crouse, & Rhodes, 1992). Belief in the fixed ability to learn was associated with less valuing of education (Schommer & Walker, 1997) and less persistence with difficult tasks (Dweck & Leggett, 1988). Belief in quick learning was associated with poor comprehension of text (Schommer, 1990) and lower grade point averages (Schommer, 1993; Schommer et al., 1992).

These findings have prompted an effort to determine the mechanisms of effect, or the processes through which epistemic beliefs affect learning. One area of focused has been the association of epistemic beliefs and various cognitive and metacognitive strategies. Some support has emerged for the hypothesis that a person's epistemic beliefs impact learning through the generation of internal standards and expectations, which in turn inform their recursive metacognitive monitoring of efforts and strategies to fit different learning tasks (Bromme et al., 2010b). The process is recursive because reflection on the outcome in turn may influence epistemic beliefs. For example, Muis (2007) has formulated a theoretical model of the reciprocal relationship of epistemic beliefs and self-regulated learning. She proposed that learners' epistemic beliefs are activated during the definition phase of a task and influence the standards that the learner sets with regard to goals, the strategies employed, and the extent of metacognitive processing engaged to complete the task. A review of the evidence regarding the relationship of epistemic beliefs to learning indicates that students who express less constructivist epistemic beliefs are more likely to engage in surface-level strategies such as memorization, while students with more constructivist epistemic beliefs are more likely to use deep-level strategies (Muis, 2007). These differences in strategies influence performance.

Efforts to determine the mechanisms or processes through which epistemological beliefs influence learning have also focused on behavioral and motivational strategies associated with self-regulated learning and academic performance. For example, studies have examined the effects of college students' epistemological beliefs on their use of educationally productive self-regulated cognitive strategies (e.g., elaboration, rehearsal, organization, and metacognition), behavioral strategies (e.g., effort regulation, time management, and help seeking), and motivational components, such as perceptions of self-efficacy and internal locus of control over their learning and strategies (e.g., intrinsic goal orientation) (Paulsen & Feldman, 2005; 2007). The findings indicated that college students with more sophisticated epistemological beliefs about learning and knowledge were more likely than those with less sophisticated beliefs to use effective self-regulated cognitive, behavioral, and motivational strategies. Moreover, the effects of beliefs about learning and knowledge on the use of self-regulated learning strategies increased with increasing sophistication in the understanding of knowledge as tentative and constantly evolving (Paulsen & Feldman, 2007). The educational implication of these findings is that one way to promote students' development and use of effective cognitive, behavioral, and motivational strategies is to help students grow in their sophistication of their epistemological beliefs about knowledge and learning.

The challenge now is to incorporate our understanding about the association of epistemic beliefs with self-regulated learning and academic performance into our educational goals and practices. As we have discussed, increasing epistemic sophistication is an educational goal in its own right and should be made explicit. In addition, epistemic beliefs and ways of knowing can be viewed as dimensions of readiness that need to be addressed in the efforts to enhance student learning in general, and with regard to domain-specific subject matter and concepts in particular. The potential impact of increasing epistemological sophistication has been recognized: "When students radically revise their notions of knowledge, would they not be likely to change their ways of going about getting it?" (Perry, 1981, p. 102). Moreover, through the process of self-authorship, personal epistemology becomes a component of one's identity such that individuals hold themselves accountable for an evaluative stance in engaging the world and making sense of their experiences. Beyond clearly articulating epistemological sophistication and evaluativist level thinking as educational goals, however, how can educational practices foster the development of personal epistemology?

EDUCATIONAL IMPLICATIONS: FOSTERING EVALUATIVE THINKING

The research on personal epistemology has implications for educational practice in terms of both learning objectives and pedagogical approaches. Higher education seeks to foster the development of intrinsically motivated, self-directed learners who are committed to the processes of inquiry, reasoned argument, evaluating evidence to discern among competing claims, and applying knowledge in the service of society. Functioning in this manner requires the evaluativist level of personal epistemology. Although there is evidence that different levels of epistemic functioning exist within the same person over time and across situations (Boyles & Chandler, 1992), the evidence also indicates that the majority of undergraduates predominately function as multiplist in that knowledge is equated with personal opinion and the commitment to tolerance is equated with nondiscrimination among competing claims (Kuhn & Weinstock, 2002). Students readily accept the need for tolerance:

> Such acceptance requires little of them. What is more difficult, however, and worthy of our attention as educators, is for students to learn to understand one another's premises and assumptions, challenge another's ideas as well as argue one's own, argue meaningfully, and learn to support one's position in such an argument (Hofer, 2006. p. 74).

The challenge is to provide an educational experience that fosters students moving from benign relativism and the "whatever" stance in relation to divergent views (Kuhn, 2005) that is, based on the belief that because everyone has the right to their own opinion, all beliefs are equal, through the recognition that some opinions are better than others, based on the strength of evidence and supporting arguments, to the realization that the goal is to replace good ideas with better ideas.

Fostering the ability to engage in reasoned argument based on judgments about the strength of supporting evidence is one of the central goals of higher education. This goal extends beyond the realm of knowledge claims to include the moral dimension of making reasoned judgments about the moral legitimacy of one's own and others views and actions (Colby, 2008). Achieving this goal, however, is dependent on students having the requisite cognitive skills, epistemic understandings, and values. In particular, functioning at the evaluative level of epistemic thinking is required and becomes an educational object in itself.

> At the heart of the evaluativist epistemological position is the view that reasoned argument is worthwhile and the most productive path to knowledge and informed understanding, as well as to resolution of human conflict (Kuhn & Weinstock, 2002 p. 138–139).

It has been suggested that commitment to the values of tolerance and acceptance may serve to inhibit the development of thinking beyond the multiplist level (Kuhn & Weinstock, 2002). Therefore, to foster development of evaluativist level thinking, attention needs to be directed toward both the individual and the larger societal context. Students "need practice in making and defending claims, especially in social contexts in which claims must be examined and debated in a framework of alternatives and evidence," and "we also need to work toward creating the kind of society in which thinking and judgment are widely regarded as worth the effort they entail" (Kuhn & Weinstock, 2002, p. 139). That is, epistemological reasoning must be expected, valued, and practiced.

Intellectual Engagement: Inquiry and Argumentation

To foster the development of evaluativist-level thinking, colleges and universities must provide the types of educational experiences that promote the value of intellectual work and the development of the requisite cognitive skills and essential dispositions including curiosity, openness, and tolerance of ambiguity; and motivation. In particular, student's must value intellectual engagement: "People must want to know, and appreciate the benefits it confers, if they are to undertake the effort it requires" (Kuhn, 2001, p. 8).

People come to intrinsically value intellectual engagement as worth the effort it entails through engaging in the *processes of inquiry* and *reasoned argument*, and discovering for themselves that these processes are empowering and useful for problem solving, deciding among competing claims, and resolving conflicts. The processes of inquiry and argument require the cognitive abilities to reason and think critically. The process of inquiry involves the formulation of a thesis, claim, or question that is capable of being disconfirmed by evidence, the construction of mental models of causality, and the processes of analysis and interpretation of the evidence. In turn, analysis involves the integration of new evidence with existing understandings and beliefs and the identification of patterns and relationships, and interpretation involves use of valid inference strategies regarding multiple causes and effects with regard to the claims under consideration. Argument is a form of inquiry. It involves a claim, counter claim, and the provision and evaluation of supporting evidence.

In seeking to promote intellectual engagement, colleges and universities must nurture the development of these two core skills of inquiry and argument (Kuhn, 2005; Kuhn, 2003; Kuhn & Udell, 2001). We know, however, that in justifying their claims, people tend to rely on explanation; that is, a plausible theory or narrative that makes sense or seems right, rather than on evidence supporting the existence of a causal relationship (Kuhn, 2005). Therefore, it is also necessary to foster the development of a personal epistemology that governs the extent to which these core skills will be acquired, applied, and practiced. Evaluativist level thinking is necessary to support and sustain intellectual engagement and view knowledge not as facts or opinions, but rather judgments that in turn "require support in a framework of alternatives, evidence, and argument" (Kuhn, 2005, p. 32). It is the necessary foundation to understand the distinction between claim and evidence and recognize the superiority of evidence over explanation as the justification for knowledge claims. It is only with an evaluativist level thinking that reasoned argument and justification of claims becomes a meaningful practice worth the efforts it entails.

THE ACADEMY AS SOCIAL CONTEXT: PEDAGOGICAL APPROACHES

From a social constructivist framework epistemic beliefs are understood as being constructed through interactions with others (Brownlee & Berthelsen, 2008), and evidence is accumulating about the influence of the cultural context on the development of epistemic beliefs (Palmer & Mara, 2008). For example, as we have already discussed, there is ample evidence that epistemic beliefs are influenced by knowledge domain and disciplinary community (Muis et al., 2006). While people may have a relatively stable general epistemology, nested within this overall general level of beliefs are domain and context specific epistemologies that may be inconsistent. That is, a person's level of epistemological thinking is dependent on the context and the knowledge domain under consideration, and people may hold disparate beliefs in different contexts.

The educational task for undergraduate education then is to create the opportunity for students to develop the epistemological sophistication and intrinsic motivation to sustain lifelong commitment to the challenging processes of evaluative thinking. For educators, valuing evaluative thinking is necessary to motivate our efforts to develop the requisite skills and commitment in our students. Values and motivation are necessary, but by themselves insufficient. We must also know *how*. That is, what educational practices and experiences should we provide to enable students to develop these skills and commitments?

A number of general suggestions emerge from studies of conceptual change about how to promote students' intellectual engagement and epistemological sophistication (Andre & Windschitl, 2003). For example, teachers should provide students with opportunities for "sense-making" in class and to express their understandings using a variety of modes. Classroom discussions should provide opportunities for dialogue with teachers and peers about how to fashion arguments, what counts as evidence, and how to support one's position. Assessment of students' performance should be designed to go beyond measuring performance and improve student learning by providing feedback on the soundness of their thinking as well as the correctness of their conceptual understandings.

Our current knowledge base enables us to move beyond these general considerations. For example, there is increasing empirical evidence that the development of epistemological sophistication is promoted by teaching and assessment approaches that encourage students to reflect on their beliefs about knowledge, the process of knowing, and their own learning (Bromme et al., 2010a); require students to critique knowledge; make the epistemology of knowledge domains explicit; and model critical thinking strategies involving analysis, weighing of evidence, and integration of evidence with preexistent beliefs (Brownlee & Berthelsen, 2008; Palmer & Mara, 2008).

Considerable evidence has also accumulated in support of the claim that knowledge and learning, ways of thinking, and methods of inquiry and discovery are in large part disciplinary specific (Beyer et al., 2007). As students progress through higher levels of education, they learn to think and act in accordance with the disciplinary framework of intellectual values and practices of specific communities of discourse, and domain-specific epistemic beliefs become more influential than general-epistemic beliefs (Muis et al., 2006). Therefore, if the learning process is conceived as inducting students into communities of practice, then it is clear that students need an understanding of the underlying epistemic assumptions about the structure and certainty of knowledge, the ways of knowing and modes of inquiry, and the standards of evidence that guide the strategies for constructing and applying knowledge in each disciple or field of study.

Beyond learning what counts as knowledge in each field and the disciplinary specific ways of knowing, exposure to domain distinctions at the epistemological level enhances student's general epistemological sophistication (Hofer, 2006). Several promising metacognitive pedagogical approaches have been developed to make these epistemic foundations of disciplines more explicit. These approaches emphasize the modeling of the higher-order thinking and strategies being employed in the inquiry, evaluation, interpretation, and argumentation processes in a discipline.

Cognitive Apprenticeship

To learn a subject, students need to learn not only the content knowledge but also how to use the conceptual tools that characterize the work of practitioners in that discipline or field. One way of learning to use these conceptual tools is through becoming an apprentice and being enculturated in a community of practice (Brown et al., 1989). Through training and supervision of the practice of essential skills, apprentices acquire the knowledge and skills needed for expert practice in a discipline, field, or profession. The *cognitive apprenticeship model* of teaching seeks to enculturate students by engaging them in authentic sense-making processes of the discipline through providing graduated and supported practice in the actual use of their knowledge and cognitive skills (Collins et al., 1989). Through modeling and coaching, faculty provide students with a scaffolding in terms of the strategies and methods of the discipline and reduce their guidance as the student acquires more independence in the understanding and use of the conceptual tools and practices of the discipline (Brown et al., 1989). Through this process students build a conceptual model of the cognitive and metacognitive processes and strategies in the discipline that are required for discovering, managing, and using knowledge. In addition to faculty modeling and coaching, opportunities are provided for students to articulate and reflect on their knowledge, reasoning, and problem solving in comparison with the model of expertise provided by the faculty (Collins et al., 1989). As the process of enculturalization occurs and expertise develops, students learn to think and act in accordance with the disciplinary framework of intellectual values and practices and come to identify with that community of practice. This sense of identity entails a personal commitment to a particular way of being in the world (Becher & Trowler, 2001).

Providing opportunities for undergraduates to undertake a faculty-mentored research project is one of the most powerful learning experiences that colleges and universities can provide. The faculty–student relationship incorporates the cognitive apprenticeship model of teaching the theoretical and methodological characteristics of the discipline with active engagement in the inquiry and discovery process around a real problem or question of interest to the student. We will consider the role of undergraduate research as a high-impact educational practice in more detail in Chapter 7.

Decoding the Disciplines

Another promising approach to making disciplinary thinking visible is the "decoding the disciplines" model developed through the History Learning Project at Indiana University (Pace & Middendorf, 2004). This pedagogical approach focuses on developing strategies for introducing students to the culture of thinking in specific disciplines and making explicit the steps students must follow to succeed. Faculty identify and explain the kinds of cognitive operations that are fundamental to their field though addressing fundamental questions:

- What are the bottlenecks to learning in this class—the points in a course where students get stuck in understanding concepts or encounter difficulty in mastering the material or tasks? What steps or operations does an expert go through to accomplish the tasks identified as a bottleneck?
- How can these steps or operations be explicitly modeled?
- How will students practice these operations and skills and get feedback?
- What will motivate the student?
- How well are students mastering these learning skills and operations?

The History Learning Project identified three primary bottlenecks to student learning (Díaz et al., 2008):

- Understanding, interpreting, and deploying evidence from primary sources
- Understanding the argumentative process and constructing arguments
- Navigating the emotional impact of historiography that could be potentially threatening and with regard to the necessity to suspend judgment

Faculty then employed various strategies to explicitly model how these practices are performed by historians, and students were provided with opportunities to practice these ways of thinking.

In particular, writing assignments tailored to the specific learning objectives and bottlenecks of the course provided students with the opportunity to practice the cognitive operations that characterize thinking as a historian. For example, a writing assignment would ask students to identify, interpret, and connect primary sources on a specific topic. Over time it has become clear that the multiple specific bottlenecks identified were actually interconnected with each other and were surface manifestations of the epistemology of History that students do not fully comprehend (Shopkow et al., 2013).

Threshold Concepts

Another pedagogical approach that aims to bring students into a disciplinary culture of practice focuses on identifying and teaching "threshold concepts" (Meyer & Land, 2003; 2005). Threshold concepts are not merely core concepts in a discipline, but constitute seeing things in a new way. Threshold concepts serve as a conceptual gateway that once comprehended results in a new way of viewing, understanding, and interpreting the subject matter, the world or oneself (Meyer & Land, 2005). Having attained the new way of seeing things, it is difficult to go back to the previous way. For example, acquiring an understanding of the concept of "hegemony" could represent a gateway for students to increase their understanding of cultural studies and recognize the implications for the ways in which their own personal choices might be culturally constrained. Another example is the concept of "opportunity cost" in the discipline of economics. The issue of choice when resources are limited is fundamental to that discipline, and opportunity costs captures the idea that choices can be compared. This understanding may also change students' way of thinking about their own choices as well as the way they interpret the choices of others.

One key insight about threshold concepts is the recognition that these concepts may also be troublesome. Knowledge in general could be troublesome because it is conceptually difficult, counterintuitive, or alien (Perkins, 1999). Threshold concepts, in particular, could be troublesome because seeing things in a new way with regard to fundamental beliefs and commitments can provoke a change in one's sense of identity which can be unsettling (Meyer & Land, 2005).

In recognition that an array of factors may be contributing to a student getting stuck at a particular point or bottleneck in the discourse of a discipline, faculty need to be sensitive and responsive to the variation within and across students in their engagement with the content and context of learning in the discipline. Awareness of the interrelatedness of learning with emotion, values, and identity, and recognition that cognitive and emotional dissonance can therefore be aroused in the process of learning, are important insights. These insights help both students and faculty to understand the resistance that may be evoked by the expectation for openness to new knowledge and calls attention to the impact of preexisting beliefs, values, and commitments on new learning. Embracing a new idea or way of thinking may require not only new learning but also altering one's values, commitments, and identity— that is, a personal transformation.

A formative liberal education seeks to transform students' ways of thinking, knowing, and understanding. The aim is for students to develop a personal epistemology that goes beyond relativism and tolerance to the evaluativist level of epistemic thinking and commitment to the processes of inquiry and reasoned argument as the best way to enhanced understanding and resolution of conflict. The evaluative level of thinking is valuable in its own right but also because it is intertwined with other cognitive and affective dimensions of functioning, and because of the integrative role it plays in conjunction with identity formation, which is the focus of subsequent chapters. However, to empower students to constructively engage difference, evaluativist level thinking is necessary, but not sufficient. It is also necessary to develop students' capacities for perspective taking and empathy, which are the focus of the next chapter.

CHAPTER 4

Empathy

This natural ability to understand the emotions and feelings of others, whether one actually witnessed his or her situation, perceived it from a photograph, read about it in a fiction book, or merely imagined it, refers to the phenomenological experience of empathy (Decety & Jackson, 2004, p. 71).

UNDERSTANDING MENTAL STATES

We have an amazing ability to quickly read and understand our own mental states and the mental states of others, including short-term emotions as well as long-term dispositions, desires, beliefs, motives, and intentions. We are social beings, and this ability to understand others as intentional agents and interpret their mental states, sometimes referred to as theory of mind (TOM), is thought to have evolved because social interactions depend on understanding and predicting the actions of others. Interpreting the mental states of others occurs on an unconscious or automatic level and also on a conscious level and includes two distinct, but interrelated, capacities: *mentalizing* and *empathy*. Mentalizing refers to the capacities to represent, interpret, and predict other's beliefs, desires, and intentions and involves the cognitive processes of reasoning, perspective taking, inference, and attribution. Empathy refers to the capacities to represent, understand, and share the feelings of another person. Inferences about mental and emotional states are based on multiple sources of information including nonverbal clues, such as facial expressions and gaze direction, and knowledge of the person's beliefs and perspective.

Understanding the basis and development of this ability to read the mental states of others has been the focus of philosophers, social scientists, and most recently neuroscientists. The basic questions relate to how we know our own mind and the subjective thoughts, desires, feelings, and intentions of another. This chapter will consider the theories and evidence about the nature and development of our ability to read mental states, with a particular focus on perspective taking and empathy. We will consider the underlying neurocortical mechanisms that enable the basic differentiation of self and other and support the cognitive and affective processes involved in interpreting and responding to the mental states of others. We will also consider the common systematic errors we make in interpreting the mental states of others. Our understanding of these mechanisms and processes and their development has implications both for the expectations we have for emerging adults and for the ways in which undergraduate educational experiences can enhance these capacities.

How Are We Able to Understand the Mental States of Others?

Several explanations or theories have been proposed. It is well recognized that we use knowledge of ourselves as a basis for making inferences and attributions about the mental states and feelings of others. There are, however, different theories about the mechanisms involved. *Social projection theory* maintains that people unconsciously perceive in others feelings, thoughts, and inclinations that are similar to their own (Dimaggio et al., 2008). Furthermore, *simulation theory* proposes that people understand the mental states of others through simulation or activation of their own mental states—that is, when we empathize or mentalize, we generate mental states that match or resonate with the states of those whom we are observing (Goldman, 2006). This theory is supported by the finding that there are mirror neurons in the brain that represent the neural basis for imitation of other's actions (Singer, 2006). These neurons fire when a person performs an action or observes another performing the action. This shared representation system is activated by emotions as well as actions, "such that the same areas are activated when we observe another person experiencing an emotion as when we experience the same emotion ourselves, as if by contagion" (Frith & Frith, 2006, p. 531). Social projection theory and simulation theory are consistent in maintaining that we tend to attribute the contents of our own experience when we think about the thoughts and feelings of others (Dimaggio et al., 2008).

Performing the same action or experiencing the same emotion, however, are not sufficient to infer the cause of another's emotion or behavior or to predict what he or she will do next. In addition to shared representation, conscious mechanisms are required. *Theory-theory* proposes that people employ general knowledge and theories about other people and apply the knowledge that they have accumulated about the world, specific people, and their own past experiences to infer the other person's mental state. Inference is dependent on the cognitive processes of perspective taking that is, adopting the psychological perspective of another, and reasoning. Learning also contributes to the understanding of the mental state of others. As we experience certain situations over time we associate thoughts and feelings with those situations. Observing others in those same situations reactivates these associations (Omdahl, 1995).

Neurocortical Mechanism Underlying Mentalizing and Empathy

The advent of neuroimaging studies has advanced our understanding by providing evidence regarding the neurocortical mechanisms underlying the theories and processes purported to be involved in understanding the mental states of others. In general, these studies ask participants to think about the mental states of others and the neurocortical networks activated under these tasks are identified through brain imaging studies using functional magnetic resonance imaging (fMRI) or positron emission tomography (PET).

The brain imaging evidence indicates that the capacities to mentalize and to empathize are distinct and rely on different neural circuits that have different developmental paths, but also interact, and undergo changes throughout life (Singer, 2006). The neural network involved in mentalizing includes three brain regions: the medial prefrontal cortex (MPFC); the temporal cortex, specifically the superior temporal sulcus (STS) and temporal-parietal junction (TPJ); and the temporal poles (Frith & Frith, 2006). In particular, the STS is activated by socially relevant visual cues, such as facial expressions or bodily movements, which convey mental states or communicate intent (Nicole et al. 2008). The neural network involved in empathizing includes the sensorimotor cortices and the limbic and paralimbic regions (Singer, 2006). Although they are distinct, it is also increasingly clear that the cognitive processes of mentalizing and the affective process of empathizing are interrelated and work together to enable us to understand our own mental states and those of others.

Empathizing and mentalizing are components of the larger domain of social cognition. Not only are both cognitive and affective processes involved, but social cognition involves dual processes, automatic and controlled, and corresponding distinct underlying neurocognitive systems (Lieberman, 2007). The controlled process include conscious awareness, intention, and effort and involve the lateral prefrontal cortex (LPFC), medial prefrontal cortex (MPFC), lateral parietal cortex (LPAC), medial parietal cortex (MPAC), medial temporal lobe (MTL), and rostral anterior cingulate cortex (rACC) (Lieberman, 2007). The automatic processes involve the amygdala, basal ganglia, ventromedial prefrontal cortex (VMPFC), lateral temporal cortex (LTC), and dorsal anterior cingulate cortex (dACC) (Lieberman, 2007). Another core processing system has been proposed to be involved in the distinction of internal mental states or external visible features or actions, both one's own and those of another (Lieberman, 2007). Externally focused processes are associated with the lateral frontotemporoparietal network, and the internally focused-processes are associated with a medial frontoparietal network (Lieberman, 2007).

Our ability to understand the mental states of others is essential not only for everyday social interactions but also for constructively engaging ethnic, religious, and political differences. With this basic understanding of the processes, we can consider in more detail the nature and development of the component capacities of empathy and perspective taking. While these two capacities are distinct, they work together and considerations of empathy typically include the cognitive component of perspective taking. The aim of this chapter is to review our current understanding of the nature and development of empathy, including the role of higher-order cognitive processes, and address how this essential capacity can be enhanced. The chapter is organized around the major research questions on empathy: What is the nature of empathy? How are we able to empathize? What biases occur in reading mental states? What is the relationship of empathy with prosocial behavior? How does empathy develop, and how can empathy be increased through education or training?

THE NATURE OF EMPATHY

Humans are thought to be "innately predisposed to be sensitive and responsive to the subjective states of other people" (Decety & Jackson, 2004, p. 77). The construct of empathy is generally considered to refer to the natural ability to share and thereby understand the emotions and feelings of others and involves three processes: "feeling what another person is feeling, knowing what another person is feeling, and having the intention to respond compassionately to another person's distress" (Decety & Jackson, 2004, p. 73). Thus whereas mentalizing refers to the process of reasoning about the mental states of others, empathy refers to a phenomenological process of sharing the feelings of another as if one were actually experiencing the same affective response. John Gardner (1963), in his book on self-renewal, captures the essence of empathy by describing it as the ability to "see life through another's eyes and feel it through another's heart" (p. 15).

In addition to having the ability to take the perspective of another, to imagine and understand how others feel, we also have the capacity to "feel felt" by another (Siegel, 2009). This sense of being understood by another person fosters a feeling of closeness to that person, and we take comfort in knowing that others are concerned about us, have compassion for our suffering and misfortune, and take joy in our triumphs (Siegel, 2009).

The origins of the concept of empathy has been traced to Theodor Lipps, who in 1897 introduced the term *Einfühlung* (feeling oneself into) into his writings about aesthetic perception; this German term was translated as *empathy* by Titchener in 1910 (Goldstein & Michaels, 1985). The concept has evolved since it was first introduced. As we have already noted, empathy is now viewed as including both the cognitive dimension of perspective taking and inferring another's emotions and feelings and the affective dimension of the observer's emotional response to another's affective state.

Although there is agreement that empathy involves both cognitive and affective processes, there is disagreement about the exact meaning of the term empathy which has been used to refer to as many as eight distinct phenomena (Batson, 2009). One reason for the application of the term empathy to so many distinct phenomena is that researchers invoke the concept of empathy to answer two different questions (Batson, 2009, p. 3):

- How can a person know what another person is thinking and feeling?
- What leads a person to respond with sensitivity and care to the suffering of another?

The first question involves an effort to explain a form of knowledge, whereas the second question involves an effort to explain a form of action and its driving motivation (Batson, 2009). We are interested in both questions but need to make clear our use of empathy as differentiated from other similar concepts, such as sympathy and compassion. Empathy involves feeling the same emotion as another person, whereas sympathy involves feeling concern or sorrow for another who is in distress or need (Eisenberg et al., 2006). Compassion denotes awareness of the suffering of another and the desire to relieve it.

Empathy is elicited in various ways and several modes of empathetic arousal have been identified (Hoffman, 2000). Some modes are automatic—essentially involuntary—processes, including mimicry, classical conditioning, and association of cues about the person or his or her situation with one's own past experiences. Empathy, however, is not just automatically triggered; it is also a motivated behavior and a conscious process involving cognitive and metacognitive processes. Cognitive processes include verbal mediation in which another person's situation in relation to one's own experiences is understood and communicated through verbal or written language. Empathy is also elicited through the higher-order cognitive process of perspective taking; imagining how another feels, or one would feel, in a particular situation. There is strong support across a number of empirical studies that "adopting the perspective of the target is the process especially likely to produce empathic concern" (Davis, 1994, p. 110). Furthermore, one of the distinctive elements about empathy is the metacognitive dimension, or "the awareness that one's feeling of distress is a response to another's distressing situation" (Hoffman, 2000, p. 49).

HOW ARE WE ABLE TO EMPATHIZE?

We understand empathy as a multifaceted process of psychological inference that requires both the ability to share the emotional experience of another person and the capacity to understand the other person's subjective experience (Decety & Jackson, 2004). It is generally agreed that there are several components to empathy: an affective response to another person that usually involves sharing that person's emotional state, the cognitive capacity and flexibility to take the perspective of another person and gain insights into that persons thoughts and emotions, and a regulatory mechanisms that enables differentiation of the self from others and control of cognition and emotion (Decety & Jackson, 2004). To understand how we are able to empathize, each of these components needs to be considered in more detail.

Affective Response and Shared Representation

The affective component of empathy is the ability to detect the immediate affective state or imagine the likely affective state of another person. This ability to understand and share the feelings of others is evoked through witnessing another's situation, but also through perceiving it from a photograph, reading about it in a book, or just imaging it.

One explanation of our capacity to empathize is based on mental simulation, or *shared representation*, of the experience of another. That is, we use our own experience as one way of understanding another's experience. But how does this work? The human nervous system has evolved the basic mechanisms to enable us to simulate emotions and behaviors, both our own and those of others. More specifically, the perception of a behavior or an emotion in another person automatically activates the neural mechanisms that are responsible for one's own representation of that behavior or emotion. This mental simulation can also be initiated intentionally as well as automatically. Shared representation occurs because the same neural systems are involved in both the recognition and expression of specific emotions.

There is ample evidence for this mechanism of shared representation. For example, infants demonstrate they are capable of "emotion contagion" by automatically mimicking and synchronizing facial expressions, vocalizations, postures, and movements with those of another person (Decety & Jackson, 2004). It is also evident that emotions can be induced by making a facial expression consistent with that emotion. Furthermore, neuroimaging studies provide support for shared representation as the mechanism underlying our understanding of others' perceptions. The evidence includes the involvement of the somatosensory cortex in the recognition of emotions; the activation of regions of the premotor and parietal cortices, associated with motor planning, both when individuals execute a simple finger, hand, or facial movement and when they see the same movement executed by someone else; and activation of regions of the anterior insula, associated with viserosensation and orofacial movement, both when an individual feels disgusted and when they see someone else expressing disgust (Ochsner et al., 2008). More specifically, reading emotional states from observable behaviors involves emotion related brain regions including the amygdala and the inferior frontal gyrus (IFG), which generates motor representations of emotions, and somatosensory cortices (SRC), which generate somatic representations of emotional states (Hooker et al., 2008).

Perhaps the strongest evidence for the mechanism of shared representations is provided from neuroimaging studies of pain perception in others and ourselves. Perceiving others in pain and experiencing pain ourselves involve both overlapping and distinct neural systems. The reason is that perceiving another individual experiencing pain activates neurocortical regions within our own brain that we use to process our own experience of pain. In terms of overlapping systems, both self-pain and perception of pain in others involve the mid anterior cingulate cortex and anterior insula. Experiencing pain ourselves, however, activates the anterior and mid-insula regions, whereas perceptions of another person in pain activates the frontal, premotor, and the amygdala regions that are implicated in emotional regulation and processing of social cues (Ochsner et al., 2008).

Another study provided evidence regarding the mechanisms involved in imagining an emotional response of another person (Hooker et al., 2008). Participants were asked to first observe the response of a person in a situation and then to predict the emotional state of that person in a different situation. The study was designed to isolate the neural mechanisms involved in predicting a future emotional response of another person and also determine whether the strength of emotion-related neural activity was related to self-reported empathy in daily life. The findings indicated more activity in the neural regions involved in mentalizing and in emotion processing when predicting the new emotional response than when recognizing the person's current emotional state. Furthermore, greater activity in the primary emotion processing regions when predicting the new emotional state was correlated with more self-reported empathy in daily life. These findings support the claim that when people predict an emotional response of another, they generate internal representations and that greater use of these representations is related to more self-reported empathy.

Once the shared representation system has been activated through interaction with another, the person must engage higher mental processes to accomplish two important steps: maintaining the differentiation between the self and the other person, and engaging in self-regulation so that the emotions aroused are not overwhelming. Thus, beyond activation, higher mental processes are needed to consciously take the perspective of another and regulate one's own emotions. This requires that cognitive and affective processes involved in perspective taking and empathy work together.

Perspective Taking: Self-Awareness and Other-Awareness

Humans have awareness of themselves, the other person, and of being the object of others' attention. Empathy involves the psychological processes of both perspective taking and differentiation between self and other. The development of the ability to represent and understand both objective and subjective aspects of self and others is dependent on the development of processes known as *executive functions* that serve to monitor, control, or inhibit thoughts, emotions, and actions and involve the prefrontal cortex region of the brain.

Perspective taking is a complex social-cognitive process that involves imagining how another feels or would feel in a particular situation, while at the same time distinguishing between one's own feelings and those feelings experienced by the other person. There is considerable evidence that the right hemisphere is involved in both self-awareness and the process of mental state attributions, which raises the question of how we distinguish between those representations activated by awareness of the self and those activated by awareness of others. The neural networks underlying self and other processing have both common and independent components (Decety & Jackson, 2004). Evidence suggests that the right inferior parietal cortex, in conjunction with the prefrontal cortex, is involved in distinguishing the self from the other (Decety & Jackson, 2004). The right inferior parietal lobe is involved in the mental stimulation of the actions of others, perspective taking, and sense of agency; that is, in distinguishing between self-produced actions and actions generated by others (Decety & Jackson, 2004).

Studies have found that when people project themselves into the situations experienced by another they report actually experiencing the feeling as if they were facing the same situation (Ruby & Decety, 2004). As we have seen, one basis for this experience is the shared representation system. In addition, people are fundamentally egocentric, and we tend to rely on our own self-perspective. This general tendency to impute our own knowledge and perspective to others is well documented and known as the *egocentric bias*, which we will consider more fully in the next section. Taking someone else's point of view requires mental flexibility and conscious effort. Thus, in order to accurately understand other's mental states, we must be able to regulate or inhibit our own perspective, which has been activated by shared representation. The evidence from a number of neuroimaging studies indicates that the frontopolar cortex is involved in the inhibition process which enables us to adopt the subjective view point of others (Decety & Jackson, 2004).

Evidence is also accumulating about the neurocortical mechanism involved in the differentiation of self and other and the interaction between emotional and cognitive processes. For example, a study investigated the brain regions that were activated when participants were asked to adopt either their own perspective (first person) or the perspective of another (third person) in response to both emotional and neutral situations (Ruby & Decety, 2004). The findings indicated that the amygdala was involved in the emotional component of the task, but not the neutral component. The amygdala is known to be involved in the basic emotions (anger, fear, disgust, happiness, sadness) and the social emotions (pride, embarrassment, guilt, shame, admiration, and jealousy). With regard to the interaction between perspective and emotional contexts, the temporal lobe was activated in the third person perspective, whereas the somatosensory cortex was activated in the self-perspective. The findings from this study enhance our understanding of the psychological process of perspective taking and empathy in showing that multiple mechanism are involved: a shared neural network that supports self and other representations and a network that support distinction between self and others.

Our understanding of the process of self and other awareness has implications for enhancing empathy and the accuracy of our efforts to understand the mental states of others. The capacity to think about one's own thoughts and feelings and the capacity to think about and make inferences about the thoughts and feelings of another are interrelated. The brain regions activated under these two processes, while not completely overlapping, are interrelated. These interrelationships suggest that enhancing self-awareness and perspective taking through self-reflection can be a path to improving empathy and promoting more sensitive judgments about the mental states of others. Since we rely on our own self-perspectives to construct the perspective of another, however, errors in assessing and inferring another's perspective are attributable in part on failure to suppress our own self-perspective (Ruby & Decety, 2004). Thus, we have to cultivate both reflection and inhibition and active evaluation of the accuracy of our appraisals of the mental states and feelings of others.

Emotional Regulation

Apprehending the affective state of another person elicits feelings that parallel those of the other person, but also affects the observer—that is, evokes emotional responses within the observer. Therefore, activation of the shared representation system that underlies empathy could lead to emotional contagion, personal distress, and being overwhelmed by the emotion aroused in observing another person's plight. Personal distress stemming from the exposure to another's negative state motivates efforts to reduce this distress (Eisenberg, 2010). Self-regulation of emotions is necessary to prevent and manage emotional arousal and involves the interaction of cognitive and emotional processes and the underlying neural networks.

The mechanism for emotional regulation depends on the interaction of the prefrontal cortex, the region responsible for cognitive and executive functions, with the amygdala, the region of the brain that is critical to the generation, expression, and experience of negative emotions. This interaction is enabled by reciprocal anatomical connections, referred to as the emotion generation-regulation circuit, between the amygdala and the anterior cingulate cortex (ACC), the orbitofrontal cortex (OFC), and dorsal medial prefrontal cortex (DMPFC) (Banks et al. 2007). The involvement of this neural network in the process of empathy was demonstrated in the findings of a study that the more effective the effort of the participants to suppress emotion through the use of cognitive reappraisal, the greater was the activation of the amygdala-OFC/DMPFC circuit (Banks et al. 2007).

Other networks are also involved in self-regulation and are components of the neural network underlying empathy. The ventromedial prefrontal cortex (VMPFC) has reciprocal connections with regions involved in emotional processing (amygdala), memory (hippocampus), and executive functions (dorsolateral prefrontal cortex), and plays a role in emotion regulation. In addition, the ACC is also part of the neural circuit involved in attention that regulates both cognitive and emotional processing (Decety & Jackson, 2004).

BIAS IN MAKING INFERENCES AND ATTRIBUTIONS ABOUT OTHERS MENTAL STATES

Being able to take another's perspective does not mean that our inferences and attributions will be accurate. Inferences and attributions about others mental states are influenced by beliefs, expectations, and cultural norms; perceived similarity between self and other; and self-knowledge and prior experience.

The accuracy of mental state attributions can be influenced by *belief-bias* in which one's reasoning conflicts with, or is overridden by, one's beliefs. Neuroimaging findings suggest that belief-bias effects may be mediated through the influence of emotional processes on reasoning (Goel & Dolan, 2003). For example, when subjects detected a conflict between their beliefs and logical inference and then inhibited the response associated with the belief-bias and engaged in reasoning, the right lateral prefrontal cortex was activated. This region of the brain supports cognitive monitoring. By contrast, when logical reasoning was overcome by belief-bias—when subjects failed to detect the conflict between their beliefs and the logical inference or failed to inhibit the response associated with the belief-bias—the ventral medial prefrontal cortex was activated. This region of the brain supports emotion processing. The finding that belief-bias was mediated by emotion processing suggest that biases could be reduced not only through increased self-awareness, but also by effortful inhibition of the impact of emotional arousal.

There is ample evidence that our default mode for reasoning about others is biased toward an egocentric or self-perspective (Decety, 2005). *Egocentric bias* refers to the tendency to over attribute our own knowledge to others, infer that others have the same knowledge and beliefs that we do, and overrate the degree to which others know our thoughts. Thus our capability for shared representation and simulating the other person's experiences can result in inaccurate inferences about others' mental and emotional states. As we discussed above, accurate simulation requires that the person inhibit his or her own perspective sufficiently to adopt the perspective of another. It is also necessary to bring evaluative processes to bear on the shared representation activated by observing, interacting with, or imagining another person's experience to ensure the accuracy of inferences and attributions that one makes.

People often make mistakes in social perception, and egocentric bias is not the only pattern of error that has been identified. Another pattern, the *correspondence bias*, is the tendency to both overestimate dispositional or personal trait factors and underestimate situational constraints (Gilbert & Malone, 1995). This tendency to attribute behavior to the person's disposition rather than to characteristics of the situation in which the person is functioning is fostered by a number of factors, including the emphasis on individual responsibility within Western culture (Gilbert & Malone, 1995). Furthermore, in Chapter 3, we considered the impact those beliefs about whether personal traits were fixed or modifiable have on social information processing, particularly with regard to stereotyping. In contrast to those holding a modifiable view regarding personal attributes, those holding a fixed view have been found to more readily endorse and apply social stereotypes and resist stereotype-inconsistent information (Molden & Dweck, 2006).

One of the most powerful influences on mental state attributions is the observers' perception of the degree of similarity with the other person. The perceived degree of similarity has been found to moderate the use of egocentric projections and stereotypes in mental state inference (Ames, 2004). When people perceive themselves to be similar to another they engage in higher levels of *projection*—assuming that others think, feel, and want as they do, whereas perceptions of dissimilarity, including that provoked by disagreements, are associated with *stereotyping* (Ames, 2004). In situations in which individuals or groups are perceived as dissimilar, judgments are not only more likely to be based on stereotypes, but the behavior of others is also more likely to be described as driven by dispositional traits and not by situational contexts (Dimaggio et al., 2008). Furthermore, erroneous judgments about others attitudes, beliefs, capabilities, traits, and dispositions errors are more frequent when the other person is from a stereotyped social group (Mason & Macrae, 2008). Even minimal exposure to a member of a stereotyped group can activate stereotypes, but once activated, the application of stereotypes depends on a number of personal and situational factors. For example, disagreements and perceived threats to self-esteem serve to increase the application of stereotypes, whereas the motivation to avoid prejudice decreases the applications of stereotypes (Kunda & Spencer, 2003).

Not only are judgments affected by perceived similarity, but people systematically respond more favorably to those who are perceived as belonging to their group than those belonging to another group. Prosocial behavior is offered more readily, arousal of empathy is facilitated and has more of an impact on prosocial behavior, information processing is more detailed and better retained, and positive behaviors for those in the in-group but negative behaviors for those in the out-group are attributed to stable characteristics of the person (Gaertner & Davidio, 2008).

People make comparisons along many dimensions, and these comparisons are frequently a source of division and conflict. In particular, people make sense of each other within the context of contrasting social status (Fiske, 2010). Appraisal of another person's social status has been found to influence appraisals of that person's intentions and predicts prejudice and prosocial behavior. More specifically, people tend to view high-status people as more competent than low-status people, attribute the cause to disposition rather than to situation or context, and respond with feelings of envy for those of higher status and scorn for those of lower status (Fiske, 2010). This "envy-up" and "scorn-down" bias affects social cognition. Particularly interesting are the findings of a study demonstrating that scorn for lower status people and groups affects social cognition not only with regard to considering them less than human, but also in terms of apparent indifference to their mental states (Fiske, 2010). However, it has been demonstrated that scorn can be moderated when the person of low status (e.g., poor, older, immigrant) acts in ways that are counter to the stereotype, such as the hard-working poor person, or through evoking empathy (Fiske, 2010).

Self-knowledge plays a role in the accuracy of attributions about the mental states of others. A person can use their self-knowledge as a basis to empathize with another and also to differentiate themselves from the other person. Self-knowledge is a basis for understanding others; however, it can also result in bias or misunderstanding. Lack of awareness of one's real or actual feelings or motivations could result in inaccurate attributions, and thus the caution that "projection may only be as valid as the introspection on which it stands" (Ames, 2004, p. 352).

The accuracy of self-knowledge in turn is influenced by the processes of self-reflection and autobiographical memory (Dimaggio et al., 2008). Self-reflection is the ability to detect one's current thoughts and feelings, and autobiographical memory is the intentional drawing on previous experiences. The abilities to understand our own minds and the mind of others, as we have seen, are distinct capabilities, but also influence one another. The more a person is able to accurately detect his or her thoughts, feelings, and motivations and draw on their own experiences, the better able the person is to understand the other person's mental states (Dimaggio et al., 2008). It is important to recognize that autobiographical memory can be inaccurate, and sometimes others recount events in our lives that we might not actually recall having experienced but we accept as having occurred. In addition, sometimes the experience we draw on was not an actual happening, but perhaps a dream or wish. Thus, we need to have the capacity for self-doubt and bring an evaluative stance to our reflections and recollections. The capacity for critical self-reflection and the ability to question one's own attributions and recall when memories were inaccurate or others remembered events differently facilitate more sensitive and accurate reading of others' mental states.

The evidence of the associations among self-reflection, autobiographical memory, and attributions about one's mental states suggests that generating a nuanced and accurate understanding of the mind of another could be facilitated through undertaking intentional efforts of three types:

- Increasing self-awareness through enhancing one's capacities for critical self-reflection and recollection
- Developing the practice of questioning and revising attributions regarding others in response to feedback and new information
- Striving to inhibit emotional arousal

The ability to reduce the effects of bias through engaging in these intentional efforts raises the question of what would motivate these efforts—or, stated differently, what would make it worth the effort. This question brings us to one of the primary basis for the interests in empathy.

RELATIONSHIP OF EMPATHY AND PROSOCIAL BEHAVIOR

One of the reasons that empathy has been the focus of so much research is the notion that empathy serves to motivate prosocial behavior. The proposed mechanism is that emotional reactions to another person who is in need or distress are causally linked with subsequent helping behavior. There is now considerable evidence at the levels of behavior, cognitive processes, and neurocircuits in support of the motivational role of empathy. Several reviews of empirical studies provide strong support for the positive and significant association of empathy with an array of prosocial or helping behaviors (Underwood & Moore, 1982; Eisenberg & Miller, 1987).

There are, however, competing hypotheses about the nature of the motivation to help. The *empathy-altruism hypothesis* proposes that empathetic concern felt for another person in need or distress elicits altruistic motivation to relieve that need. The *egoistic hypotheses* proposes that the helping behavior is motivated by self-benefits, including the reduction of negative emotions aroused by witnessing another in need, avoiding punishments or self-disapproval for not helping, and seeking reward or approval for helping. A recent review concludes that the evidence clearly supports the empathy-altruism hypothesis: "emphatic concern produces altruistic motivation" (Batson, 2010, p. 23).

Empathy has been linked to the inhibition of aggression and specific types of prosocial behavior. For example, empathy has been associated with a considerate social style (tactful, tolerant, greater cooperation, affective support for others), and more tolerant attitudes toward stigmatized groups (Davis, 1994). Similarly, the tendency to spontaneously adopt the psychological point of view of others in everyday life—perspective taking—has been associated with less interpersonal friction reflected in conflict avoidance and conflict management (Davis, 1994).

Empathy has also been linked with the development of moral reasoning (Hoffman, 1978) and the construction of moral judgments (Eisenberg, 2005). In fact, multiple associations have been found among empathy, perspective taking, moral reasoning, and prosocial behavior. For example, moral reasoning was found to mediate the relationship of empathy to prosocial behavior (Eisenberg, 2005), and the association of perspective taking with prosocial behavior was found to be mediated by empathy and moral reasoning (Eisenberg et al., 2006). Moral reasoning and perspective taking effected prosocial behavior through increasing empathy. It has also been argued that moral behavior is not internalization of fiat or fear of punishment, but rather an expression of empathy through identification with the plight of others (Rifkin, 2009).

These multiple relationships between empathy and prosocial behavior attest to the intertwining of cognitive and affective processes in prosocial behavior. How these cognitive and affective processes of mentalizing and empathy interact is addressed in two different models of helping behaviors (Betancourt, 1990a). The *empathy model* proposes that the cognitive process of taking the perspective of the person in need gives rise to empathic emotions, which, in turn, increases the probability of helping behavior. The *causal attribution model*, however, proposes that this relationship between the cognitive process of perspective taking and empathetic emotions and prosocial behavior is moderated by another cognitive process. More specifically, the cognitive appraisals that an observer makes of the degree to which the cause of the other person's need in a particular situation is under volitional control gives rise to affective reactions, which, in turn, influence helping behavior. Attribution of the person's need to a cause that should be under the person's control elicits anger and lowers the probability of helping, whereas attribution of need to uncontrollable causes elicits empathy and increases the probability of helping.

An integration of the attribution and empathy models has been proposed (Betancourt, 1990a) through which the relationships between the cognitive processes of both attribution of controllability and empathic perspective taking with helping behavior are mediated by (that is, operates through) empathic emotions: "Part of the effect of empathy on prosocial behavior is attribution-mediated and part of the effect of attributions is mediated by empathic emotions" (Betancourt, 1990b, p. 210). Evidence in support of this proposed integration has been provided by studies that found that attributions regarding controllability significantly influenced emphatic concern, which in turn significantly influenced actual offers of help (Betancourt, 1990a). More specifically, perceived uncontrollability elicited positive feelings of empathy, which in turn increased the likelihood of helping; perceived controllability elicited negative feelings of anger, which in turn decreased the likelihood of helping. Furthermore, inducing empathic perspectives in the participants increased the likelihood of viewing the victim's need as uncontrollable, which demonstrated that perceived controllability differs depending on whether the observer approaches the situation with an empathetic or nonempathetic perspective.

Empathy also has a role in improving intergroup relations. A number of studies have demonstrated that eliciting empathy results in more favorable attitudes and behaviors toward out-groups, including racial minorities (Stephan & Finlay, 1999; Finlay & Stephan, 2000). One important finding is that both the cognitive, perspective taking, and the affective components of empathy play a role. Perspective taking serves to reduce prejudice through coming to understand the worldview of others and their cultural practices, norms, and beliefs. The positive feelings of concern and the negative feelings of distress elicited for the person or group can arouse a sense of injustice. In turn, a sense of injustice can lead to changes in attitudes, cognitions, and evaluations about the out-group and lead to a reduction in prejudice, particularly if the prejudice is based on the belief that the world is just and therefore people get what they deserve (Stephan & Finlay, 1999). When "empathy creates a sense of injustice on behalf of the out-group, in-group members may be stirred to social action" (Stephan & Finlay, 1999, p. 738).

Not only does inducing empathy directly influence attitudes and behaviors toward the out-group, empathy is also "a significant mediator by which other factors, such as intergroup contact and perceptions of common identity, influence intergroup attitudes and behaviors" (Dovidio et al., 2010, p. 394). For example, research findings provide support for the mediating role of empathy in response to antibias interventions to improve intergroup relations (Dovidio et al., 2010). It has also been demonstrated that while empathy sensitizes people to the needs of others and to concerns about injustice, it can also promote punitiveness toward those who are perceived to be unjustly causing the suffering of others (Dovidio et al., 2010). Because empathy has been shown to directly influence intergroup relations and mediate the influence of other factors, it has become an important target for interventions designed to improve intergroup relations (Dovidio et al., 2010). We will discuss this further in a subsequent section on enhancing empathy.

RELATIONSHIP OF EMPATHY AND LEADERSHIP

Empathy not only motivates prosocial behavior, but is also an essential capacity for effective leadership in our knowledge-based economy and globally interconnected world of the twenty-first century. This era has the characteristics of complex adaptive systems involving interactions among multiple interdependent agents in which change is rapid and adaptation is nonlinear and emergent (Plowman et al., 2007; Uhl-Bien et al., 2007). Problem-solving in such an era requires the formation and integration of teams of individuals with diverse talents, skills, and knowledge. Effective leadership is no longer a matter of "command and control," but requires the skills to "connect and collaborate" and the ability to "enable and empower" others to maximize their contributions to team functioning. In this complex systems model, leadership is not fixed but is an emergent phenomenon; that is, leaders emerge to fit the needs of the situation (Avolio et al., 2009). In this model effective leaders engender support, trust, and confidence and inspire performance by understanding the interests, values, and intensions of others. Effective leadership requires both cognitive skills and emotional intelligence.

The concept of emotional intelligence (EI) has been the focus of scholarship as well as considerable attention in the popular press. The concept was introduced by Salovey and Mayer (1990), and refers to a set of interrelated abilities involving the processing of emotional information (Côté et al., 2010). Emotional intelligence was conceptualized as a dimension of individual difference: "EI includes the ability to engage in sophisticated information processing about one's own and others emotions and the ability to use this information as a guide to thinking and behavior" (Mayer et al., 2008, p. 503). It includes a rough hierarchy of four skills: perceiving our own and other emotions accurately, using emotions to facilitate thinking, understanding the meaning of emotional signals, and managing emotions to attain goals. These skills are considered to serve "adaptive functions that potentially benefit themselves and others" (Mayer et al., 2008, p. 503). Thus, the capacity for empathy is one of the fundamental abilities that comprise emotional intelligence (Wolff et al., 2002).

People high in EI tend to be more socially competent, to have better quality of relationships, and to be viewed as more interpersonally sensitive than those low in EI (Mayer et al., 2008). High levels of emotional intelligence have also been associated with better relationships at work as well as at home and more effective business performance. These differences in relationships and performance are attributed to people with higher EI as being "better able to recognize and reason about their emotions, as well as about the emotional consequences of their decisions, and the emotions of others" (Mayer et al., 2008, p. 512).

Emotional intelligence has also been found to be associated with emergent leadership in small groups over and above the contribution of intelligence and personality characteristics (Côté et al., 2010). In particular, the ability to understand emotions was the most consistent predictor of leadership emergence. Others have found that the capacity for empathy improves the ability to accurately perceive and understand the emotions and needs of other team members (Wolff et al., 2002). Furthermore, there is evidence that there are two distinct routes through which individuals are perceived as leaders in a small group: from displays of empathetic skills and from displays of cognitive skills, particularly perspective taking (Kellett et al., 2002).

Several reasons have been postulated for the association of the capacity for empathy with effective leadership. First, the capacity for empathy enables others to feel valued as individuals (Kellett et al., 2002). Second, sensitivity to others emotions may enable identification of unstated needs (Côté et al., 2010). Furthermore, empathetic skills, along with perspective taking skills, enable the leader to understand how to empower and support other team members (Wolff et al., 2002). The capacities for perspective taking and empathy, self-awareness and self-reflection, are essential for leadership in a world increasingly characterized by both multicultural engagement and collaborative team functioning.

THE DEVELOPMENT AND ENHANCEMENT OF EMPATHY

Empathy is generally thought to be a natural ability that is shaped through socialization processes: "The basic building blocks are hardwired in the brain and await development through interaction with others" (Decety & Jackson, 2004, p. 71). There is ample evidence to support the notion that emotional responsiveness to another's distress is an innate capacity. The importance of social intelligence in human functioning, however, is also clear, particularly with regard to the abilities to take another's perspective and to anticipate the response that our behavior will elicit from others. Furthermore, as we have seen, the processes of perspective taking and empathy are linked. Evolutionary pressures are viewed as having selected for development of the human capacity for emotion sharing and the cognitive capacity to imaginatively adopt the psychological point of view of others (Davis, 1994). Furthermore, Jeremy

Rifkin (2009) argues in *The Empathetic Civilization* that evolutionary pressures continue. More specifically, advances in technology and communications have brought more diverse peoples together and heightened empathetic sensitivity, which acts as an "invisible hand" with the potential to extend the sense of awareness of the vulnerability we all share and our common desire to live to the entire human race and other species. Increasing our understanding of how this capacity of empathy develops and can be enhanced within the individual has been the focus of an extensive body of research.

It is beyond the scope of this chapter to summarize and integrate the many theories and findings about the development of the cognitive, affective, and motivational components of empathy and their underlying neurocortical foundations. Rather, our purposes are best served by considering the developmental progression of the increasing sophistication of empathetic response to the distress of others.

Emotional Reactivity

Individual differences in the capacity for empathy are based on the interaction of innate differences in emotional reactivity and the environmental socialization processes. Emotional reactivity is one of the dispositional dimensions of infant temperament, and individual differences in emotional reactivity are evident at birth. This innate difference in emotional reactivity both shapes, and is shaped by, socialization experiences that differ across cultures and subcultures with regard to parenting practices and societal emphasis on prosocial behaviors and social responsibility. The influences of the social environment are evident very early in life, such as with an infant's emotion contagion when they automatically mimic and synchronize their facial expressions, vocalizations, postures, emotions, and movements with those of others (Decety & Jackson, 2004). Infants begin to interpret facial expressions as emotional cues in the second half of their first year and demonstrate rudimentary awareness of the subjective states of others around a year of age (Decety & Jackson, 2004). Midway through their second year, infants react with concerned attention and helping behaviors that suggests the emergence of the capacity for empathy (Decety & Jackson, 2004).

Cognitive and Emotional Development

Beyond mimicking and the socialization of empathetic reactivity, the development of cognitive processes plays a key role in the development of empathy. More specifically, the way we mentally conceptualize others moves through levels of increasing sophistication and impacts our capacities for empathy

(Davis, 1994). In Piagetian terms, our ability to conceptualize moves through levels of increasing sophistication from the preoperational level through concrete operations to formal operational thought. During the first year of life infants are acquiring the awareness of a stable sense of self and others as different from the self. Around two to three years of age, as language skills develop, rudimentary role taking and perspective taking skills emerge and empathy can be observed in the prosocial behaviors of helping or comforting others.

The advances in understanding others mental states also become apparent around this time as demonstrated in the "false beliefs test" (Wimmer & Perner, 1983). In this test children are shown a box of crayons and asked what they think is in the box, and they typically respond "crayons." The box is opened and shown to contain candy instead of crayons. Then if asked what another child, who has not seen the actual contents of the box, would think was inside, children two to three years of age respond "candy." It is not until about four years of age that children understand that what they know would not be apparent to the other child who would have a false belief about what was in the box.

The development of empathy has also been linked to the adoption of moral principles, particularly with regard to caring or concern for the well-being of others and justice; that is, society's criteria for allocating resources based on considerations of merit, need, and equality (Hoffman, 2000). This association of empathy with moral principles is reflected in the stages in children's view of fairness (Damon, 1977; 1988). For example, by four years of age most children have developed an understanding of the obligation to share with others, but as they progress into childhood they increasingly endorse need-based and equality-based distribution and their support for "need" is enhanced by empathetic arousal (Hoffman, 2000). Further support for empathy as a moral emotion that both activates moral reasoning and motivates moral behavior is provided by the evidence that empathy has both a direct influence on prosocial behavior and an indirect pathway through its association with moral reasoning (Eisenberg, 2005).

The child's developing cognitive abilities interact with the increasing sophistication and differentiation in emotional reactivity that is also occurring. Corresponding to this progression in conceptualization of the self and others is the transformation from generally undifferentiated distress in response to the distress of others to more specific feelings of sympathy and compassion (Davis, 1994).

Along with the progression in cognitive conceptualizations of self and others and emotional differentiation, there is also progressive development in social cognition, more specifically in perspective taking. Robert Selman (1980; 2003) formulated an influential model that describes the gradual development of social cognition and perspective taking that occurs through interactions with others. A recent revision of Selman's model (Elfers et al., 2008) provides a clear description of the progression in perspective taking beginning with the *undifferentiated/egocentric* stage that characterizes early childhood during which the child differentiates individuals as separate physical entities but does not appreciate that these entities have their own separate points of view. At the *differentiated/subjective* stage, typically evident around six to eight years of age, the child realizes that different individuals can have different perspectives about the same situation but does not put differing perspectives in relation to each other. At the *self-reflective/reciprocal* stage, typically evident around 8-10 years of age, the child is able to switch between his or her own and others perspectives, sequentially but not simultaneously. The ability to take on the multiple perspectives simultaneously is characteristic of the *third person/mutual* stage, evident typically around 10-12 years of age, in which the child can take the perspective of a third person on both his or her own and another's perspective. At the *societal and conventional systems* stage, typically evident around 12-15 years of age, the child can also understand and apply the generalized perspective of a societal group and society in general.

The development of the ability to represent and understand both objective and subjective aspects of self and others is functionally linked to the development of the executive functions that monitor and regulate thoughts, emotions, and actions (Decety & Jackson, 2004). Increasing sophistication in these skills is apparent in early adolescence. The adolescent views others as having stable identities and internal states that persist beyond the immediate situation, is able to anticipate other's reactions in different situations, and responds empathetically to the distress of people as a group as well as an individual (Goldstein & Michaels, 1985).

Although interrelated, the emotional and cognitive dimensions of empathy have different developmental trajectories. The brain structures involved in empathy mature earlier than those involved in cognitive perspective taking. The dorsolateral prefrontal cortex in particular is not fully mature until age 25 and given its possible role in the modulation and control of affective responses "might suggest that the full capacity for effective and adaptive empathic responding is not developed until late adolescence" (Singer, 2006, p. 861).

Selman's model of development of social cognition has recently been extended into adulthood with the addition of two metareflective stages of advanced thinking in search of means of reaching consensus or resolution of disparate views (Elfers et al., 2008). The stage of *idealized perspective taking* is characterized by the motivation to create conditions such as trust, fairness, and respect that are conductive to possible solutions of problems arising out of strongly divergent perspectives. The stage of *dialogical engagement with others* posits that in the absence of any formal conditions, "the only way to come to a joint understanding of radically divergent perspectives is to persevere with patience and openness to locate possibilities of truth in each of the competing perspectives" (p. 253). Beyond serving as possible pathways to moving beyond seemingly incommensurable positions and perspectives, these two metareflective stages provide direction for educational interventions in terms of salient learning objectives. First, students could be made aware of these advanced levels of perspective taking that "hold transformative potential for their communities and societies, as well as for themselves" (p. 255). Second, development of these advanced levels of perspective taking could be fostered through providing educational experiences that engage students in critically considering a wider range of perspectives in the context of debate and problem solving around contemporary social and moral issues such as poverty, climate change, and religious or ethnic conflict.

The Process of Socialization

Research on the socialization of empathetic responding has focused on three dimensions: the affective quality of the child's relationship with the parent, parental empathy, and parental discipline techniques (Davis, 1994). The findings suggest that the more secure and affectionate the family relationships, the greater the level of empathetic disposition of the child. That is, the child's emotional responsivity is associated with the experiences of close and secure family relationships (Davis, 1994). Similarly, parental warmth and expressiveness have been associated with empathy-related responding (Eisenberg, 2005). With regard to parenting discipline practices, an inductive style that emphasizes the negative impact and social consequences of a child's actions is thought to lead the child to adopt an other-oriented view. Modeling is one of the proposed mechanisms for the impact of family relationships and parenting practices on the development of empathy.

One approach to enhancing empathy with school age children, Roots of Empathy, uses observation of mother-baby interactions to evoke caring and enhance perspective taking. This program was developed by Mary Gordon (2009) and implemented in school systems across Canada with a curriculum for kindergarten classes and grades 1–3, 4–6, and 7–8. The program involves monthly visit to the classroom of parents and their baby starting when the baby is two to four months of age and continuing throughout the school year. The relationship between the parents and her child is viewed as a template for positive empathetic relationships. The visits provide an opportunity for a trained instructor to focus the children's attention on the development of the baby and the parent child relationship which in turn is an opportunity for developing the social and emotional competence of the children through instructor prompted questions and reflection about the temperament of the baby, their own temperament, and that of their classmates. Children are coached in taking the perspective of the baby and of the parents, and learn strategies for engaging the baby and for comforting crying babies. The curriculum involves previsit and postvisit exercises through which instructors make connections to popular children's literature to illustrate themes such as loneliness, sadness, and inclusion. A number of outcome studies have been conducted, including two randomized control trials, and findings based on teacher pre–post reports indicate that children who participated in the Roots of Empathy Program had greater gains in perspective taking and prosocial behavior and decreases in aggression and other antisocial behaviors than comparison children who did not participate in the program (Gordon, 2009).

Enhancing and Fostering Empathy

Beyond the socialization of empathy, questions arise about whether, and to what extent, empathy can be enhanced and taught. The desire to enhance empathy stems from the association of empathy with prosocial behavior and moral development in general, and as a basis for understanding and engaging religious, ethnic, and political differences in particular. Although empathy is considered an innate ability, it is a complex phenomenon that is triggered voluntarily as well as automatically, and thus is potentially modifiable. More specifically, empathy "is susceptible to social-cognitive intervention" (Decety & Jackson, 2004, p. 94), and this susceptibility provides an opportunity to enhance empathetic capacity through education (Hoffman, 2000).

Much of our understanding of how to enhance empathy stems from the professional training of health care and social service providers and educators. In these professions, the capacity for empathy is viewed as essential for establishing and maintaining effective therapeutic and learning relationships. With regard to professional training, it has been useful to distinguish between empathy as a dispositional trait and empathy as a clinical skill. The focus of training is to enhance the professional practitioner's empathetic skills by building on the natural disposition of empathy through practice and training (Alligood, 1992). A recent review of the medical education literature, for example, found support for the effectiveness of a range of education strategies, including communication skills training and reflective writing exercises, in promoting empathy in medical students compared to controls not receiving this training (Stepien & Baernstein, 2006).

In general, efforts to enhance empathic concern for someone in need focuses on increasing perspective taking, either through having the person imagine how another person perceives their situation and would feel or how they themselves would feel if they were in that same situation (Batson et al., 1997). Efforts to enhance empathetic understanding typically focus on fostering *empathetic accuracy* through sensitive, nonjudgmental listening. In addition, communication is another component of critical importance in extending the impact of empathy beyond prosocial behavior. *Empathetic communication* is the expression of empathy in a way that "would be experienced as understanding, accepting, and supportive by the person undergoing the emotional distress" (Goldstein & Michaels, 1985, p. 45). Communicating understanding of the mental states and feelings of a person in distress can benefit the person directly without being accompanied by overt helping. Therapist, teachers, and parents frequently have beneficial impact with others in distress by accurately and effectively communicating empathy without intervening directly to alleviate the cause of the person's distress.

Carl Rogers (1975) advocated a central role for empathy in his approach to effective psychotherapy and humanistic education, and emphasized that empathy involved more than just sensitivity to the other person's affective world but also the capacity to communicate this understand to the other person. Correspondingly, didactic-experiential training programs were developed to enhance empathy in which the principles were taught in supervision training sessions and practiced in counseling and role play situations (Carkhuff, 1969; Traux & Carkhuff, 1967). In the late 1970s, a number of approaches were developed to enhance empathy and human relations skills such as encounter groups, and sensitivity training or "T" groups. These approaches combined training in a spectrum of psychological and interpersonal skills through a group experience in which the skills were practiced in a supportive and affirming context.

Beyond professional training of care providers and educators, findings from a number of studies indicate that it is possible to increase levels of empathy through a variety of training programs. As a result, empathy has been incorporated into many intergroup relations and dialogue programs, including conflict resolution workshops and multicultural education programs (Stephan & Finlay, 1999). The approaches to fostering empathy typically include engagement with information about group values, beliefs, and norms to enhance perspective taking, and the induction of empathy by inviting participants to identify with members of the other group through attending to the feelings expressed in narratives, writings, or role playing. Not only do these intergroup relations program demonstrate that empathy can be enhance, they also provide additional support for the role of empathy in prosocial behavior by demonstrating the effects that enhancing empathy have on intergroup relations. Part of the effectiveness of intergroup relations and dialogue groups comes about through bringing groups together. There is considerable empirical support from research in the field of social psychology for the contact hypothesis, which maintains that contact among members of different groups lowers hostility, prejudice, and stereotype, primarily through reducing intergroup anxiety associated with negative expectations of rejection and discrimination during an intergroup encounter (Crisp & Turner, 2009). Intergroup relations and dialogue programs go beyond the benefits of bringing together members of different social groups through using various techniques to promote perspective taking and arouse empathetic concern. These programs have proven effective in reducing prejudice and improving intergroup relations (Stephan & Finlay, 1999) and provide support for the notion that the dialogue programs improved interpersonal relations through increasing empathy.

Empathy can also be enhanced outside of formal training programs. Cross-group friendships are particularly effective in reducing intergroup prejudice, and this relationship is mediated by the process of mutual self-disclosure which generates empathy (Turner et al., 2007). Furthermore, increasing empathy for a member of a stigmatized group not only produces a more positive attitude for that person, but can also generalize to a more positive attitude about the stigmatized group as a whole (Batson et at., 1997). Moreover, the benefits have also been demonstrated to occur when the experience of contact is not direct, but vicarious through knowing people in one's social network who engage in positive interactions with members of outgroups (Crisp & Turner, 2009). This research provides empirical support for higher education's commitment to campus diversity and inclusiveness as ways to foster positive attitudes toward other groups through enabling contact and cross-group friendships that generate empathy.

Recently, it has been demonstrated that these positive effects of engagement with difference can also occur thorough imagined interactions. That is, mentally simulating a positive encounter with an outgroup activates cognitive-behavioral processes similar to actual contact, reduces intergroup anxiety, and leads to improved outgroup attitudes and reduced impact of negative stereotypes on performance (Crisp & Turner, 2009). These extensions of the positive benefits of intergroup engagement through simulation indicates that opportunities to vicariously experience positive interactions with outgroup members might also be a mechanism to enhance empathy when opportunities for direct contact with outgroups or specific situations are limited. For example, given the number of different ethnic, religious, and political groups in a community, it is not possible to have direct contact with each and every group. Furthermore, from an educational perspective, imagined intergroup contact has the potential to be an efficient and effective means to promote more positive perceptions of outgroups and prepare students for engagement: "The value in imagined contact is in its ability to encourage people to seek out contact, to remove inhibitions associated with existing prejudice, and to prepare people to engage outgroups with an open mind" (Crisp & Turner, 2009, p. 231).

We previously discussed the similarity bias that works to elicit projections for those viewed as similar to ourselves and stereotypes for those perceived as different. Thus, it is not surprising that there is also an empathy bias in favor of those who are perceived as being similar to ourselves: "People empathize with and help others who they are led to believe share their preferences, attitudes, interests, life goals, and chronic concerns" (Hoffman, 2000, p. 294). Similarity bias can be understood in relation to the normal human process of social categorization of people into in-groups and out-groups: "People respond systematically more favorably to others whom they perceive to belong to their group than to different groups" (Gaertner & Dovidio, 2008, p. 111). Furthermore, the process of social categorization enhances perceptions of similarities of members within groups and exaggerates differences between groups. This understanding suggests that attempts to eliminate similarity based bias should be directed toward shifting the basis for categorization to an alternative that is more inclusive. One strategy is *recategorization* as common members of a more inclusive or superordinate group. For example, it is a common experience to unite disparate groups under a larger umbrella, such as Americans or veterans. Another strategy is *decategorization*, such that former in-group and out-group members are induced to perceive themselves as distinct individuals. Both strategies target social categorizations by altering perception of group boundaries to reduce bias (Gaertner & Dovidio, 2008). We will consider these categorization strategies in more detail in relation to our discussion of identity and what colleges and universities can do to reduce intergroup bias and promote intergroup relations in Chapter 6.

Direct educational efforts can also be undertaken to combat empathy bias that favors those who are similar and against those who are perceived as different through intentionally identifying and focusing on commonalities among individuals and cultural groups rather than surface differences. It has been argued that as our society becomes increasing multicultural, there is an increased need for such direct educational approaches by parents and teachers to create a sense of human oneness:

> This may require identifying empathetic bias and showing children that while it is natural to empathize with people who share one's life experiences, a certain amount of empathic impartiality is necessary. It also requires pointing out that despite people's social, cultural, and physical differences, there are important similarities in emotional responses-responses to being treated unfairly, for example, and to life crises like separation, loss, and aging (Hoffman, 2000, p. 23).

In addition to working to identify and combat empathetic bias that favors similarities, it is also necessary to enlarge the interpretative frame to accommodate differences. Globalization and immigration have lead to increasing diversity across the world and thus encounters of people with different cultural backgrounds. Fostering empathy across cultural differences requires cultural empathy: understanding of how a person's behavior is linked to the values, assumptions, and expectations of his or her culture (Pedersen & Pope,

2010). The same behaviors can have different meanings across cultures, and likewise different behaviors can have the same meaning. Therefore, accurate interpretation of behaviors requires an understanding of the cultural expectations regarding those behaviors. To develop the ability to "interpret another person's behavior accurately in the context of that person's culturally learned expectations" (Petersen & Pope, 2010, p. 849), increased multicultural awareness is necessary.

> The underlying principle of multicultural awareness is to emphasize at the same time both the culture-specific characteristics that differentiate and the culture-general characteristics that unite (Petersen & Pope, 2010, p. 846).

In our globally interconnected world, multiculturalism in now a generic component of competence needed to explain and understand expectations, intentions, and behaviors within a cultural context (Petersen & Pope, 2010). The implication is that colleges and universities have to ensure that their students develop multicultural awareness, knowledge, and competencies.

There is evidence that the empathetic capacity of undergraduates can be enhanced through various educational or instructional approaches. For example, college students who participated in peer facilitation skills training involving instruction in nonjudgmental and emphatic listening improved significantly more in perspective taking and empathetic concern than students who did not receive the training (Hatcher & Nadeau, 1994). With regard to undergraduate education, however, community service programs in general and service learning in particular have demonstrated the most promise for enhancing the capacity for empathy. The evidence about the impact of service learning in enhancing empathy, and in turn moral development, is best considered in the context of identity formation which is the focus of the following chapter.

CHAPTER 5

Identity and the Process of Self-Authorship

The most important fact about humans is that they are naturally self-constituting creatures. Their capacities for self-reflective awareness afford them a subjective perspective on themselves and permit them to construct for themselves a self for which they are responsible and that gives meaning to their lives (McKinnon, 2005, p. 59).

The concept of identity refers to the distinctly human capacity to reflect on and make sense of ourselves. As we have discussed, identity formation is a major developmental task of emerging adulthood and therefore an integral focus of a formative education committed to fostering the development of the whole person. Moreover, along with personal epistemology and the capacity for empathy, developing an integrated sense of oneself that includes agency for personal and social responsibility is essential for constructively engaging difference. Before considering the role of higher education in fostering the development of identity, this chapter will review our current understanding of the nature of identity, its functions, and the factors and processes that contribute to identity formation.

THE NATURE OF THE SELF AND IDENTITY

The concept of *self* has a long history in psychology, with varied meanings involving self as known (object) and self as knower (subject). The objective self includes knowledge of our characteristics, emotional tendencies, and motives. The subjective self involves the conscious experience of our agency, self-direction, and responsibility for self-management and also appropriation;

that is, the conscious process of owning or disowning and integrating aspects of the self "in order to shape and modify the reality of who we are" (Blasi, 2004a, p. 15). These appropriations, in turn, are manifested and validated through our commitments. Identity can be understood as an individual's response to the question, "Who am I?"

Identity as a social-psychological construct is based on the view of individuals as social beings with needs for a personal sense of uniqueness and significance and also a sense of belonging and mattering to significant others (Adams & Marshall, 1996). That is, an individual needs a sense of self-esteem and needs to know that he or she makes a difference and counts in some way. This view leads to conceptualizing identity as the intersection of two complementary developmental processes (Adams & Marshall, 1996; Adams et al., 1987): *differentiation*, the process of highlighting various aspects of the self and asserting oneself as an unique individual; and *integration*, the process of becoming part of a larger group and connected to others, and fitting in with familial, social, cultural norms (Schwartz, 2001). Two dynamics are at work: to be special and unique through the process of individualization and to belong through the process of integration (Adams & Marshall, 1996).

Identity can also be understood in terms of the functions or the roles that identity serves in the person's life (Adams & Marshall, 1996). Identity is essentially a self-regulatory system that serves to direct attention, filter or process information, manage impressions, and select appropriate behaviors. Moreover, identity serves as the integrating structure for self-understanding, a sense of personal control and free will, and giving meaning and direction to our lives through our commitments, values, and goals. Identity also motivates a striving for consistency, coherence, and harmony between values, beliefs, and commitments and enables the recognition of potential through a sense of future possibilities and alternative choices.

Identity Status: Exploration and Commitment

The study of identity has been particularly influenced by the theoretical work of Erikson (1963; 1968) who viewed identity as a self-constructed synthesis of components "into a coherent and autonomous self that guides the unfolding of one's adult life course" (Montgomery, 2005, p. 347). There are two major components. *Personal identity* refers to the goals, values, beliefs, and other aspects of the self that distinguish a person from other people. *Social* or *group identity* refers to a sense of inner solidarity with a group's ideals and consists of elements that have been integrated into one's sense of self from groups to which the person belongs.

The process of identity formation is central to Erikson's theory of personality development which continues throughout the life span. Erikson postulated eight stages of psychosocial development, with each stage having a characteristic crisis or central issue, the resolution of which was critical to subsequent development. Erikson considered identity formation as the major developmental task of adolescence, a period characterized by actively questioning and exploring various possibilities before committing to particular goals, values, and career choices. Advances in cognitive abilities that occur in adolescence and early adulthood bring new capacities for perspective taking, alterations in beliefs, and a sense of increased vulnerability that constitutes a crisis with regard to identity. How the person manages these crises has implications for the person's subsequent development (Schwartz, 2001).

Identity in Erikson's theory is represented by a single bipolar dimension anchored at one end by *identity confusion* and at the other end by *identity synthesis*. The more the multiple facets of identity such as career, religion, and political ideology come together to form a consistent mosaic, the greater is the identity synthesis (Schwartz, 2001). A coherent, well-integrated identity structure provides a sense of purpose and direction, and a basis for effectively coping with and adapting to the demands and challenges of life. Individuals at any point in their lives can be placed at some point on the identity confusion-identity synthesis continuum.

James Marcia (1996) extrapolated from Erikson's theory two dimension of identity. *Exploration* refers to the processes of learning about oneself, trying out of alternative choices, and ways of living and being in the world, particularly in the areas of ideology, beliefs, love, and work. *Commitment* refers to choosing among alternatives and adoption of a set of goals, values, and beliefs. A person's position along Erikson's identity–confusion continuum can be characterized in terms of the intersection of these two processes of exploration and commitment, which yields the four identity statuses (Marcia, 1966) as depicted in the chart below:

	Commitment	
	Low	High
High **Exploration**	**Moratorium**	**Achievement**
Low	**Diffusion**	**Foreclosure**

- *Identity diffusion* is an apathetic state characterized by the relative lack of both exploration and commitment.
- *Identity foreclosure* is the state characterized by having made commitments to a set of goals, values, beliefs, or career choices, or uncritically adopting those of others, in the relative absence of prior exploration.

- *Identity moratorium* is the state of open-mindedness and active exploration in the relative absence of commitment.
- *Identity achievement* is considered the most mature state and is characterized by commitments that are made following a period of exploration
  (Schwartz, 2001).

Identity statuses are not considered stages of development, but rather as
different phases in the process of identity formation. These phases do not follow a unidirectional developmental sequence, and individuals may repeatedly
recycle through these phases.

A summary of the large body of research regarding the relationship of
these four identity statuses with other dimensions of development (Kroger,
1993) indicates that individuals characterized in the identity achievement status demonstrate the highest levels of moral reasoning, internal locus of control,
self-esteem, performance under stress, and intimacy in interpersonal relationships. In addition, identity status has been related to personality characteristic,
including openness, which refers to tolerance and exploration of the unfamiliar,
and conscientiousness, which refers to organization, persistence, and motivation
in goal-directed behavior. Consistent with expectations that openness would be
related to exploration and conscientiousness with commitment, adolescents in
the foreclosure status have been found to have lower levels of openness than
those in the moratorium and achievement statuses, and those in the foreclosure
and achievement status have been found to have higher levels of conscientiousness than those in the diffuse and moratorium statuses (Luyckx et al., 2005).

While descriptively useful, subsequent research has revealed some limitations of the identity status model, including the need for additional statuses
beyond the original four and the recognition that individuals could be at different levels of identity across different domains of career, relationships, and
values (Moshman, 1999; Fadjukoff et al., 2005). Furthermore, the identity status model conceptualizes personal identity as static rather than as a dynamic
process of constructing and revising one's sense of self (Schwartz, 2001).

With regard to the need for additional statuses, Luyckx and colleagues
(2005; 2006) have provided evidence for an expansion of Marcia's original two
dimensions, which they refer to as *exploration in breadth* and *commitment making*, with the addition of two new dimensions, *exploration in depth* and *identification with commitment*. With these expanded dimensions, achievement status
is characterized by high exploration in both breadth and depth, and the highest identification with commitment. The foreclosure status is characterized
by low exploration in breadth but moderate exploration in depth and high
commitment making, although to a lesser extent than achievement status.
The moratorium status is characterized by exploration in breadth but not in
depth, as individuals in this identity configuration explore various social roles
and ideologies and exhibit a low to moderate level of commitment making

and identification with commitment. The diffusion status is characterized by low to moderate exploration in breadth and depth, low commitment making, and the lowest identification with commitment. Employing these new dimensions, Luyckx and colleagues provided support for the original four statuses but also generated an additional status they labeled *carefree diffuse*, which is characterized by low to moderate levels of exploration in depth and breadth and moderate levels of commitment but better adjustment than typically associated with diffusion status.

In Marcia's model identity statues represent outcomes of how the adolescent resolved the developmental task of identity formation and is based on the idea that exploration precedes commitment. In a more recent conceptualization, the focus is on how adolescents manage their commitments, and identity formation is considered as involving the interplay of three dimensions: commitment, in-depth explorations, and reconsideration (Meeus et al., 2002; 2010). In-depth exploration involves the ways in which adolescents maintain and validate the commitments they have already made by reflecting on them, looking for information, and talking with others about them. Reconsideration refers to the process of comparing current commitments with possible alternative commitments when the current commitments are no longer satisfactory. This model also results in identity statuses that are similar to Marcia's. The clearest differences in conceptualization are apparent in contrasting the foreclosed and achievement statuses of Marcia, which are based on the level of exploration before commitment, with the statuses of closure and achieving commitment, which make no claims about the past but rather describe the exploration of the present commitment. Closure is characterized by high commitment and low exploration, and achieving commitment is characterized by high commitment to which the adolescent explores and give a lot of attention. Some support for this conceptualization is provided by a study of Dutch adolescents, which examined the relationship of exploration and commitment over a three-year period across the two domains, personal relationships and societal identity, as reflected in school and work (Meeus et al., 2002). The findings indicated that adolescents with strong commitments also explore them frequently, whereas those with low exploration in general have weak commitments. As expected, relational identity showed a greater stability of commitment than of exploration, which was not the case for societal identity. In neither identity domain, however, was commitment predictive of exploration three years later, nor was exploration predictive of commitment.

The models developed by Luyckx and colleagues and Meeus and colleagues share a dual-cycle conceptualization of identity formation (Meeus, 2011). In the Luyckx model the first cycle involves identity formation through explorations in breath followed by making commitments, and the second cycle involves explorations in-depth that enable identification with commitment. The order of both cycles is exploration in-breadth, commitment making, explorations in-depth, and identification with commitment. In the Meeus model, identity formation involves the continuous interplay between commitment, reconsideration, and in-depth exploration. The first cycle involves identity formation through forming and reconsidering commitments, and the second cycle involves identity maintenance and consolidation through exploring identity commitments in depth. The order of both cycles is reconsideration, commitment, and in-depth explorations.

The issue of the developmental sequence and stability of identity statuses has also been addressed. A recent review of the longitudinal evidence (Meeus, 2011) indicates that personal identity maturation progresses slowly during adolescence and takes many forms reflecting increases in explorations and commitments and a decrease in reconsideration of alternatives, but many adolescents do not change statuses; the high commitment statuses, foreclosure and achievement, have greater stability than the diffuse and moratorium statues; and the stability of identity is higher in adulthood than adolescence. Furthermore, it is argued that the identity status continuum has the order diffuse > moratorium > foreclosure (early closure or closure) > achievement. Within this progression, two sets of transitions have been identified: diffuse > foreclosure (early closure) > achievement and diffuse > moratorium > closure > achievement. While transitions are predominately progressive, some adolescents exhibit regressive patterns characterized by reconsidering commitments (achievement> moratorium) or movement with less active consideration (achievement > foreclosure). The statuses reflecting high commitment, achievement and foreclosure (early closure and closure), are the most frequent end points in adolescent identity formation.

While additional refinements of identity dimensions and statuses are likely, characterizing an individual's resolution of identity issues or current engagement in the process of identity formation in terms of relative engagement with the processes of exploration and commitment has proven useful. Furthermore, the two dimensions are not orthogonal, but rather are directly related within specific identity domains and statuses derived from these dimensions are reliably associated with other aspects of development. In particular, achievement statuses are generally associated with higher levels of moral reasoning, the personality dimensions of openness and conscientiousness, and an evaluativist epistemic stance.

Collective Identity

Individuals inhabit a social ecology and in constructing their sense of identity are influenced by the groups with which they associate and have some characteristics in common, such as ethnicity, gender, occupation, religion, or political affiliation. *Collective identity* is that component of a person's identity that is derived from membership in a group and is shared with the other members of the group (Simon & Klandermans, 2001).

Several psychological processes operate to strengthen members' sense of belonging to a cohesive group that provides them with respect and the collective strength to act efficaciously (Simon & Klandermans, 2001). More specifically, stereotyping at the cognitive level and conformity at the behavioral level accentuate intragroup similarities and intergroup differences. Similarly, prejudice at the affective level and discrimination at the behavioral level foster viewing the in-group positively compared to the out-group, induce efforts to secure a privileged position for the in-group, and spur intergroup competition for power. In turn, collective identity heightens, and is reinforced by, the awareness of shared grievances (Simon & Klandermans, 2001).

Collective identity has cognitive, affective, and behavioral dimensions (Ashmore et al., 2004). Cognitively, the most basic element is self-categorization; that is, identifying oneself as a member of a group. Although others may refer to someone as a member of a particular social group, it is the subjective claim of membership that is determinative for identity. Another cognitive element is evaluation. The person attaches personal meaning, positive (self-esteem) or negative (stigma), and makes judgments about other's perceptions of the favorability of the groups to which he or she belongs. Individuals belong to multiple groups. The affective dimension of collective identity involves the person's sense of emotional attachment or felt closeness to a group and sense of interdependence or shared fate. The behavioral dimension refers to the influence a group has on one's social behavior and the degree to which the person's behavior expresses actions, such as cultural or religious practices, that are reflective of group membership.

Collective identity, like identity in general, serves important psychological functions related to our needs for belongingness and distinctiveness, such as respect and esteem, understanding and meaning, and agency (Simon & Klandermans, 2001). Collective identity provides a perspective or interpretative lens on the social world and our place in it, and can motivate individual and collective social actions (Simon, 2004). For example, a person's sense of collective identity can influence concerns about social justice and willingness to engage in social change processes (Simon & Klandermans, 2001). Collective identity could, however, also motivate conformity and stereotyping of oneself and others (Simon, 2004) and intergroup bias such as evaluating one's own group more favorably and other groups less favorably, which intensifies under threat (Deaux, 1996). How one's group is treated by others matters. For example, procedural justice—that is, being treated fairly—communicates respect and importance that in turn influences people's attitudes and feelings and willingness to act on behalf of the group (Tyler & Smith, 1999).

The relationship of collective identity to social behavior is very complex. Beyond the cognitive, affective, and behavioral dimension, several elements in particular are important to the influence of collective identity on social behavior: the goodness of fit, or how typical one views himself or herself to be of the group; the centrality or salience, or the importance of the group membership to the person's overall self-concept; and embeddedness, which refers to the degree to which a person's everyday social interactions and social network involve other members of the social group (Ashmore et al., 2004). These elements interact with each other and with situational characteristics and different combinations have been found to be important for an array of outcomes including academic achievement, physical and psychological well-being, and civic and social engagement (Ashmore et al., 2004). Furthermore, people identify with multiple social groups, and these multiple social identities exist simultaneously under the overall umbrella of identity. Thus, across time and situations, different identities may come into play as a function of the interaction of person variables, such as readiness, and social context characteristics, such as prejudice (Simon & Klandermans, 2001). In our increasingly pluralistic and globally interconnected world, the influences that group identities have on social behavior attest to the necessity for enhancing our understanding of collective identity and how fostering multiple identities could serve to lessen intergroup conflict:

> If we can learn how the integration of multiple identities takes place and can be promoted, we can perhaps show that ethnocentrism and intergroup conflict within a society is not a necessary concomitant of pluralism (Phinney, 1993, p. 56).

IDENTITY FORMATION AS A DEVELOPMENTAL TASK

Each culture has relatively distinct periods in the life cycle with socially recognized expectations that a maturing individual is expected to accomplish. Along with developing competencies, interpersonal relationships, autonomy, and the capacity for self-regulation of attention, emotions, and behaviors, the process of formulating a sense of identity is one of the primary developmental tasks of adolescence and emerging adulthood in the United States and other modern societies (Chickering, 1969). As we discussed in Chapter 2, emerging adulthood is the period occurring after the dependency of childhood and adolescence but before the responsibilities that are normative of adulthood, roughly ages 18 to 25 (Arnett, 2000), that offers the most opportunities for identity explorations of possible life directions and commitments in the areas of love, work and education, and worldview. Emerging adulthood is essentially a time of self-authorship that spans the undergraduate years, and thus, in a very real sense, the university serves as a lab for identity development.

Within the overall developmental task of identity formation, developing the capacity for long-term intimate relationships of trust and mutuality is a key developmental task of adolescence and emerging adulthood. Erikson conceptualized intimacy as "the willingness to participate in a supportive, tender relationship without losing one's self in the relationship," and argued that having a sense of identity was necessary for the development of psychosocially mature intimacy (Montgomery, 2005, p. 347).

Humans have a lifelong propensity to seek physical and psychological closeness to another (Montgomery, 2005). The capacity for intimacy emerges through transactions of the person with her or his social environment. These transactions give rise to expectations about relationships and ways of engaging with others that constitute a pattern that is perpetuated across time and successive developmental periods, but modified through the processes of assimilation and accommodation to new experiences and situations (Collins & Sroufe, 1999). Earlier transactions influence later transactions. For example, the quality of interpersonal relationships through childhood and adolescence has been found to be associated with the quality of early attachments and relationships (Collins & Sroufe, 1999).

Intimacy involves maintaining a secure sense of self while connecting with another person, establishing mutuality of emotional involvement and understanding, and committing to the processes of compromise and self-sacrifice entailed in an intimate relationship (Paul et al. 1998). The development of the capacity for intimacy occurs within the context of changes in social, emotional, physical, and cognitive domains that are mutually influential. Developmental changes also promote transitions in type of relationships. For example, a focus on romantic relationships frequently occurs in the context of other transitions, such as the entry into college, and the success or failure of romantic relationships has been found to be a predictor of academic success, satisfaction, and mental health (Paul et al. 1998). A mature capacity for intimacy, based on a solid sense of self, reflected in the desire and ability to engage in close, committed relationships is considered essential for fulfilling the developmental tasks of adult life, especially marriage and parenthood. Unfortunately, for some, the development of identity and intimacy are compromised in some way with negative consequences for their well-being. One factor that can interfere with developing the capacity for intimacy is the experience or fear of rejection.

People vary both in their experiences of rejection and their sensitivity to rejection. For example, some people may carry their previous experiences of rejection by parents, peers, romantic partner, or arising from their group status into relationships and social situations and are prone to readily perceive and over react to rejection. Sometimes rejection-sensitivity leads to avoidance strategies and other times to overinvestment strategies as individuals endeavor to protect themselves from rejection. Rejection-sensitivity is self-perpetuating. That is, because a person expects rejection, he or she may interact in ways that elicit rejection (Downey et al., 1999). Overcoming rejection sensitivity is essential to succeeding with the developmental task of developing the capacity for intimacy.

Identity and Autonomy

Identity also intersects with the developmental task of *autonomy*. More than achieving independence, autonomy reflects the development of the capacities for self-motivation and self-regulation and is fostered by contexts that the person perceives as affording choices and freedom from external pressure toward behaving or thinking in a certain way (Ryan & Deci, 2000).

Cultures differ in the levels of choice they provide in the construction of the mature self, and one's sense of identity is both assigned and selected. In most modern societies, identity is increasingly selected (Adams & Marshall, 1996).The process of globalization has contributed to a reduction in identities that are assigned or conferred through one's birthrights, family social position, and religion and has fostered increased freedom, range of role models and opportunities, and expectations for individuals to construct their own identities. However, individuals continue to experience a range of social pressures, constraints, and rewards during this process of identity formation. As a consequence, some aspects of a person's identity are *extrinsically motivated* in that these arise from and are maintained by expectations, rewards, and punishments in one's environment. Other aspects of a person's identity are *intrinsically motivated* in that these evolve out of one's interests and are inherently enjoyable and satisfying.

There is a large area between these two poles that constitutes a continuum of relative autonomy (Ryan & Deci, 2003). Some external expectations and values can become internalized or personally endorsed and assimilated into the self because they have instrumental value for the person (Ryan & Deci, 2003). That is, the person adopts and maintains a role not because it is assigned or personally meaningful but for some other reason, such as to enhance self-esteem or avoid feelings of anxiety or guilt. For example, this continuum can be observed with regard to religious identity. For some people religious identity is assigned not chosen, and participation in religious practices is extrinsically motivated to maintain approval of parents and others in their community. For others, religious identity has been internalized and participation in religious practices serves to avoid feelings of anxiety and guilt, whereas for others participation is completely volitional and personally meaningful.

THE DETERMINANTS OF IDENTITY DEVELOPMENT

Identity development involves a continuous transaction in which the social context influences, and is influenced by, the developing person (Bosma & Kunnen, 2001). Individuals are actively involved in shaping their opportunities and eliciting support from their environment, and the degree of environmental support for change and exploration and the range of expectations and available opportunities in one's social world influence identity development. Thus, identity is both personally and socially constructed (Vignoles et al., 2011). The construction of identity takes place through discourse, and therefore the development of identity can be understood as a collaborative enterprise that takes place within the context of relationships. Consequently, any consideration of the determinants that influence identity development must address both personal and social context factors and relationship processes.

Personal Factors: Cognition, Motivation and Personality

Cognitive development is clearly important to the process of identity formation. It is not just the level of operational thinking, concrete versus abstract, but rather epistemic cognition that is the critical link in the cognition-identity relationship (Moshman, 1999). As we discussed in Chapter 3, the transition from concrete operational thought to formal operational thinking in adolescence brings with it the possibility to think about knowledge in a different way that in turn influences one's personal epistemology. Children at the concrete operational level of thinking lack the capacities for reflective thought and making abstractions. They understand different knowledge claims as different interpretations of facts and view knowledge as true facts. With maturation of thought, differences in knowledge claims are recognized and it is understood that "different persons not only may know different things but sometimes also may know the same thing in different ways" (Chandler, 1988, p. 403). At this level of maturation, however, differences are still viewed as able to be set right by the authority of objective facts.

The movement from concrete to formal operational thinking is a gateway to more sophisticated epistemological thinking, and the person is able to view knowledge as a construction around which a consensus can be reached on the basis of supporting evidence and subsequently altered with new or better evidence. It is only with the movement to formal operational thinking, and the ability to abstract from individual cases, that differences in knowledge claims call into question the possibility of objective truth and give rise to epistemic doubt. The capacity for and experience of epistemic doubt is potentially disruptive and has been posited as a "stepping stone" to higher levels of identity achievement (Boyes & Chandler, 1992). Support for this contention is provided by studies that link epistemic development and identity status. In an early study, viewing knowledge as certain was associated with both diffuse and foreclosed statuses, whereas a skeptical view of knowledge was associated with either diffuse or moratorium statuses, and viewing knowledge as an interpretative but rational choice among alternatives was associated with achievement status (Boyes & Chandler, 1992). In a more recent cross-sectional and longitudinal study of German adolescents (Krettenauer, 2005), identity diffusion was associated with absolutism, and identity moratorium was related to multiplism, but identity foreclosure was not related to epistemic level. However, attaining epistemic evaluativism was associated with an increase in identity achievement scores 18 months later.

Another way of understanding identity development is with regard to what motivates it. People construct individual and collective identities that provide them with a sense of self-esteem, distinctiveness, belonging, efficacy, meaning, and continuity (Vignoles et al., 2006). Different motives and multiple combinations of motives contribute to identity construction at various times. For example, striving for a sense of personal agency or efficacy and a sense of belonging have been identified as motivators of the processes of identity exploration and commitment (Bosma & Kunnen, 2001). Similar to the role of epistemic doubt, conflict in the perceived fit between a person's commitments and needs can also motivate identity development or adaptation to one's social context through the processes of assimilation and accommodation (Baumeister & Muraven, 1996). Assimilation involves efforts to change the situation itself or the interpretation of the situation, and if successful, identity commitments are reaffirmed. If assimilation is not successful, accommodation involves changes in self-perception and identity commitments.

Some commitments and activities are personally expressive—they are particularly authentic to the "true self" and evoke a sense of meshing with the activity, an intense feeling of being alive or being complete or fulfilled while engaged in an activity, and the impression that this is what one was meant to do and who one really is (Waterman, 1984; 1993). This notion of true self derives from the philosophical and ethical system of *eudemonism* that refers to the person's obligation and efforts to recognize and live in accordance with their daimon; that is, "those potentialities of each person, the realization of which represents the greatest fulfillment in living of which each is capable" (Waterman, 1990, p. 52).

Living in accordance with one's true-self or daimon involves a commitment to both goals and principles by which one chooses to live. The feeling accompanying behavior consistent with one's true potential is referred to as eudemonia, "a feeling of doing not just what one wishes to do, but what one must do (and) a conviction that what one is striving for genuinely matters" (Waterman, 1984, p. 16). The cognitive-affective sense of eudemonia incorporates notions of flow, peak experiences, and self-actualization arising from situations in which environmental challenges are high and engage high levels of personal skills in fulfilling one's highest potential and purpose in living.

This consideration of true self brings into awareness the existential difficulties inherent in choosing who one is to be from among all of the available options. To address this issue of choice, Waterman (2004) has argued that personal expressiveness be considered a third dimension, along with exploration and commitment, in identity formation. Personal expressiveness can serve as the internal criterion for discerning "better" identity options. Those activities and commitments that are personally expressive—that is, that engage and further those potentialities that are integral to one's daimon or purpose in living—are seen as better identity choices.

Personality characteristics also influence identity development. In particular, openness to change and exploration of alternatives are seen as important for adaptation and developmental change in one's identity (Bosma & Kunnen, 2001). Another personality dimension of importance is ego-strength or resilience, particularly in terms of being able to tolerate the anxiety that can be aroused by epistemic doubt, conflict, or transitions in one's sense of self and commitments.

The Role of Social Context: Globalization

As we have discussed, the social context of late-modern life is characterized by fewer assigned roles and increased freedom to make one's life choices. In turn, individuals have the responsibility for finding within themselves meaningful ways to endow their life with values and a basis for making life choices. Modern Western industrial cultures "demand that individuals actively explore and develop their identity" (Bosma & Kunnen, 2001, p. 45). There are societal expectations for individuals to cultivate their talents, to pursue self-understanding, self-interest, and self-actualization, and to be special and unique (Baumeister & Muraven, 1996).

Although it is recognized that individuals are afforded increased freedom and fewer expectations with regard to forming their formation, it has been argued that it is now more difficult for the individual to establish a stable identity that is based on community commitments and that there is less support and guidance in making developmental transitions (Côté, 1996). As a consequence, the transition from identity moratorium to identity achievement is more difficult to accomplish (Côté & Schwartz, 2002). That is, there are pressures to perpetuate the period of exploration without making commitments:

> Late-modern normative pressures seem to be pushing people to engage in more management of their social identities, more projection of situationally appropriate images, and a greater need for flexibility so as not to diminish future options (Côté & Schwartz, 2002, p. 584).

The current cultural period is also characterized by globalization, the "process by which cultures influence one another and become more alike through trade, immigration, and the exchange of information and ideas" (Arnett, 2002, p. 774). Globalization, in turn, impacts identity formation in several ways. In addition to their national identity, increasing numbers of people are developing a global identity that "gives them a sense of belonging to a worldwide culture and includes an awareness of the events, practices, styles, and information that are part of the global culture" (Arnett, 2002, p. 777). In a sense, many individuals are constructing *bicultural identities*, not merely in the customary sense of dual identities as immigrants or members of ethnic minorities and also members of the dominant culture, but rather as a reflection of having a global consciousness as well as a local consciousness (Arnett, 2002).

Globalization also carries with it the potential for an increase in identity confusion and also for identification with transnational religious, ethnic, or ideological groups and movements. Globalization also calls attention to the dynamic, mutually informing interaction of different groups and cultures and the corresponding need to revise our conceptualizations of fixed boundaries between groups. For example, our conceptualizations of identity often reflect a "container theory" in which nations contains cultures which contain religion which contains persons and their identities (Fletcher, 2008). Identity, however, can no longer be regarded as discrete and formed within the boundaries of national and cultural containers. Instead, identity is better understood as constructed and reshaped through multiple engagements with people from multiple cultures who have different views, beliefs, and experiences.

It has been argued that to successfully navigate the challenges of modern society, individuals need to develop identity capital (Côté, 1996). Identity capital is comprised of cognitive skills, personality attributes, and the multiple and context specific identities necessary to deal with a complex and changing social milieu. The concept of identity capital goes beyond the concepts of human capital, with the assumption that knowledge and skills generate economic activity, and cultural capital, with the assumption that knowledge of high culture gains one access to the reward structures of the upper class. Identity capital includes tangible assets, such as educational credentials, fraternity/sorority/social club and vocational networks, and parental social status; and intangible assets, such as cognitive flexibility, critical thinking skills and moral reasoning abilities, internal locus of control, and self-efficacy. These identity capital resources provide the individual with the wherewithal to understand and negotiate personal, social, and occupational challenges and opportunities commonly encountered throughout adult life (Côté, 1997).

Colleges and universities in particular offer opportunities for the development of both the tangible and intangible dimensions of identity capital (Côté, 1996). Institutions of higher education, however, have been criticized for educational practices that are based only on human capital assumptions; that is, focusing on skill oriented knowledge, and thus as not adequately preparing their students for the challenges of the late modern period (Côté, 1996). To be more responsive to societal needs, colleges and universities can foster the development of identity capital by supporting engagement with the developmental tasks of exploration and commitment regarding one's beliefs, values, and capabilities; encouraging the formulation of a life plan and goals; promoting the development of the skills of critical thinking and self-reflection; and providing opportunities for developing a sense of self-efficacy and active agency for moral and civic engagement.

IDENTITY FORMATION: A PROCESS OF SELF-AUTHORSHIP

With an understanding of the role of personal factors and social context, we can consider how these components interact in the process of identity formation. There are two perspectives on the underlying process. The self-discovery perspective contends the existence of an optimal self, the daimon, which as we discussed above represents the individuals' set of unique potentials, talents, skills, and capabilities, and to which the person is naturally drawn, "intuitively choosing from among these possibilities those that 'feel right' and appear to correspond to one's true self" (Schwartz, 2002, p. 321). These potentials are already present but unrecognized and need to be discovered, through engagement with the environment, and manifested for the person to live a fulfilled life (Waterman, 1984; 1990; 1993; 2004). Through the processes of making choices and intentionally engaging in activities, individuals come to understand their unique potentials that led them to pursue those particular activities.

The self-construction perspective rejects the notion of a preexisting self and views identity development as a shared, reciprocal process between individuals and their social and cultural environments and as dependent on both competencies and opportunities. The individual, viewed as an active and self-directed agent, chooses from identity alternatives available in a specific cultural and temporal context and is responsible for those choices and the consequences. Self-direction involves appropriation, the more or less conscious taking-over of aspects of oneself, not merely to represent ourselves but "in order to shape and modify the reality of who we are" (Blasi, 2004a. p. 15). The constructivist approach calls attention to the role of the social context in promoting identity development through providing opportunities for the development of cognitive and psychosocial competencies (Schwartz, 2001), which is a role that higher education in particular can play in our society.

Arguing for either a self-construction or self-discovery view is a false dichotomy. Discovery does not have to be conceptualized as identifying a preexisting self but instead can be viewed as "finding oneself" in the sense of learning about one's personal characteristics, capabilities, and limitations and actualizing one's potentials through engaging with the environment, identifying options, and making choices among alternatives using both rational and intuitive criteria (Schwartz, 2002). Thus, individuals both construct an identity path and evaluate it in relation to realization of their true self. The process of formulating an identity involves both reflection and social interaction with alternatives chosen as a function of one's capabilities and one's social and cultural context. The formulation of identity, therefore, involves both creation constrained by external social forces and discovery constrained by realities within ourselves to which we need to be true (Moshman, 1999). One mechanism through which identity is formulated is the process of self-authorship.

Self-Authorship

Beyond the processes of construction and discovery, identity formation can be understood as *self-authorship*: the self-directed process of making-meaning of oneself. Self-authorship is the essence of Marcia Baxter Magolda's (2008) view of identity formation that involves the interconnectivity of three dimensions (Kegan, 1994): the *epistemological*, or how we view the world; the *intrapersonal*, how we view ourselves; and the *interpersonal*, how we view social relations. Through a several decades-long longitudinal study of 18-year-olds upon entering college, Baxter Magolda (2008) has identified a nonlinear increase in complexity in this meaning-making system of self-authorship that involves two essential dynamics: consciously creating a framework to synthesize one's beliefs and intrapersonal and interpersonal identities into "the core of one's being," and moving from understanding one's commitments to living them. Baxter Magolda (2008) has advocated a role for higher education in fostering the development of the capacity for self-authorship through encouraging exploration; fostering students' reflection and sense-making of their experiences with people with diverse beliefs, ideas, values, and worldviews; and promoting students efforts to align their commitments and actions.

The Role of Narrative Processing

Consistent with the notion of self-authorship, one way in which individuals make sense out of their life is through engaging in *narrative processing* and *autobiographical reasoning* about their life experiences. That is, individuals serve as biographers by building a narrative about their past, current, and future that incorporates familiar story devices including settings, plots, characters, intentions, outcomes, and themes (Singer & Bluck, 2001). In forming their life story, people reason about, evaluate, and interpret their memories, which leads to inferences, lessons, and insights (Singer & Bluck, 2001).

These autobiographical reasoning and narrative processes are the basis for the life story theory of identity (McAdams, 2001) in which narratives are viewed not merely as portals to understanding a person, but rather as forming the actual structures and foundations of the self. One's life story is a coherent narrative that creates a sense of unity, meaning, and purpose in one's life that in turn is internalized as one's identity.

There is a developmental trajectory to the formulation of life stories. The process begins in adolescence when the increase in cognitive capabilities enables self-reflection and autobiographical reasoning (Bluck & Habermas, 2001). The process of self-reflection is not merely reminiscence, but rather entails subjecting the reconstruction of life events to further analysis in terms of explanation and evaluation and thereby generates insights (Staudinger, 2001). In composing their life stories individuals bring back memories and attribute significance to some life events but not others, identify themselves with specific issues and values, and in making these choices reveal the ways in which they organize their relations to the social world (László, 2008). Once begun, formulating the life story is a recurring process as new experiences and the acquisition of new knowledge and understanding evoke reconstructions and reframing of past experiences and future goals and options.

People select and interpret certain memories, and not others, as self-defining particularly with regard to explanations of causality that serve to create coherence of the life story (Pals, 2006). Turning points in one's life are central to the identity narrative, and it has been suggested that the narrative construction of the meaning of these turning points, rather than the experience itself, provides self-understanding (Mclean & Pratt, 2006). Several prominent narrative themes have been identified in people's life stories, such as commitment, redemption, and triumph over adversity (McAdams, 2001).

The process of sense-making through the construction of narrative operates on a number of levels. We have been focusing on the level of the construction of individual identity, but personal narratives link an individual life story to a narrative of social, political, or religious groups that is also constructed. Thus the process of identity development is culturally and historically contingent. In particular, individuals must make meaning of their culture and master narratives of national identity regarding race, gender, religion, and ideology (Hammack, 2008). The story of a culture involves master narrative themes such as struggle, resistance, and vulnerability, and these become incorporated into the individual's narrative and identity. The forces of history present different challenges to personal and collective identity at different times. Whereas the modern period was characterized by a focus on nationalism, the postmodern period is characterized by globalization, a defining characteristic of which is increasing interactions of multiple cultures, which increases the possibilities for identity conflicts as individuals negotiate multiple national and cultural identities and perceptions of threats to collective identity (Hammack, 2008).

Conflicts among groups defined by ethnicity, nationality, religion, or other social identities are a major concern in the beginning of the twenty-first century (Eidelson & Eidelson, 2003). Beliefs are a central component of one's personal and collective identity and are one source of intergroup conflict. We discussed in the previous chapters on personal epistemology and empathy the role that beliefs play in reasoning, interpretation of others mental states, and prosocial behavior. Beliefs also influence the ways in which individuals interpret and give meaning to their experiences, which in turn affects their processing of information and behavior. For example, some individuals view fundamental personal attributes such as intelligence or personality as relatively fixed, whereas other view these attributes as incremental and able to be modified (Molden & Dweck, 2006). Those holding a fixed view tend to view threats or setbacks as inability and in response employ avoidance strategies whereas those holding an incremental view interpret failure as reflecting lack of effort and/or the need for improvement and engage in efforts at mastery (Molden & Dweck, 2006). In contrast to those holding an incremental view, those holding a fixed view also have been found to more readily endorse and apply social stereotypes and resist stereotype-inconsistent information (Molden & Dweck, 2006).

Core beliefs or worldviews at both the personal and group levels reflect entrenched ways of understanding, interpreting, and making sense of the world and influence emotions and behaviors (Eidelson & Eidelson, 2003). Moreover, parallels between the worldviews individuals hold about superiority, injustice, distrust, vulnerability, and helplessness and the collective worldviews of groups have been identified as playing important roles in triggering or constraining conflict between groups (Eidelson & Eidelson, 2003). The belief of *superiority* includes a sense of specialness, deservingness, and entitlement. The *injustice* mind-set is based on actual or perceived mistreatment by others and can lead to a sense of legitimacy of grievances or to the identification "as unfair that which is merely unfortunate" (Eidelson & Eidelson, 2003, p. 185). *Distrust* reflects a presumption that others are hostile and untrustworthy, and *vulnerability* involves catastrophic thinking based on assessment of the world as dangerous and oneself as weak and unprotected and can lead to preemptive actions to ensure safety. *Helplessness* refers to the conviction of powerlessness and dependency which tends to be self-perpetuating because it diminishes motivation. In terms of a broad simplification, superiority, injustice, distrust, and vulnerability appear to operate primarily as triggers whereas helplessness may instead serve as a critical constraint on group conflict (Eidelson & Eidelson, 2003).

In this analysis, core beliefs at both the personal and collective level are viewed as arising from narratives within the family, interpersonal relationships, and broader cultural understandings. These core beliefs can reflect biases that interfere with consideration of alternative meanings and lead to problems in individuals' lives and intergroup conflict (Eidelson & Eidelson, 2003). As we discussed previously, personal beliefs are resistant to change, but collective worldviews may be even more resistant to change because they are consensually validated by in-group members and new or discrepant information is discounted or reinterpreted to fit prevailing views. The implication for our efforts to constructively engage difference and understand and prevent conflict is that the master narratives that give rise to and sustain these core beliefs need to be reconstructed or transformed.

When there is intractable conflict between groups, as currently is the case for example between the Israelis and Palestinians, a contributing factor can be master narratives characterized by mutual perceptions of identity threat and negative interdependence, such that intergroup conflict is constructed as a "zero-sum" (Hammack, 2008). Intractable conflicts become entrenched and self-sustaining and new or discrepant information is discounted or reinterpreted to fit, and may even intensify, prevailing views (Vallacher et al., 2010). Resolution of these intractable conflicts requires a reconstruction of these master narratives through a transformation from negative to positive interdependence (Hammack, 2008) and reconfiguring the elements to promote a more benign coherent story (Vallacher et al., 2010).

Constructively engaging differences also requires leadership. The abilities to formulate, communicate, enact, and embody the narrative of a people, institution, or organization has been recognized as an important element of strategic leadership (Morrill, 2007). As we discussed in Chapter 4 on empathy, effective leadership in the twenty-first century involves the empowerment of others. Narratives play a role in this empowerment. By giving meaning to the history, defining moments, and core values of an institution and by reflecting the beliefs, desires, and aspirations of the members, narratives serve to inspire, to motivate, and to guide and create a shared sense of commitment (Morrill, 2007).

In summary, consistent with the constructivist perspective a life story always reflects a process of joint authorship of the person and the individual's social world within which his or her life has meaning (McAdams, 2001). Life stories link an individual's life story to larger cultural and historical narratives and serve to bring a sense of coherence and meaning to one's life. There are many elements to the life story, and the story evolves and is reconstructed many times over the life course as the person develops and has different experiences. One's life story is not a single narrative but includes multiple self-stories nested in larger and overlapping stories, "creating ultimately a kind of anthology of the self" (McAdams, 2001, p. 117).

The issues of continuity and change are important in human development, and particularly salient with regard to identity. One of the central aspects of the concept of identity is a continuing subjective sense of oneself as a unique individual. While one's sense of personal and social identity has continuity over time, we have also seen that there is a developmental trajectory to identity that reflects the transactions among emerging cognitive capabilities and changing social expectations, opportunities, and life circumstances. We can consider the issues of continuity and change in terms of adaptations of one's sense of identity in response to these transactions.

In modern life, fewer identities are assigned and identity boundaries are more flexible and permeable. Individuals have the opportunity to create and refashion their identity many times over. Willingness or unwillingness to engage in the identity exploration process is a function of both abilities and skills, such as critical thinking, problem solving and perspective taking, and orientations and attitudinal factors, such as rigidity and procrastination (Grotevant, 1987). In particular, the degree of satisfaction or dissatisfaction with one's current identity serves to motivate the process of exploration (Schwartz, 2001). With repeated periods of exploration, commitments are likely to change over time along a number of dimensions. Commitments could become stronger or weaker, more or less flexible, and the areas of commitment can change as well. One way to view identity development is in terms of the strength and quality of commitments (Bosma & Kunnen, 2001).

Across the life course, individuals experience recursive periods of relative stability and periods of crisis characterized by consideration of new ways of being and making sense of the world and new or renewed commitments that may result in a temporary phase of regression or disorganization (Kroger, 2004). During such a period of crisis the person is endeavoring to work through identity questions and striving to make important life decision about personal goals, values, or beliefs. The identity adaptations associated with making sense of and responding to new internal and external realities typically reflect a rebalancing, but sometimes involve a major transformation in the theory of oneself. Resolving a crisis requires tolerance for ambiguity and anxiety, openness, and sufficient strength to move away from previous definition of the self. Thus, identity is better understood not as static but as a recursive process of stability, crisis, and rebalancing across the phases of one's life.

IDENTITY DOMAINS

Individuals construct increasingly differentiated notions of themselves as they engage in identity explorations and make identity commitments across many different life domains. The centrality and importance to one's identity of any specific domain varies across individuals and within individuals over their life span, and individuals can be at different status levels of identity achievement on different domains. With these considerations in mind, we examine several identity domains around which identity explorations and commitments typically occur and that are particularly relevant for our focus on the major developmental tasks of the undergraduate years and preparing students to constructively engage differences.

Sexual Identity

Sexual identity involves the interrelationship of biological, psychological, behavioral, and social components and an array of terms as our understandings of these processes have become more differentiated. *Sex* refers to the person's biology and anatomy and involves chromosomes and genes, hormones, brain physiology, and external genitalia. Based on these factors, sex determination is made as male, female, or intersexed (mixed biological characteristics). *Gender* or *gender identity* refers to a person's psychological sense of being male, female, or something else. The terms transsexuals or transgendered refer to those whose gender identity is at variance with their sex (often expressed as feeling that they have the wrong body). *Gender roles* refer to social functions which society deems suitable for males and females to engage. *Gender expression* refers to the way a person communicates gender identity to others through behavior, clothing, hairstyles, voice, or body characteristics. *Sexual orientation* refers to an enduring pattern of emotional, romantic, or sexual attractions to men, women, or both sexes and typically considered (exclusively, predominately, or incidentally) as heterosexual, homosexual, or bisexual; and a person's sense of identity based on membership in a community of others who share those attractions (American Psychological Association, 2011).

A detailed consideration of the biological and psychosocial aspects of development is beyond our scope. In general, we know that infants can differentiate male and female voices and faces and that by three years of age gender identity emerges as children express awareness of themselves as girls or boys (Fausto-Sterling, 2012). Socialization of gender roles continues throughout childhood and adolescence, and as part of the overall identity formation process individuals construct their sexual identity and navigate gender role expectations. These individual developmental processes occur in the context of societal expectations and response to variations from the norm of heterosexuality that are continually evolving.

The focus of some investigations of sexual identity has been on elucidating experiences and processes unique to gay, lesbian, and bisexual sexual identity subgroups. However, this research has been characterized as primarily descriptive of the coming out process rather than a general model of sexual identity development (Dillon et al., 2011). Recently, it has been argued that research needs to be directed to the commonalities in sexual identity development across subgroups, including heterosexuals, and a unifying model of sexual identity as a universal process has been proposed (Dillon et al., 2011). This unifying model focuses on the individual and social processes by which all individuals acknowledge and define their sexual values, needs, and orientation. The model proposes *compulsory heterosexuality* as an externally imposed status and common starting point such that individuals of any sexual orientation operate within the culturally prescribed norm that individuals identify as male or female and are heterosexual in their sexual preference. From this common starting point, the sexual identity process involves active exploration, commitment, and synthesis reflected in experiencing "little or no self-stigma or internalized heterosexism/homophobia" (Dillon et al., 2011, p. 664).

Sexual identity calls attention to the dynamics of difference from the norm and the meaning and attributions ascribed to this difference by the individual and by society. Divergences from the norm have at times been framed as disorders or moral failings and have evoked rejection, prejudice, and discrimination from the majority. The power of beliefs, biases, and stereotypes and the needs for openness and evaluative level thinking to revise beliefs in the face of new evidence and understandings, that we have been considering regarding engaging with difference in general, are evident with regard to sexual identity. We currently are in a period of change in beliefs and practices that are resulting in broader and more inclusive conceptualizations of what constitutes the norm with regard to human sexuality. There are particular challenges for members of some religious groups that express moral convictions regarding sexuality, sexual identity, and sexual orientation that their members are expected to adopt and practice. There are also challenges for others who do not hold these beliefs in engaging with those who do.

Sexual identity is a core issue for colleges and universities not only because identity formation is a key developmental task of emerging adulthood, but because of their fundamental respect for individual differences and value commitment to diversity, social justice, and promoting human flourishing. Colleges and universities also engage the issues of sexual identity in accordance with their societal roles to generate and apply knowledge and understanding and educate youth in the service of society. Furthermore, sexuality is an area of academic scholarship and education. Genetic, hormonal, and brain studies are elucidating the biological contribution to variations in sex, gender, and sexual orientation, and sexuality studies programs are increasing understanding of the psychological and sociocultural processes. Correspondingly, colleges and universities have established centers for gay, lesbian, bisexual, and transgendered (LGBT) students that serve to recognize and celebrate their collective identity and provide individual support and guidance.

The primary mechanisms of engagement are through: articulating the values of the academic community, which is often a more inclusive norm than students may have experienced previously; recognizing and treating LGBT individuals and the community with respect; reducing prejudice through increasing empathy and understanding brought about by promoting contact and friendships; and expecting evaluative level thinking about claims regarding human sexuality as with any area of inquiry. This continues to be a work in progress on college and university campuses as well as in our larger society.

Social Identities

Just as our understanding of sexual and gender identity is becoming more differentiated, so too is our understanding of social identities—that is, categorical grouping of peoples based on ancestry and geography including race, ethnicity, culture, and national identity. It had been customary to consider race as biologically based and reflected in physical characteristics such as skin color, hair, and bone structure, and ethnicity as a sociological construct involving behavioral and cultural practices. However, with advances in genomics and the forces of globalization, these traditional categories have less meaning. Advances notwithstanding, race, ethnicity, culture, and national identity continue to matter in terms of the contributions of collective social identity to one's overall identity and as a basis for intergroup conflict. Our purposes are served by considering several key dynamics that influence the self-categorization process and the ways in which social identities, formed on multiple bases, interact to promote increasing heterogeneity within and across categories.

Ethnic identity is a term that encompasses three aspects of group or collective identity: ethnic heritage, racial phenotype, and cultural background (Phinney, 2006). Development of ethnic identity has been examined in relation to Erikson's identity diffusion-achievement continuum and Marcia's (1966) identity statuses. In an early study, Phinney (1989) examined the ethnic identity development of American-born black, Asian, and Hispanic high school students and found about half could be categorized in the diffuse or foreclosed status and a quarter in both the moratorium and achievement statuses, with no significant differences in proportions across ethnic subgroups. While the task of making sense of one's ethnic identity begins early in childhood, it is highly salient in adolescence and emerging adulthood, particularly in culturally diverse settings (Phinney, 2006). With increasing cognitive development, young people are able to take the perspectives of both dominant and minority ethnic groups and develop a multicultural viewpoint. Developing a sense of one's ethnic identity is even more complex for those who are multiracial or multicultural, as they must determine to what extent they identify with ethnic or racial groups and the larger society. The setting, such as whether the campus culture is organized around specific ethnic groups or has a multicultural focus, is often an important factor in the resolution chosen (Phinney, 2006).

Individuals formulate their social identities in the broader context of the value society has placed on one's group membership, and groups are valued differentially within and across social contexts. Individuals who belong to groups that are devalued by society have identity challenges that those belonging to more highly valued groups do not have to face. In particular, racial and ethnic identity is thought to be more central for members of minority groups than for majority groups (Phinney, 2006). When faced with a context that devalues one's racial or ethnic group, the person may internalize the negative evaluation of the larger society or work to foster a positive sense of their collective group identity.

In multicultural societies, through social interactions within and between cultural groups, cultural elements are borrowed, blended, and reinterpreted and cultural boundaries are negotiated. As a result of this dynamic process, "race," "ethnicity," and "culture" are not experienced in the same way, and over time labels become less fixed and more dynamic. In addition, historical elements of time and place add to the heterogeneity of experience and become readily apparent when we consider the experiences and perspective of those within a cultural group during different time period and geographical places.

Racial, ethnic, and cultural identities are often influenced by broader national identities such as an American, German, Israeli, or Palestinian, and, as we discussed previously, master narrative themes such as struggle, resistance, and vulnerability. Knowledge about in-group history and relations with other groups contributes to the sense of national identity. History education in particular contributes to the formation of national, ethnic and religious identities, and intergroup relations (Korostelina, 2008). In particular, a history of conflicts between groups and how these conflicts are portrayed with regard to "chosen glories" and "chosen traumas" contributes to the saliency of national identity to one's social identity (Korostelina, 2008).

A central issue in the process of national identity formation is the interrelation between subgroups, including the majority and minority subgroups, and those who are natives and those who are immigrants. For example, Korostelina (2008) has argued that alternative conceptualizations of national identity, based on how minorities are perceived, influence attitudes and behavior toward ethnic groups within the nation and approaches to other nations.

Perceiving one's nation as having been built around a core ethnic community yields a monoethnic and monolingual view of the nation into which ethnic minorities are expected to assimilate, and the corresponding belief that those who have inherited or assimilated the values and attributes of the ethnic core should have higher status within the nation. This view of national identity is likely to foster discrimination and intergroup conflict.

Perceiving one's nation as multicultural, with equal rights for all ethnic groups, leads to viewing the cultural heritage of the various ethnic groups as part of the national heritage. Correspondingly, different ethnic groups are provided an opportunity to receive education in their own language and resources are provided to maintain their ethnic culture and communities. The multicultural conceptualization is likely to decrease the potential for conflict between the majority and minority groups, but may lead to conflicts between and among minority groups (Korostelina, 2008).

Perceiving one's nation as having been built on a civic culture, in which citizenship is viewed as a contract between the people and the state concerning both rights and obligations, results in decreasing the significance of ethnicity and connecting the concept of national identity to civic responsibility and coexistence. It has been argued that the civic concept of national identity is likely to decrease the possibility for intergroup conflict (Korostelina, 2008).

With this brief consideration of social identities, we gain an appreciation of the extent to which individuals personalize their social identities, which in turn results in a high degree of heterogeneity of social identity within groups (Ferdman, 2000). Most important, perhaps, is the recognition that constructing a social identity involves more than self-categorization. It also involves explaining why one came to claim particular identities and the meaning attributed to those choices.

Moral Identity

Morality refers to prescriptions of right and wrong that are not based on consensus or authority, but rather stem from conceptions of fairness, justice, rights, and human welfare (Nucci, 2001). There is an extensive literature on character and moral development that is beyond the purview of this book, and the interested reader is directed to excellent integrative reviews (Lapsley & Power, 2005; Turiel, 2006). The focus of our attention is on the more specific concept of moral identity and its proposed role in motivating moral actions.

Morality is generally considered to involve three components: standards of behavior, moral judgments, and moral actions. A major emphasis has been on the linkage between making moral judgments and acting on those judgments, with a particular focus on identifying the motives for moral action. Some approaches emphasize the role of cognition, in terms of moral reasoning, and others emphasize the role of emotion and empathy in motivating moral action. Both moral reasoning and moral emotion have been empirically associated with moral action but only moderately, indicating that there are other factors that contribute to moral action (Hardy & Carlo, 2005). Among these other factors, moral identity has been proposed as playing a central role in motivating moral action.

Moral identity reflects the importance or salience of morality to an individual's identity (Hardy & Carlo, 2011). The premise is that "the more individuals see moral virtues and values as important to their sense of self, the more likely they are to engage in moral behavior" (Hardy & Carlo, 2005, p. 252). Moral identity has been conceptualized from a character perspective as a trait-like individual difference that reflects the extent to which the self is organized around values and moral commitments. Moral identity has also been conceptualized from a social cognitive perspective in terms of accessible cognitive schemas or conceptions about what it means to be a moral person (Hardy & Carlo, 2011). Situational factors play a role in activating a person's moral schemas and therefore in one's sense of moral identity (Aquino et al., 2009).

Augusto Blasi (1980; 1983; 2004a; 2004b) has formulated the most fully developed model linking moral identity, which reflects the integration of moral understanding into one's personality, to moral action. Blasi's self-model has three components (Walker, 2004; Hardy & Carlo, 2011): the importance of moral values in one's identity, a sense of personal responsibility for taking moral action, and self-consistency or integrity manifested by congruence between judgment and action. A key tenant of the Blasi model is that the responsibility for connecting judgments about the morally correct action with the personal obligation to undertake that action is integral to a person's identity. Perhaps Blasi's greatest insight is the contention that the desire for integrity—that is, the desire to live consistent with one's moral commitments—is the primary mechanism in motivating the person to ensure the congruence between judgments and actions. It seems intuitively apparent that fidelity to self has more motivational power than fidelity to abstract principles (Bergman, 2004).

> The best answer to the question, Why be moral?, may thus be, Because that is who I am, or, Because I can do no other and remain (or become) the person I am committed to being (Bergman 2002, p. 123).

Empirical support is emerging for the proposed association of the sense of moral identity with both moral reasoning and moral action, typically defined as social responsiveness to the needs of others (Bergman, 2004; Hardy & Carlo, 2005). For example, in a series of studies undergraduate and high school students' sense of moral identity was related to both self-reported volunteering (e.g., at a local homeless shelter, or mentoring troubled youth) and actual prosocial behavior in the form of donations to a food drive (Aquino & Reed, 2002).

An individual's sense of moral identity has also been shown to contribute to intergroup relations. One proposed mechanism is that a sense of moral identity decreases out-group hostility through generating a more expansive "circle of moral regard": a broader conception of the in-group toward which a person feels morally obligated (Reed & Aquino, 2003). Support for the role of moral identity in expanding the circle of moral regard was provided in a series of studies with undergraduates that investigated the relationship of self-reported moral identity and attitudes and behaviors toward both in-groups and out-groups in the aftermath of the September 11, 2001 attacks on the World Trade Center and Pentagon (Reed & Aquino, 2003). Students with a strong internalized sense of moral identity reported a stronger moral obligation to share resources with four out-groups (people from another country, strangers, people with different ethnicities than oneself, people who practice a different religion than oneself); were more likely to favorably perceive the worthiness of relief efforts to assist two distinct out-groups (Afghan, Turkish); and were less willing to accept civilian deaths as a result of military attacks against Afghanistan. Another study demonstrated the interaction of moral identity with national identity in motivating behavior. Those with a higher level of moral identity were more likely to allocate a larger portion of a $3 donation to the out-group (UNICEF Emergency Effort for Afghani Children and Families) than to the in-group (NY Police and Fire Widows and Children's Benefit Fund), whereas those with a strong American identity were more likely to restrict the donations to the in-group (Reed & Aquino, 2003).

Another series of studies with undergraduates provided support for the hypothesis that moral action is a joint function of the centrality of moral identity and the extent to which situational cues evoke moral self-schemas (Aquino et al., 2009). The idea is that the greater the centrality of moral identity, the greater is the activation potential for moral self-schemas and the stronger the desire to maintain self-consistency. Individuals, however, have multiple values and goals, and situational cues can activate both moral and self-interested schemas. Only under the combination of high centrality of moral identity and the presence of a moral prompt was cooperative behavior sustained in the face of the selfish actions of others (Aquino et al., 2009). The implication of these findings is that a sense of moral identity is important but must not be taken for granted, and using situational cues to prompt the salience of moral values and goals is important in promoting moral and prosocial behavior.

The development of moral identity is a function of the transactions between personal capabilities and social experiences and is a progressive process that extends from adolescence into adulthood. Moral reasoning—the way that people understand and make judgments about moral issues—is dependent on the evolving mental capacities that support cognitive functioning, and the same progression is seen in reasoning about moral issues as with the sophistication of epistemic beliefs, from absolute to relative to evaluative. Through their social experiences, individuals "actively construct and reconstruct their understandings of moral concepts like justice, rights, equity, and welfare" (Colby, 2008, p. 393). While dependent on the development of mental capacities and cognitive functioning, the importance of engagement in social experience as an instigator of moral development is increasingly recognized. For example, Blasi remarks that the ideal of social justice

> as psychologically felt, is neither constructed by learning the concept of justice and the various norms of fairness nor by being exposed to speeches about justice, even though all of this may help; rather it is formed by concretely experiencing in oneself and others the positive consequences of small and concrete actions of fairness and the damaging results of concrete injustices (Blasi, 2004b, p. 343).

Religious Identity

For many people, morality acquires meaning only within the context of their religious commitments. For these individuals, religious beliefs are central to their identity. Increasingly, religious identity has become a selected component of one's identity, as individuals choose their religious identity rather than have it assigned to them. Although different, conceptualizations of religious identity and spirituality are intertwined. Religious identity refers to a commitment to a particular faith tradition or set of institutional beliefs and practices, whereas spirituality refers to the subjective experience of connectedness with an ultimate reality, higher power, or community and with one's inner life and sense of life's meaning or purpose (Roehlkepartain et al., 2011).

Religion serves a number of functions. Because notions of the supernatural, an omnipotent deity, and an afterlife have been consistently part of the human experience over time, geography, and cultures, some have argued that humans are predisposed to these beliefs which must have been evolutionary advantageous (Bering, 2006). One proposed function, for example, is to foster social relations through an all-knowing deity that would punish deviance from social expectations and moral norms and reward prosocial behavior, either in this life or hereafter. As we discussed in Chapter 4 on empathy, we attribute our own thoughts, feeling, and perspectives to others, and this projection also maybe a basis for conceptualizing the deity in human like form with similar mental states and as interested in human affairs, albeit with supernatural powers.

Another function of religion is as a coping device to alleviate the existential anxiety that accompanies self-consciousness and with it the recognition of our own mortality: "We built religious systems to make the world we live in and the life we live make sense" (Spong, 2009, p. 121). Religions point to larger realities that transcend the person (Emmons & Paloutzian, 2003) and provide a view of what people should be striving for and the ultimate purpose and meaning in life rituals through which to express community beliefs. Religions not only encourage morality, but they also prescribe actions, and religious movements in particular have demonstrated the ability to mobilize collective action in pursuit of social justice (Gill, 2001).

As a country without an official national religion, the United States has a tradition of a commitment to religious freedom and tolerance that also includes nonbelief. Religious tolerance has been part of our national identity, but now there are increasing references to religious pluralism. It is important to recognize, however, that a commitment to religious pluralism as part of our national identity would mean more than accommodating a range of different religious traditions, values, and practices. This difference has been eloquently articulated:

> Religious pluralists hold that people believing in different creeds and belonging to different communities need to learn to live together. Religious pluralism is neither mere coexistence nor forced consensus. It is a form of proactive cooperation that affirms the identity of the constituent communities while emphasizing that the well-being of each and all depends on the health of the whole. It is the belief that the common good is best served when each community has a chance to make its unique contribution (Eboo Patel, November, 2006).

In the pluralistic world of today, religious identity is clearly a major source of difference and conflict. However, for most of the twentieth century, higher education has been largely secular (Jacobsen & Jacobsen, 2008a) and religion has largely been left out of the multicultural movement on college campuses. In part this is because of the perception of the inadmissibility of faith and revealed truth in an academic culture that prizes reason and evidence: "If you commit yourself to intellectual openness and scientific inquiry, you must give up dogma" (Wolfe, 2006, p. 11).

There are indications that higher education is entering a new period, characterized as the postsecular age (Jacobsen & Jacobsen, 2008a) in which issues of faith and reason are to be engaged not only to prepare students for citizenship in highly pluralistic, globally interconnected world, but also as part of the educational mission to promote identity development. Some of the most significant issues of meaning and purpose occur at the intersection of faith and reason, and to foster the development of an integrated identity the college campus needs to be a space in which this intersection can be explored. Engagement does not predetermine the outcome. Commitments can be made stronger or weaker by being exposed to other claims. Having to clarify, critically analyze, and defend one's religious and moral positions—just as one would do with claims about science, economics, or political theory—is part of the learning experience and identity formation process.

College students are likely to encounter two major challenges with regard to religious identity. First, for many students making the transition into college religious beliefs constitute an ascribed rather than a chosen identity and a foreclosed identity status reflecting incorporation of family values, traditions, and commitments without much exploration. Explorations raise the potential for doubt, and different commitments which may carry with it the perceived risk of alienation from family and faith community. Second, as we discussed in Chapter 3 on personal epistemology, the college years are a period of intense engagement with beliefs about knowledge and ways of knowing, and the movement from absolutist and relativistic stances to an evaluativist approach to the construction and justification of knowledge. For many students their identity crisis will be how to reconcile a commitment to naturalism, fallibility, and the provisional nature of knowledge as one part of their identity with notions of the supernatural, infallibility, and knowledge as authoritatively known as another part of their identity. John Shelby Spong captures well the dilemma: "I do not want to abandon the wisdom of the past, but neither do I want to be bound by that wisdom, since wisdom itself is ever changing" (Spong, 2009, p. 144). In contemporary life there are prominent examples of eminent scholars who reflect different resolutions ranging from those who find commitments to evaluativist perspectives incompatible with religious commitments, to those whose commitments to reason and evidence lead them to religious commitments, to those who began at one position and moved to another. The argument being made here is that achieving an integrated identity requires intentional engagement with the issue rather than avoidance as the person strives in the process of self-authorship for coherence and a holistic sense of himself or herself.

Work and Career Identity

Emerging adulthood is the time period in which individuals in our society begin to achieve self-sufficiency through the important step of making commitments to work and careers. The undergraduate years in particular are a time for preparing for and making these commitments. In turn, work commitments are important to identity:

> Identity, who we are and who we will become, is channeled and expressed in part through the kinds of work we do, just as the work of our lives lends definition to who we are as persons (Hoare, 2006, p. 347).

Work provides a sense of worth, validation, and self-affirmation. It provides the social context in which one can feel coherent, unique, and valued. For many, their work and career provides a way of relating to the world and expressing ideals and values to which they are committed. Work also provides a community of discourse through which individuals are enculturated in ways of viewing knowledge and the justifications for knowledge claims that are characteristic of the group. Furthermore, work and career are domains through which moral identity is expressed. For example, within each profession, there are explicit ethical codes that express the value commitments and standards of behavior that members are expected to abide by and internalize. It has been noted that "over time each adult becomes more of what he or she does for a living" (Hoare, 2006, p. 348).

The importance of work to one's sense of identity is reflected not only in the evidence of the negative impact of involuntary job loss on identity and self-esteem, but also the association of higher levels of identity integration with career development. There are various dimensions to work and both complexity and autonomy of the work are important to overall work satisfaction and identity development (Hoare, 2006). Although work is an important identity domain, the centrality of work to one's sense of identity varies from person to person and within an individual over time as identity continues to be reconstructed throughout adulthood.

INTEGRATED IDENTITY

We have been considering identity as the response to the fundamental question: "Who am I?" We have understood identity as the lifelong, discursive process of self-authorship, driven by the intersection of basic human needs for distinction and differentiation with the needs to belong and matter, as comprised of assigned and selected elements, and realized through the basic processes of exploration and commitment. We have also come to appreciate that identity is the way in which individuals make sense, give meaning and purpose to their lives, and hold themselves responsible for acting with integrity to their commitments. We also have recognized that identity is multifaceted, and that individuals have multiple personal and social identities across different domains, times, and situations. Given these understandings, we can appreciate the self-authorship challenges that individuals face in formulating an integrated identity—that is, experiencing one's identity as a unitary phenomenon.

Contemporary culture allows young people to postpone permanent employment, marriage, parenthood, and other adult roles, and thus the task of consolidating a coherent identity is extended into the early adult years. For many, higher education is the context in which opportunities are provided to explore various identity alternatives and develop a coherent sense of self. Some students enter college or the university developmentally ready to engage the many opportunities inside and outside of the classroom and navigate the identity-formation process. Other students, however, may be less developmentally ready and may need assistance with the identity exploration and commitment processes. It is the premise of this book, however, that colleges and universities need to be intentional in providing an educational experience for all students that fosters identity development as well as cognitive development. Such intentionality would constitute a return to earlier conceptualizations of the role of higher education in promoting the development of the whole person. The question then becomes: In what ways could colleges and universities intentionally foster the development of identity?

INTERVENTIONS TO FOSTER IDENTITY DEVELOPMENT

It is well understood that deep learning requires students to be actively and emotionally engaged in their work. Two types of experiences in particular, community service and service learning, provide students with authentic problems that have the potential to evoke emotional engagement and the motivation to acquire the knowledge and expertise to address the problems and make a difference in the lives of others.

Community Service

From a developmental perspective, the theoretical rationale for promoting student involvement in community service has been clearly articulated:

> When youth are given opportunities to use their skills to redress social problems, they can experience themselves as having agency and as being responsible for society's well-being. When they participate as a cohort and when participation is encouraged by respected adults, youth begin to reflect on the political and moral ideologies used to understand society. It is this process of reflection, which takes place publicly with peers and adults, as well as privately, that allows youth to construct identities that are integrated with ideological stances and political-moral outlook (Youniss & Yates, 1997, p. 36).

As we have seen, identity is more than self-understanding. It involves becoming part of a larger society. In particular, community service provides an opportunity for the self-society link in identity construction (Youniss & Yates, 1997). More specifically, participating in community service has been linked to a greater sense of social responsibility, personal agency, and commitment to act politically for social change (McIntosh et al., 2005). The effects of community service, however, have been found to vary by the type of service. For example, community service that involves a social cause, such as remedying specific problems such as drug abuse or racial intolerance or direct contact with the needy, was associated with a greater increase in social concerns than participating in services such as tutoring, coaching, or performing manual labor (McIntosh et al., 2005).

There is also increasing empirical evidence that involvement in community service is developmentally formative in promoting a sense of agency and responsibility that continues across time. For example, findings from a longitudinal multiinstitutional study that controlled for students' precollege propensity to engage in service found that participating in volunteer service during college was associated five years after graduation with participating in community service, helping others in difficulty, socializing with other races, and promoting racial understanding (Astin et al., 1999).

Service Learning

Service learning refers to a wide range of experiential learning activities that involve participation in projects of benefit to the community as a component of a course or academic program. The term service learning was coined in 1967, but the principles have been traced back to Dewey's views on the educational value of experiential learning and reflective thinking about one's experiences (Giles & Eyler, 1994). In 1989 the Wingspread principles of good service-learning practice were developed, and the central tenant was clearly articulated (Honnet & Poulsen, 1989, p. 1): "Service, combined with learning, adds value to each and transforms both."

Service learning is now considered as one of the *pedagogies of engagement* that, along with internships and participation in research, focus on learning as an active process (Colby et al., 2003). The aims of service learning include both educational objectives and personal development (Waterman, 1997):

- Enhancing the learning of academic material through praxis: applying academic concepts, understandings, and methods in a real life context
- Fostering a sense of civic responsibility through identification and involvement with community institutions
- Promoting personal development, particularly self-efficacy arising from the experience of making a difference in the lives of others or the community environment
- Contributing to the community

The educational learning objectives include enhancing students' ability to think clearly and sophisticedly about complex civic and moral issues. The personal development objectives are implicitly formative, and can be conceptualized as enhancing student's capacities for moral commitments and a sense of personal responsibility to act through fostering their development of moral identity, which involves an integrated sense of one's values, commitments, agency, and purpose. Service learning builds on the emotional and empathetic engagement engendered by the service experience, and helps students expand their circle of moral regard and connect their experience of individual suffering and injustice to both larger social issues and actions they could undertake to improve social conditions. Making this connection can motivate a commitment to social justice understood as both reducing human suffering and promoting human values of equality and justice (Vasques, 2012).

Thus, one aim of service learning is to develop students' critical consciousness about the systemic issues underlying social, political, and economic inequities and their sense of personal and collective agency and efficacy in addressing these issues (Youniss & Yates, 1997). The process of becoming aware of and reflecting on the underlying cause of inequities can result in a questioning of one's own values, attitudes, and commitments and having the experience of making a difference in the lives of others can contribute to a sense of efficacy and agency which are important components of identity.

It is this potentially transformative impact through the development of critical consciousness, empathy, and identity formation that makes service learning particularly salient as a way of fostering the development of capacities needed to engage difference.

A Transformative Experience

There is evidence from national research projects that involvement in service learning is associated with a number of positive outcomes, including a reduction in negative stereotypes, an increase in tolerance for diversity, and an appreciation of other cultures as well as a deeper understanding and ability to apply subject matter (Eyler & Giles, 1999). In particular, service learning has an impact on how students see themselves and others (Eyler & Giles, 1999), and for many students, service learning is truly a transformative experience.

As with community service in general, there is also empirical support for the long-term impact of service learning. For example, Hill and colleagues (2005) conducted a longitudinal study of students who had participated in a summer service-learning experience and a matched control group 10 years after graduation. The findings indicated that the participants in the service-learning program were rated significantly higher than the control group on three dimensions: commitment to serving those who are disadvantaged; relationship to society reflected in a sense of one's role in the world, connection to others, and awareness of how one may give as well as receive support; and growth reflected in an orientation to active learning and participation in activities that enhance personal development (Hill et al., 2005).

Although the potential for positive impacts is evident, it is also recognized that service learning could do more harm than good (Boyle-Baise & Efiom, 2000). Students construct meaning from their experiences in the community through the conformation or disconfirmation of prior knowledge and understanding (Boyle-Baise & Efion, 2000). Service learning can foster increased awareness and acceptance of cultural diversity, but also could reinforce negative stereotypes and biases. Thus we need to ensure that the service-learning experience incorporates current knowledge about attitude change and prejudice reduction (Erickson & O'Connor, 2000).

Research on the impact of service learning is beginning to examine the mechanisms of effect that is, determining how the experience of diversity contributes to student outcomes. This understanding is critical to guide the design of effective programs. A recent example is the study by Bowman and Brandenberger (2012) that tested three hypotheses that are consistent with the theoretical framework of Gurin and colleagues (2002) about the impact of diversity experiences: Students who interact with diversity are often experiencing the unexpected; these unexpected experiences often challenge students' beliefs; and belief challenge is associated with attitude change. Study participants included students at a medium-sized Catholic university in the Midwest who completed a service-learning course. The outcome measure was an orientation toward equality and social responsibility (ESR) survey, which assesses a set of attitudes and values regarding the recognition and denunciation of societal inequality and the importance placed on helping others. The findings indicated that both positive and negative diversity experiences were positively related to experiencing the unexpected, that experiencing the unexpected was associated with greater belief challenge, and both experiencing the unexpected and belief challenge were associated with increased orientation toward equity and social responsibility. Furthermore, there was evidence of an accentuation effect. Students who were more sensitive to issues of equality and social responsibility tended to interact with diverse people in a way that lead to fewer negative and more positive encounters. The implication of these findings is that "higher education practitioners and faculty should facilitate diversity experiences that are contrary to students' expectations" (Bowman & Brandenberger, 2012, p. 196).

Essential Principles, Practices, and Processes

Over the course of 40 years since the term was coined, service learning has evolved in terms of its conceptualization, objectives, and corresponding practices. Butin (2010) argues that there is no single service-learning model, but rather that service learning is a pedagogical strategy that can be enacted in multiple ways and a framework within which to understand the linkages across teaching, learning, and research in the classroom and local community. As service learning has become part of the undergraduate experience, we are accumulating knowledge about essential components of effective courses and programs.

Two fundamental principles have emerged. First, service is understood as working with and empowering others and not as paternalistic helping of others. Second, reciprocity and mutuality are key characteristics such that both parties not only benefit, but also are involved in the development and implementation of the project.

A number of specific practices have been designed to ensure the educational value of the service-learning experience. First, specific learning objectives are formulated for the community service experience component of the course or program. The service experience is designed and supervised to achieve these objectives and evaluated with regard to attainment of these learning objectives as well as with regard to the benefits to the community. Second, students are afforded some degree of choice as to the nature of the service-learning experience activity, and the experience needs to be linked to a period of critical reflection (Nucci, 2006). Third, the service-learning experience is integrated into the student's course or program, which is structured to enable students to bring their experiences and reflections back into the classroom or some other forum for discussion.

The quality of the personal reflection process, in particular, has been found to influence educational outcomes (Eyler & Giles, 1999). First, it is recognized that there are several different forms and levels of reflection (Hatton, & Smith, 1995). It is critical reflection in particular that is emphasized as an essential educational process of service learning. Critical reflection is more that constructive self-criticism. It is a deliberative cognitive process that involves thinking about the effects that one's actions have on others with consideration of moral and ethical criteria (Hatton, & Smith, 1995). Second, this process of critical reflection must be structured to accomplish several key functions. Students need to be able to identify and share their feelings engendered by the community service experience and connect the experience to their own values, sense of efficacy, and sense of responsibility. The critical reflection process also needs to stimulate the consideration of potential underlying issues such as stereotypes, fairness, and social inequality, and include evaluation of the assumptions of service agencies (Nucci, 2006). Finally, critical reflection serves the function of linking the service experience to academic learning. In particular, writing assignments such as keeping a journal and personal reflection papers provide opportunities for students to make connections between their experiences, their reaction to the experience, and the theories and knowledge that are the focus of the course or academic program.

With regard to methods for structuring critical reflection, the model developed by Kolb (1984) aims to integrate feelings and action with abstract and systematic thought. This approach structures critical reflection as a cycle. The first step is to ask students to describe their concrete experience through reflective observation. With these observations as a base, the next step is to ask students to make abstract conceptualizations through which to derive meaning and integrate knowledge from other sources. The last step is to ask students to formulate hypotheses or action strategies that can be tested in the community through active experimentation (Eyler & Giles, 1999).

Another approach to structuring reflection exercises is to ask students to address three interrelated questions: What? So What? Now What? (Eyler & Giles, 1999). In particular, writing courses and writing assignments that encourage the process of self-reflection help students not only become better writers, but also to extract meaning and integrate themes from their service experiences.

> Properly taught, writing can make an important contribution toward identity. Such teaching provides formative occasions for becoming a reflective and engaged person—that elusive end to which both liberal and professional education aspire (Sullivan & Rosin, 2008, p. 123).

Whatever methods are used to foster the process, critical reflection is most fruitful when students are engaged in service learning with inspiring role models with whom they can identify and within a campus community context that supports the development of moral identity and civic engagement (Colby, 2008).

As the movement for promoting civic engagement has advanced across higher education, concerns have emerged about the scholarship that is needed to improve the quality of these efforts and provide supporting evidence for the claims of personal, institutional, and community benefit (Butin, 2010). The concern now is that the rapid expansion of service-learning "has overtaken the field's ability to examine and account for the implication of its successes" (Butin, 2010, p. xvi). The danger is in overreaching and not ascertaining the limits of service-learning, as well as its possibilities. Service-learning needs to be the object of inquiry and critique, consistent with any other academic endeavor, with regard to theory and practice and personal, institutional, and community impact. As well as participating in service learning, undergraduates can be encouraged to contribute to this scholarly process of inquiry. Structures are emerging to facilitate such involvement. For example, the *Undergraduate Journal of Service Learning & Community-Based Research* was recently established, and is dedicated to publishing the intellectual and reflective work by undergraduates on service learning and community engagement activities.

THIS IS WHO WE ARE, AND THIS IS WHAT WE DO

It is clear that colleges and universities have the opportunity to promote students' development of an integrated identity that includes moral identity and agency for civic engagement. However, institutions need to be more intentional and systematic in this process. We know that the experience of community, that sense of being part of something bigger than ourselves, is a strong motivational force. Therefore, the place to start is for colleges and universities to articulate the core values and commitments that characterize the academic community in general, and their institution in particular, and make explicit the connections between these values, what is taught, and how the range of undergraduate experiences provided at the institution fulfill the moral aspirations of the community: This is "who we are" and "what we do" (Davidson, 2005).

Faculty and administrators need to view fostering identity as one of their educational goals and through their teaching and administrative policies and practices provide the metacognitive scaffolding to enable students to integrate the values and norms of the academic community with their lived experiences inside and outside of the classroom. It is also essential that colleges and universities provide students with opportunities for guided critical reflection on the consonance of their individual identity with the community identity. That is, the undergraduate educational experience needs to be structured to encourage the intentional process of self-reflection that is essential for the successful completion of the major developmental task of emerging adulthood: self-authorship and identity formation. Through fostering engagement with the values of the academic community, colleges and universities can provide an optimal environment for the development of moral identity and promotion of civic engagement. The next chapter will focus on the role of campus culture in fostering identity and developing students' capacities and dispositions to constructively engage differences.

CHAPTER 6

Campus Culture

Developing the Capacities to Constructively
Engage Difference

Institutions of higher education need to build structures—academic and social, formal and informal—in which students not only can interact but can hardly avoid interacting with those who are different from themselves (Beyer et al., 2007, p. 142).

To be responsive to the societal needs of the twenty-first century, higher education must prepare students to constructively engage ethnic, political, and religious differences. To accomplish this task, colleges and universities must provide an undergraduate experience that enables students to develop a personal epistemology that includes a commitment to evaluative thinking and their capacities for perspective taking, empathy, and an integrated identity that includes a sense of agency for engaging differences. Having reviewed the nature and development of these essential capacities, and targeted approaches to promoting identity development, we now turn to a consideration of the role of the overall campus culture in fostering the developmental transformations that are the focus of this book, with particular attention to the impact of diversity, advances in our understanding about how to reduce prejudice and promote intergroup relationships, and policies and practices with regard to residential and social life.

IMPACT OF DIVERSITY

The university has been recognized as the place where "the diaspora of human thought and identity, aspiration and purpose, method and procedure is given a home" (Nixon, 2011, p. 29). There has been a remarkable increase in the diversity on college campuses along ethnic/racial, religious, and socioeconomic dimensions. The educational potential of diversity, however, is not achieved by the mere presence of a diverse student body, but depends on whether or not this diversity results in greater interaction across differences. Research has focused primarily on the impact of racial diversity but it can be argued that the findings about the processes that moderate and mediate the impact may guide our understandings regarding political, gender, religious, and other differences as well.

The theoretical rationale for the educational value of diversity and supporting evidence regarding the impact of diversity on educational outcomes have been presented in a seminal report (Gurin et al., 2002). The claim is that promoting interaction among students from diverse racial and ethnic backgrounds, through both the curriculum and informal interactions, positively impacts students' modes of thought and intellectual engagement and social growth. The impact of engagement with diversity is believed to be especially important during the late adolescent period of development when experimentation in the process of forming a sense of personal and social identity is occurring. The supporting evidence is provided from two longitudinal databases. The Michigan Student Survey (in conjunction with the Michigan Mandate) was completed by students (1,129 white, 187 African American, 266 Asian American) entering the University of Michigan in 1990, and a follow-up survey four years later. The multiinstitutional Cooperative Institutional Research Program (CIRP), an national survey conducted by the Higher Education Research Institute at UCLA (Astin, 1963), included 11,383 students (10,465 white, 216 African American, 496 Asian American, 206 Latino/a) from 184 institutions who were surveyed upon entering college in 1985, and again four years later. Across both databases, the findings indicate that diversity in terms of classroom diversity experiences and informal interactions such as multicultural events and intergroup dialogues were positively associated with learning and citizenship engagement outcomes. The research findings supported the claim that the racial diversity of a campus operates through students' experiences (Gurin et al., 2002). Subsequent studies have endeavored to better understand contributing factors. Research findings in general provide support for two claims: that students who attend campuses that are more racially diverse report higher frequencies of cross-racial interaction, and that cross-racial interaction plays an important role in achieving the educational benefits associated with racial diversity. For example, Chang et al. (2004) refer to studies that have linked higher levels of cross-racial interaction to greater cognitive development, more positive academic and social self-concepts, growth in leadership skills, cultural awareness and understanding, higher graduation rates, and higher levels of civic interest and college satisfaction. The findings regarding the association of cross-racial interactions with educational benefits have in turn led to research to identify the conditions that foster cross-racial interaction among undergraduate students.

A longitudinal study by Chang et al. (2004) addressed both the impact of diversity on educational outcomes and also the mechanism through which the impact occurs. The sample was comprised of approximately 9,703 students who entered 134 different four-year colleges and universities. The students completed the Cooperative Institutional Research Program (CIRP) (Astin et al., 1994) survey as incoming freshmen in 1994 and a follow-up survey four years later that asked how often (not at all; occasionally; frequently) they engaged in the following activities at the college:

- Studied with someone from a different racial/ethnic group
- Dined with someone from a different racial/ethnic group
- Dated someone from a different racial/ethnic group
- Interacted in class with someone from a different racial/ethnic group

The findings indicated that experiencing cross-racial interaction during the undergraduate years positively affected a range of student outcomes, including intellectual ability, civic interest, and social skills. As expected, one factor that promoted cross-racial interaction was the racial diversity of the student body: "The larger the proportion of students of color in the student body, the more cross-racial interaction" (p. 539). Another contributing factor was the extent of the student's reported commitment to "promoting racial understanding" at the time they entered college. Those students who endorsed this commitment were more likely to report seeking out cross-racial interactions during college than students who were not as strongly committed. A third factor was the amount of time students spend on campus. When the student body is diverse, the more time students spend living and working on campus, the greater their frequency of interaction with someone of a different race or ethnicity.

However, the findings of this and other studies also indicate that simply enrolling more students of color does not always result in increased interaction of nonwhite students. The impact of diversity is much more nuanced for students of color, and as the diversity of the study body increases some factors, such as more students living and working off campus, serve to blunt cross-racial interaction (Chang et al., 2004).

To realize the full individual and community benefits of diversity, putting students in a diverse environment is necessary but insufficient. Engagement with difference is necessary to realize the benefits of diversity, and this recognition focuses attention on the factors that promote engagement, particularly the universities' policies and practices with regard to social and residential life.

FACTORS THAT INFLUENCE INTERACTION ACROSS RACIAL GROUPS

The Preparing College Students for a Diverse Democracy Project (DDP) at the University of Michigan has been the basis for a number of studies on the factors that contribute to interactions across racial groups (Hurtado, 2003; Hurtado et al., 2003). The sample included African American, Asian American, Latino, and white students (n>4,000) from 10 public universities who completed surveys at entry to college in fall 2002, and again two years later in spring 2002. Positive cross-race interaction was assessed through seven survey items that asked students to indicate the extent to which they engaged students of other racial/ethnic backgrounds in dining and sharing meals, having discussions about racial/ethnic relations outside of class, sharing personal feelings and problems, studying and preparing for class, socializing and partying, having intellectual discussions outside of class, and attending events sponsored by other racial/ethnic groups.

The findings of one study (Saenz et al., 2007) indicated that the frequency and extent of interactions with diverse peers in high school and opportunities for intensive dialogue in classes were significant predictors of positive interactions across race in college for all four racial/ethnic groups. There were, however, differences across the four groups in the contribution of precollege and in-college variables to interactions across race in college. For example, participation in a Greek organization was associated with less engagement for white students, while faculty interest in student development was associated with more engagement for African American and white students.

The findings of another study (Saenz, 2010) provided additional support for the perpetuation of precollege socialization experiences on cross-race interactions in college, even after controlling for a variety of other precollege measures (e.g., precollege interactions with diverse peers, studying with diverse peers, anxieties over interacting with diverse peers) and precollege expectations (e.g., expecting to get to know diverse peers, expecting to enroll in a diversity course). However, the findings also indicated the potential of college diversity experiences to interrupt such perpetuation effects. In particular, students who lived with others from different backgrounds, compared to students who lived in less diverse settings on campus, were very likely to report greater levels of positive interaction across racial groups. One implication of the findings was that:

> In spite of students' segregated precollege environments and experiences, public universities that are more structurally diverse and that foster more diverse curricular and cocurricular activities can positively affect students' levels of interactions with diverse peers (Saenz, 2010, p. 30).

Although there has been a substantial increase in the degree of racial diversity on college and university campuses, and there is evidence that campus culture can positively affect students' levels of interactions, concerns have been expressed about whether the benefits of this increased diversity are being realized in terms of students actually engaging differences.

BALKANIZATION AND SELF-SEGREGATION

The tendency for students to associate with members of their own race/ethnic group on campus is a phenomenon that is readily recognized in terms of dinning, residential, and social life on campus, with references for example to the "Asian table" or the "Latino house" or the "black sorority." Along with this recognition there have been efforts to understand the underlying processes. More specifically, *balkanization*, the tendency for students from different racial and ethnic groups to associate primarily with others within their group has become an increasing concern and is frequently attributed to a process of *self-segregation*.

A recent study sought to answer several critical questions: To what extent do students perceive racial balkanization on a diverse campus; to what extent do students' closest friendships reflect balkanization; and how influential are these friendship groups in students' development of racial understanding, cultural awareness, and interracial interaction (Antonio, 2001)? The study sample consisted of UCLA students (n = 677) who completed the Cooperative Institutional Research Program's (CIRP) annual freshman survey in 1994 and again as third-year students. Part of the survey asked respondents to list the names of fellow students whom they identify as those "with whom you spend most of your time and consider to be your best friend(s) at UCLA." *Friendship group diversity* was defined by the percentage of the largest racial or ethnic group represented in the friendship group: homogeneous, the largest racial/ethnic group, makes up 100% of the friendship group; predominantly one race/ethnicity, the largest racial/ethnic group, makes up 75–99% of the friendship group; majority one race/ethnicity, the largest racial/ethnic group, makes up 51–74% of the friendship group; and no majority, the largest racial/ethnic group, makes up 50% or less of the friendship group.

The study found that only 26.7% of the students reported a homogeneous (17.1%) or predominately one race/ethnicity friendship group (9.6%), and 27.6% reported friendship groups consisting of a majority of one race/ethnicity. The most common friendship group, described by almost half of the sample (45.8%), was racially mixed in that no racial or ethnic group constituted a majority. Men and women did not differ on the degree of racial diversity in their friendship groups. However, in spite of this high degree of interracial friendships, the students still perceived the campus as balkanized as reflected in the percentage endorsement of two survey questions: Students on campus are predominantly clustered by race/ethnicity (92.9%), and students rarely socialize across racial lines (51.9%). Significantly more men than women students in this study perceived UCLA as a racially segregated campus, but there were no significant differences in responses by friendship diversity group type.

These findings suggest that there are two dimensions of campus diversity, the behavioral and the perceptual or psychological. On the behavioral level students reported a high degree of interracial friendships, but on a psychological level students overwhelmingly saw their campus as racially and ethnically segregated. The perceived norm was balkanization, and students with diverse friendship groups think of themselves as the exceptions (Antonio, 2001, p. 81).

One implication of these findings is that it is important for institutions to address the psychological dimension of campus culture diversity. Colleges and universities need to be aware of the perceptions regarding campus culture and regularly monitor and provide information on key makers of diversity that go beyond the demographics of the entering class and capture dimensions of engagement and interaction. In addition, colleges and universities need to continuously articulate their diversity values and commitment to establishing a campus culture that fosters the engagement with difference. The most salient avenues available to institutions to support diverse student interactions are through their social and residential life policies and practices with regard to racial/ethnic/cultural groups.

PERSPECTIVES ON IMPACT OF RACIAL/ETHNIC/ CULTURAL GROUPS

The prevalence of racial/ethnic/cultural student organizations on campus is one of the factors often claimed to contribute to segregation (Sidanius et al., 2004). However, many students derive valued academic and social benefits from being members of such groups. Consequently, colleges and universities are confronted with formulating policies and practices with regard to the establishment and support of these groups and the associated issue of whether to allocate social and residential space to these groups and if so, where on campus. There are two competing theoretical perspectives with which to view the impact of racial/ethnic/cultural groups on intergroup attitudes and relationships on campus that institutions can draw on to inform and guide their policies.

The *multicultural perspective* argues that ethnically oriented student organizations serve as a support system and "safe harbor" from which to reach out to the larger community (Sidanius et al., 2004). The limited empirical evidence suggest that "students join minority racial or ethnic organizations for the purposes of identity enhancement, and increased comfort with one's identity may, in turn, lead to greater interests in cross-cultural contacts, a greater sense of belonging to the university community, and a greater integration into broader campus life" (Sidanius et al., 2004, p. 96). While there is evidence in support of positive impact on minority academic achievement and retention rates, there has been little investigation of the impact of student organizations on intergroup attitudes and behaviors (Sidanius et al., 2004).

In contrast to the multicultural perspective, *social identity theory* argues that in-group identification is causally related to intergroup bias and therefore steps that increase the degree of ethnic identity may increase rather than decrease the amount of intergroup tension and bias (Sidanius et al., 2004). It has been argued that attention to collective group identity should not be limited to minority groups. More specifically, consideration of the impact of student groups should be extended to include the largely white fraternities and sororities that comprise the Greek system, which have been found to be associated with high levels of ethnocentrism and prejudice (Sidanius et al., 2004). To address the impact of group membership on intergroup attitudes, a longitudinal study undertaken at UCLA with 2,132 incoming students examined the hypotheses that (1) both minority membership in ethnic organizations and white membership in Greek organizations contribute to increased levels of in-group identifications and more negative intergroup attitudes; and (2) increases in negative intergroup attitudes are mediated by increases in levels of in-group identity (Sidanius et al., 2004).

The findings supported both the multicultural and social identity theory perspectives. Consistent with the multicultural perspective, the decision of minorities to join an ethnically oriented student organization was associated with high levels of ethnic identification and activism and sense of being part of the larger university, and membership in turn increased their level of ethnic identity and desire to be politically active on behalf of the group. Consistent with social identity theory, however, membership did not increase the students' sense of common identity with members of other groups or their sense of belonging to the wider university community, but it did increase feelings of victimization by virtue of one's ethnicity and the perception that ethnic groups are locked into a zero-sum competition with one another. Furthermore, increases in ethnic identity mediated increases in the sense of zero-sum competition. Similarly, membership in the Greek organizations functioned as "ethnic clubs" for white students. Membership was significantly related to precollege levels of white ethnic identity and intergroup bias, membership increased their sense of white ethnic identity, and the increase was associated with other attitudes including increased opposition to an ethnically diverse campus, belief that ethnic organizations promote separatism, and sense of ethnic victimization. These findings led the investigators to conclude that:

Altogether then, the effects of both minority and White ethnic organizations appear to be substantially more antagonistic and less benign than has been suggested in past research (Sidanius et al., 2004, p. 108).

In general, research findings indicate the association of racial/ethnic/cultural groups with both positive and negative impacts with regard to intergroup attitudes. These organizations offer minority students a sense of safety, but "membership in these organizations has a tendency to increase perceptions of group victimization, intergroup bias and perceived zero-sum conflict between groups" (Sidanius et al., 2004, p. 108).

RESIDENTIAL LIFE

While some colleges and universities randomly assign students to residential spaces, often the residential life systems enable some degree of student choice, and many have mixed systems with random assignment in the first year followed by choices in subsequent years. Thus, it is common practice across colleges and universities to have separate residence dormitories or floors set aside for subgroups of students. For example, separate resident spaces for athletes and members of theme groups, such as the French Language House, and living–learning communities, such as those centered on community service. Sometimes separate residences are established for cultural groups or religious groups. In particular, it is the separate residences around racial/ethnic/cultural groups that have evoked the most concern about self-segregation.

Students often make the choice to live in particular residences because they want to be with their friends, and feel they will be more comfortable with members of their own groups. Colleges and universities are confronted with the dilemma of wanting to foster comfort and positive group identity of minority students and also interaction across groups. Arguments have been made against enabling racially and ethnically based housing. Arguments have also been made in support of enabling student choice, even if it results in ethnic enclaves. Although this has been an issue for some time, there is surprisingly little empirical research about the extent of self–segregation, its impact, or comparison of different residential practices with regard to various dimensions of academic and student engagement.

Although there is a widespread impression that there is a high level of residential self-segregation among African American students, this impression is not empirically supported. A study reported in the *Journal of Blacks in Higher Education* (1997–1998) is a good example. The study examined the percentages of students residing in African American residences at ten highly ranked universities and liberal arts colleges selected on the basis of reputations for intense self-segregation on the part of blacks. The findings indicated that less than one-third of all black students on these campuses lived in the African American theme houses, and at half of the campuses surveyed less than 10% of the black students lived in these program houses. Thus, two-thirds to 90% of all black students chose to live in fully integrated housing.

In the absence of empirical research, policies and practices are guided by three major theoretical approaches (Bocian, 1997). The *integration model* emphasizes people relating to each other as individuals rather than as members of groups. The aim is not to erode cultural particularities, but to foster interaction between people of different races, cultural, and religious groups. Advocates of this approach argue for random assignment. The *multicultural model* emphasizes the plurality of cultures and seeks to promote the recognition and nourishment of distinct cultures to prevent being subsumed by the dominate culture. Advocates of this approach argue for ethnically and culturally based housing as a way to promote both recognition and student comfort in the context of ample opportunity for interaction inside and outside of the classroom. The *diversity within unity model* promotes the allegiance of individuals to their own subgroup and also to the greater society in which they live. Advocates of this model argue that students should be able to live and learn in their subgroups but subgroups should be required to interact with each other to explore and foster common bonds and commitments, typically through some common activity.

Colleges and universities generally try to be responsive to student preferences, but student preferences are viewed as contributing to self-segregation. However, there have been very few empirical studies of the actual impact of student preferences. One recently reported study explored the role of preferences in producing racial separation through a case study of a university housing system in the southeast that experienced an increase in the residential separation between black and white students during the period of 1988–1998 (Koehler & Skvoretz, 2010). The housing system asked students to rank their residence hall preferences and made housing assignments based upon these preferences in a completely "color-blind" fashion. Yet over time, black and white students became increasingly separated. The findings indicated that the percent black composition of the residence hall positively affected a residence hall's ranking by both black and white students. Although the percentage of black composition increased the ranking given to a hall on student applications, the fact that the effect size was three times greater for black students as compared to white students resulted in the potential for separation of white and black students into different buildings: "Hence, it is possible that when assignments are made, black students are disproportionately assigned to halls with greater percent black, because those halls attract higher ranks from black students" (Koehler & Skvoretz, 2010, p. 21).

This research demonstrates just how difficult it is to achieve residentially integrated outcomes even when the assignment of residence is color-blind. In fact, the findings suggest that to avoid such outcomes and the resulting opportunity costs in terms of interaction across racial groups, race would need to be taken into account during the assignment process. However, to justify intervening in the housing assignment process would require a community consensus that diversity within residence halls is a valued goal. Given the different goals of respecting student preferences, promoting the recognition of distinct cultures, and fostering intergroup interactions, such a consensus is difficult to achieve. Therefore most institutions will function, intentionally or by default, with a residential model that enables some level of racial/ethnic/cultural housing.

The challenge for colleges and universities with regard to racial/ethnic/cultural social groups and residential life is to balance the multicultural and integration approaches, and in particular to mitigate the potentially negative impacts though other policies and practices that encourage intergroup engagement. In particular, attention has focused on theoretical perspectives and research evidence regarding effective approaches for addressing the underlying processes involved in reducing bias and promoting positive intergroup relations.

REDUCING INTERGROUP BIAS AND PROMOTING INTERGROUP RELATIONS

Exposure to others who are different than oneself is not automatically beneficial, and it can elicit negative reactions and avoidance of interactions. Therefore, attention has been directed toward understanding the factors that contribute to negative interactions. Much of our knowledge about the basis of negative interactions between groups stems from the research on intergroup racial bias. There are cognitive, affective, and behavioral components to bias (Engberg, 2004):

- *Prejudice* refers to negative attitude that includes both a cognitive component of thoughts and beliefs and an affective component of feelings and emotions.
- *Stereotypes* are beliefs about members of racial, ethnic, gender, religious, and age groups that are activated relatively automatically. Stereotypes involve over attributing the extent to which a particular group shares a trait and the tendency for individuals to perceive their own group positively, as unique and heterogeneous, but other groups negatively and as homogeneous.
- *Discrimination* refers to negative behavior toward members of a particular group that is unjustified.

In Chapter 3 on empathy, we previously discussed the existence of several specific biases that work to elicit positive appraisals for those viewed as similar to ourselves and negative stereotypes for those perceived as different. At the most basic level, there is the similarity bias reflected in people responding systematically more favorably to others whom they perceive to belong to their group than to different groups (Gaertner & Dovidio, 2008). Thus, it is not surprising that there is also an empathy bias in favor of those who are perceived as being similar to ourselves: "People empathize with and help others who they are led to believe share their preferences, attitudes, interests, life goals, and chronic concerns" (Hoffman, 2000, p. 294). In situations in which individuals or groups are perceived as dissimilar, judgments are not only more likely to be based on stereotypes, but the behavior of others is also more likely to be described as driven by dispositional traits and not by situational contexts (Dimaggio et al., 2008). Furthermore, erroneous judgments about others attitudes, beliefs, capabilities, traits, and dispositions errors are more frequent when the other person is from a stereotyped social group (Mason & Macrae, 2008).

We also considered the contribution of two other types of biases to prejudice and stereotyping. The correspondence bias refers to the tendency to attribute behavior to the person's disposition rather than to characteristics of the situation in which the person is functioning (Gilbert & Malone, 1995). We also saw that belief about whether personal traits were fixed or modifiable have an impact on social information processing. In contrast to those who view personal attributes as modifiable, those holding a fixed view more readily endorse and apply social stereotypes and resist stereotype-inconsistent information (Molden & Dweck, 2006).

To overcome these biases, it is necessary to address the cognitive, affective, and behavioral components. Accurate knowledge about others, as individuals and groups, is essential. However, biases influence social information processing and thus transformative or corrective experiences are necessary to foster openness to new information and new interpretations. We discussed the role of engagement with others in developing one's capacities for perspective taking and empathy as a way of enhancing understanding of, and regard for, others. Therefore, colleges and universities must provide opportunities for students to develop multicultural knowledge and competencies through experiences inside and outside of the classroom, and students must hold themselves accountable for evaluative thinking and intentional efforts to engage difference. The primary way that colleges and universities endeavor to promote these transformations is through contact with diverse others.

THE CONTACT HYPOTHESIS

The commitment to providing opportunities for contact with diverse others stems in large part from the intergroup contact theory which maintains that under optimal conditions intergroup contact facilitates learning about the out-group, and this new knowledge in turn reduces prejudice (Allport, 1954). In this original formulation, the optimal conditions were specified in terms of four features of the contact situation: equal status between the groups; common goals; intergroup cooperation; and the support of authorities, law, or custom.

In the 50 years since the original formulation of this theory, many studies have been conducted that in general provide support for the contact hypothesis. For example, a large meta-analysis of 713 independent samples from 515 studies found that intergroup contact clearly reduces intergroup prejudice (Pettigrew & Tropp, 2006). Furthermore, these contact effects have been found to occur across a broad range of contact settings and extend beyond racial and ethnic groups to other out-groups, including the physically and mentally disabled, groups based on sexual orientation, and the elderly. Although 94% of the samples in this study showed an inverse relationship between intergroup contact and prejudice, only 19% of the samples involved situations structured in line with the four optimal conditions specified by Allport (1954). Thus the findings of this meta-analysis indicate that these optimal parameters are facilitative but not necessary.

As the evidence in support of the contact hypothesis has accumulated, the focus is now on identifying the mechanisms of effect. The question being asked is whether the reduction in prejudice is just a matter of exposure, or a function of some other mechanism. In particular, four proposed mechanisms have been considered.

One proposed mechanism is cross-group friendship. That is, it is not just exposure to other groups but rather the formation of friendships that matters. In support of this idea, cross-group friendships have been found to reduce prejudice (Pettigrew et al., 2007; Pettigrew, 2008). A second proposed mechanism is that contact serves to reduce the feelings of anxiety that are considered likely to arise as a consequence of expectations of rejection or discrimination during cross-group interactions: "These feelings grow out of concerns about how they should act, how they might be perceived, and whether they will be accepted" (Pettigrew & Tropp, 2006, p. 767). The evidence indicates that contact reduces prejudice through lessening feelings of anxiety and threat (Pettigrew & Tropp, 2006; Crisp & Turner, 2009).

A third proposed mechanism is that contact increases empathy. In another series of meta-analyses of 81 samples from 63 studies, Pettigrew and Tropp (2008) tested the significance of three widely studied mediators of contact effects on prejudice: new knowledge about the out-group, anxiety reduction, and increased empathy for the out-group. The findings indicated that all three serve as mediators but the affective process of empathy and perspective taking were more important than the cognitive process of knowledge about the out-group.

A fourth proposed mechanism is self-disclosure, which has been found to mediate the effects of two types of intergroup contact, cross-group friendship and extended contact, on out-group attitudes (Turner et al., 2007). Self-disclosure works in several ways to improve out-group attitudes. One way is by generating empathy. For example, studies indicate that the more participants had experienced reciprocal self-disclosure with out-group members, the more they empathized with the out-group, and, in turn, the more positive was their attitude toward the out-group attitude (Turner et al., 2007). Another way through which self-disclosure improves out-group attitudes is by promoting reciprocal trust, an expression of confidence that one will not be harmed by another person or groups actions. Studies indicate that those who trusted and felt trusted by the out-group held a more positive out-group attitude (Turner et al., 2007).

Although the preponderance of evidence supports the positive impact of intergroup contact, negative outcomes, including prejudice, distrust, and conflict, can result from threatening contact situations. For example, in the previously discussed meta-analysis (Pettigrew & Tropp, 2006), 5% of the studies found intergroup contact associated with greater prejudice (Pettigrew, 2008). Determining the individual factors and context conditions that lead to, and mitigate, these negative outcomes needs more study.

In addition to focusing on mechanisms of effect, attention is also being directed to addressing some of the limitations of the contact hypothesis framework (Dixon et al., 2005). These include expanding studies beyond the optimal forms of contact to those that characterize intergroup relations and contact as lived and practiced in everyday life; moving beyond employing formal typologies of contact to recover participants own constructions of their interactions and the meaning and implications they ascribe to these interactions; and expanding beyond a focus on the rehabilitation of the prejudiced individual to other outcomes such as political attitudes, support for policies regarding inequalities, and resistance to discrimination (Dixon et al., 2005). Recognizing that the lived experience of both contact and desegregation may differ according to group membership, historical time period, and location within a social systems calls attention to the need for comparative studies that seek to understand how different groups come to hold disparate understandings of what constitutes equality, cooperation, and integration (Dixon et al., 2005).

The research evidence certainly indicates colleges and universities can reduce bias and prejudice through policies and practices that not only promote contact across groups, but make it inevitable and incorporate those mechanisms through which contact has a positive effect: cross-group friendships, self-disclosure, reducing interactional anxiety, and increasing empathy and reciprocal trust. In addition, knowledge about the impact of collective identity can be another source of guidance for institutional policies and practices.

In response to increasing diversity, colleges and universities seek to promote the well-being and flourishing of students from different backgrounds. In addition to promoting contact across groups and fostering the underlying process of increasing empathy and reducing anxiety, attention has also been directed to promoting collective identity. Not surprisingly, the theories and research evidence with regard to the role of collective identity in intergroup engagement are often in conflict, but yet have the potential to provide a firm basis for guiding university social and residential life policies and procedures with regard to ethnic/racial/cultural and religious groups.

As we discussed in the section on collective identity in Chapter 5, group identifications serve the important functions of belonging and distinctiveness. Social identity theory maintains that people have a need for a positive social identity, and one way to achieve this positive identity is through the distinctiveness of one's own group in comparison to other groups. This need is viewed as motivating efforts to enhance the distinctiveness of one's group and reduce the distinctiveness of other groups (Turner & Reynolds, 2001). Group identifications provide individuals with a sense of belonging and self-worth that give rise to beliefs about the importance of their group and feelings of group solidarity, which tends to reinforce perceptions of intergroup differences and competition. Individuals affiliate with many different groups, and their group identifications vary in strength and how central they are to the person. Social identity theory holds that strong in-group identification gives rise to strong out-group antipathies, but not under all circumstances. The relationship of intergroup identification and out-group conflict is more likely when the differences between groups are pronounced and viewed as zero-sum. Moreover, advances have been made in identifying the processes involved when strong group identities result in conflict. For example, viewing other groups as potentially threatening leads to intolerance and conflict (Gibson, 2006).

Social categorization theory builds on these ideas to explain the psychological basis of group processes. The act of self-categorization with a particular group is viewed as the mechanism that fosters in-group positive bias and out-group prejudice. This process of self-categorization, therefore, has become the focus for efforts to reduce prejudice between groups. The research findings about categorization are sufficiently consistent to yield a few general principles consistent with social identity theory (Crisp & Hewstone, 2007):

- There is a positive correlation between the degree of category differentiation and the degree of discrimination.
- Under high category differentiation, differences between categories tend to be exaggerated and difference within categories minimized.

- Differentiating or making a category more salient serves to increase discrimination such as in-group favoritism and out-group prejudice.

Although people strive to maintain a positive and distinct social identity, this does not inevitably result in intergroup prejudice and conflict. If students are encouraged to engage this self-categorization process in a flexible way, intergroup relations can be enhanced. For example, students can shift how they categorize themself to an alternate, more inclusive social identity or shift how they categorize someone else. With this recognition, three general approaches have evolved regarding changing self-categorizations to reduce prejudice and improve intergroup relationships.

- *Decategorization* emphasizes individual identity over group identity such that former in-group and out-group members are induced to perceive themselves as distinct individuals.
- *Recategorization* urges thinking of people from different groups as part of one superordinate group. There are two specific strategies that have evolved (Gaertner et al., 2000). The common in-group identity model is based on the idea that one can change their categorization from "us" and "them" to a more inclusive, superordinate "we," and thereby reduce intergroup bias. The dual identity model also proposes forming a common identity, but recognizes that the salience of the original categorization can be retained alongside this new common identity.
- *Cross-categorization* emphasizes the members of two groups are also members of a third group.

As part of their extensive review of interventions to reduce prejudice, Paluck & Green (2009) conclude that each of these approaches has achieved some measure of success in reducing prejudice and that the integrative and crossed categorization models claim the most empirical support.

One implication of these findings for universities is to balance the salience of distinctive social categorizations through increasing the relative salience of common identities (Crisp & Hewstone, 2007). In doing so, it needs to be recognized that those who are strongly committed to a group are motivated to differentiate their group from other similar groups in order to maintain group distinctiveness and positive social identity. They are likely to react negatively to blurring of intergroup boundaries and may feel a threat of loss of distinctiveness if subsumed into a superordinate group which could lead to increased efforts at differentiation and thus increased intergroup bias. Therefore, when identification with a group is high, the strategy would be to foster dual identifications and simultaneously bring groups together on a second cross-cutting dimension (Crisp & Hewstone, 2007).

University Identity

To enhance intergroup relationships, what common-in-group or superordinate group identity should universities foster? One obvious candidate is university identity. Levin and colleagues (2009) undertook a study to test the hypothesis that university identification could be an effective common-in-group identity for promoting relationships among ethnic groups on campus. The study followed an incoming class at UCLA and assessed the extent of university identification on the basis of student's responses to three questions:

- How often do you think of yourself as a UCLA student?
- To what degree do you experience a sense of belonging or a sense of exclusion at UCLA?
- How likely is it that you would consider dropping out of UCLA before earning a degree?

The findings indicated that whereas ethnic identification was related to desires for status differentiating group-based hierarchies and ideologies that foster conflict and inequities, university identification was virtually unrelated to these outcomes. One implication is that fostering university identification could promote more positive relations between ethnic groups on campus (Levin et al., 2009).

Normative Beliefs

Beyond promoting common group identities, another way to improve campus climate is to reduce the tendency to form status hierarchies among groups. Individuals vary in their social dominance orientation—that is, in their desire to establish and maintain power differences between groups—which is often expressed through denigrating subordinate groups and engaging in acts of prejudice. In light of the evidence that social dominance orientation drives ethnic and cultural group prejudice, Levin and colleagues (2012) undertook a study with college students to determine whether this orientation could be influenced by the types of beliefs that were presented as normative. In particular, they were interested in the potential influence of acculturation beliefs. They proposed that the relationship between social dominance orientation and prejudice would be stronger when hierarchy enhancing acculturation ideologies are considered to be the norm than when hierarchy-attenuating ideologies are considered as the norm. Three types of acculturation ideologies were examined. *Assimilation* is considered a hierarchy-enhancing ideology because it uses the cultural characteristics of majority group members to define the national identity. *Multiculturalism* is viewed as hierarchy-attenuating, because it promotes the maintenance of each ethnic group's cultural heritage. *Colorblindness* is also considered as hierarchy-attenuating, because it promotes equal treatment regardless of group membership. In the study, students read an article that reported findings from a survey regarding which acculturation condition is considered normative in American society. The experimental manipulation in this study was to vary which ideology was reported as normative.

The findings indicated that hierarchical social dominance orientation can be enhanced or attenuated by the ideology that is presented as normative. Portraying the assimilation ideology as normative was positively associated with both social dominance orientation and prejudice, whereas portraying the multiculturalism and colorblindness ideologies as normative was negatively associated with both orientation and prejudice. The implication is that one way universities can reduce prejudice is through establishing and promoting the hierarchy-attenuating ideologies of multiculturalism and colorblindness as normative for the university community.

Procedural Fairness

Another way in which colleges and universities can facilitate both identity development and the engagement with difference is through establishing a culture of procedural fairness. As we have seen, people enhance their self-esteem through making comparative judgments about their group in relation to other groups. When those in a position of authority treat social groups fairly this leads to members of those groups feeling self-esteem and respect, having positive attitudes and feelings toward the group, and being willing to act on behalf of the group (Tyler & Smith, 1999). In particular, establishing a culture of procedural fairness can create positive social identities associated with being a member of a social group and lessen the need to feel better through comparative judgments with other groups (Tyler & Smith, 1999).

EDUCATIONAL INTERVENTIONS

In addition to aspects of the campus culture, educational interventions have been undertaken to reduce bias and promote intergroup relations. Engberg (2004) conducted a review of the research literature to determine the effectiveness of various types of educational interventions that have been designed to reduce racial bias among students in higher education. The interventions included multicultural courses, both required and optional; diversity workshops and training programs; service-based interventions; and peer-facilitated training and instruction including intergroup dialogue, collaborative learning, and living learning communities. Of the 73 studies reviewed, findings from 52 were positive, 14 were mixed, and seven were nonsignificant. Support was provided for the effectiveness of the four types of interventions in reducing racial bias. However, many of the educational interventions produced mixed or nonsignificant results, and conceptual and methodological limitations were identified across a number of the studies (Engberg, 2004). More specifically, many studies were not grounded in a theoretical framework that enabled testing of formal hypotheses about the explicit links in terms of underlying processes between the intervention and the intended student outcomes, and the measures employed in many studies lacked sufficient conceptual clarity and rigor. The most prevalent limitation, however, was related to the research design, particularly lack of appropriate controls.

The limitations of the current research on interventions to reduce bias and promote intergroup relations were also evident in another review. Paluck and Green (2009) conducted a review of 985 intervention studies, of which 72% are published. Of the 985 studies, 60% are nonexperimental studies in the field (which constituted 55% of the published studies), 29% are experimental studies in the laboratory, and 11% are experimental studies in the field. The interventions reflected a broad array of ideas including multicultural education, sensitivity training, cooperative learning, as well as interventions based on intergroup contact. Although the number and scope of studies is impressive, because of the general lack of methodological rigor the authors conclude that "the literature does not reveal whether, when, and why interventions reduce prejudice in the world" (Paluck & Green, 2009, p. 360).

Engberg (2004) made a number of recommendations to improve the quality of interventions studies including an emphasis on identifying the underlying psychological processes that mediate change, expansion of measures beyond prejudice to include other aspects of racial bias, and determination of the role of developmental effects, such as cognitive and identity development, in fostering change in racial bias. For example, the findings of a number of studies "suggest that changes in racial bias are dependent on students' level of cognitive and identity development" (Engberg, 2004, p. 501). Furthermore, more rigorous research design and analytic methods are needed to address more refined research questions, including: differential effects, or determining who benefits from various types of educational interventions; comparative effects of the magnitude of the effects across types of interventions or whether certain interventions are more effective at targeting certain types of bias; long-term and cumulative effects of various interventions; and mechanism of effect regarding how the various elements of a particular intervention actually work to enact change in racial bias (Engberg, 2004).

An example of a study that addressed both long-term effects and mechanisms of effect followed college students into their mid-thirties, and examined the impact of having taken an ethnic studies course or participated in a racial/cultural awareness workshop while in college (Bowman et al., 2011). The overall findings indicated that engagement with racial/cultural diversity had a positive, indirect effect on personal growth, purpose in life, recognition of racism, and volunteer work 13 years after graduation. More specifically, participating in the workshops had a significant effect, and taking an ethnic studies course had a marginally significant effect, on personal growth and engaged purpose in life and both effects were mediated by the extent of prosocial orientation in the senior year. The authors suggest that structured college engagements of this type may place students on a trajectory of helping others through fostering the internalization of a prosocial orientation, which leads to attitudes and behaviors that are congruent with these core values (Bowman et al., 2011).

INTERGROUP DIALOGUE

Some campuses have developed student run centers to promote leadership development specifically with regard to engaging with differences. For example, on my own campus, Duke University students organized a Center for Race Relations in 2003 to foster interaction among diverse groups. This center held forums to promote sustained dialogue and developed an experiential learning component in the form of a four day retreat experience called Common Ground. This student-led retreat incorporated elements of human relations skills training based on approaches such as encounter groups and sensitivity training or "T" groups, which were originally developed in the early 1970s. This consciousness-raising experience was designed to empower participants to explore their own identities and inspire respect and understanding of others in their communities. The curriculum for the retreat included films, and student and faculty led small group sessions addressing the intersection of race, ethnicity, culture, gender, sexual orientation, and power hierarchies. Participants reported that these Common Ground retreats were powerful transforming experiences. More specifically, the findings of a student research project indicated that the participants reported significant increases in measures of self-esteem, self-efficacy, and identity (Lazarus, 2004).

Student-led dialogues, through centers or other mechanism such as religious-life group retreats, are becoming part of the landscape on college and university campuses and national networks are now emerging to provide students with leadership training in these consciousness-raising experiences. For example, the Sustained Dialogue Campus Network (www.sdcapmusnetwork.org) is made up of students from a number of colleges and universities, and its mission is to train, mentor, and connect student leaders who then initiate and sustain dialogues to build cohesive, engaged, and diverse campus communities.

Another example of a national effort is the Interfaith Youth Core (www. IFYC.org). Established in 2002 by Eboo Patel, the IFYC is motivated by two questions: What if people of all faith and traditions acted together to promote the common good? What if young people led the way? IFYC seeks to make interfaith cooperation a social norm on college campuses by working with students, faculty, and staff to positively engage religious diversity and to express their common values, typically through working together in service projects. The IFYC provides skills and resources to empower students through leadership training institutes for students from across colleges and universities, as well as workshops on individual campuses. In addition, IFYC has also established partnerships with colleges and universities to undertake holistic campus transformations as models of interfaith cooperation and provided assistance with program planning, implementation, evaluation, and sustainability.

Across these examples, we see the recognition by students and institutions not only of the need for engagement with difference but also the need for policies, practices, and structures, within and across campuses, to provide students with the opportunities to develop the requisite skills and dispositions. More specificity about what universities can do to reduce intergroup prejudice will be dependent on advances in the quality of the research. In particular, theoretically driven experimental field studies are need to build our knowledge base about intervention approaches that are effective in impacting the processes that mediate intergroup contact and enhanced intergroup relationships. It is this understanding that is needed to guide initiatives to enhance campus culture and more fully realize the promised educational and developmental benefits of diversity.

CHAPTER 7

Providing a Formative Undergraduate Liberal Education

We can count on a sustained process of intellectual development only when people are engaged in work that demands it (Anderson, 1993, p. 94).

In the preceding chapters it has been argued that a transformation of undergraduate education goals and practices is necessary to meet the societal needs of the twenty-first century and empower students to constructively engage ethnic, religious, and political differences. This transformation involves a reaffirmation of the value of a formative liberal education committed to fostering the development of the whole person as not only practical, but necessary to prepare students to confront the challenges of our knowledge-based, globally interconnected, and increasingly conflicted world.

To realize the goals of a formative liberal education, colleges and universities must adopt a developmental model of education to guide and structure the undergraduate educational experience to go beyond a focus on enhancing students' capacities for reasoning and tolerance. Opportunities must also be provided for students to develop a personal epistemology that includes a commitment to evaluative thinking, their capacity for empathy, and an integrated identity that includes values and a commitment to constructively engage differences.

The aim of this book is to provide a developmental science basis to inform this transformation in undergraduate education, through reviewing and synthesizing our current understanding about the nature of these essential capacities and dispositions and the evidence about how these capacities can be enhanced through campus culture and educational practices. Now, we need to consider how the undergraduate experience as a whole, inside and outside of the classroom, can be reshaped and aligned in accordance with a developmental model of undergraduate education as a process of intellectual and personal growth, involving empathy as well as reasoning, values as well as knowledge, and identity as well as competencies.

AGENDA FOR UNDERGRADUATE EDUCATION

Any reshaping of the undergraduate experience must begin with the college or university formulating a clear agenda that includes a well-articulated educational philosophy, specific student learning objectives in terms of intellectual and personal skills and dispositions, and a plan for how to use the resources of the entire institution to accomplish these objectives. The responsibilities for the undergraduate experiences are typically shared across academic and student affairs divisions of the institution, and the plan must address components both within and across these units. Matters of the curriculum and pedagogy are the responsibility of the faculty, and are the main areas of focus within academic affairs. Residential life, social and cultural groups, and religious life are the main areas of focus within student affairs. Adopting a developmental model of education provides a basis for integrating academic and student life dimensions of the undergraduate experience specifically around learning objectives and developmental tasks. For example, living and learning groups link academic and residential life, and experiential pedagogies such as service learning link the classroom and community service around common learning objectives. Furthermore, a developmental model can guide the intentional sequencing of experiences, both inside and outside of the classroom, that promote readiness for successive challenges across the undergraduate years. The institution must engage the academic community in the process of formulating the agenda for undergraduate education that will guide decisions about the curriculum, residential and social life, and their interrelationship.

It is through the formulation of their intellectual agenda that colleges and universities differentiate themselves. Liberal education is not a generic product that is interchangeable across institutions. Colleges and universities do little to differentiate their values, commitments, and intellectual strengths by claiming to provide a liberal education. Furthermore, very few institutions can achieve excellence in all areas of endeavor. Rather, colleges and universities need to formulate their unique intellectual agenda by delineating their core areas of intellectual strengths, values, commitments, and those opportunities that vary across departments and fields. The intellectual agenda needs to address key questions such as:

- What are the core intellectual commitments and values of the institution around which it will recruit and retain faculty strength?
- What does the institution want to be known for as the "go-to place"?

The answers could be a field such as biomedical engineering, neuroscience, or history, or a cross-field theme such as social or ecological justice, or a process such as interdisciplinarity or globalization. The point is to formulate the intellectual agenda of the institution in a way that sharpens its intellectual profile and commitments, and then align the undergraduate education experience in terms of curriculum, pedagogical practices, and cocurricular experiences with the intellectual agenda.

CURRICULUM

The curriculum of a college or university is more than the array of courses offered. It is the scaffolding to accomplish the intellectual agenda of the institution. The curriculum reflects the mission, values, and traditions of the institution and the aspirations of its students, faculty, and alumni. Any effort to reshape the undergraduate experience must include an appraisal of the extent to which the curriculum reflects the institutions' distinguishing values and commitments, takes advantage of the institution's unique resources and areas of excellence, responds to innovations in the field, achieves current student learning objectives, and prepares students for the societal challenges of today and tomorrow. Based on this appraisal, learning objectives can be reformulated as necessary and corresponding changes in the curriculum can be implemented.

The trends in curricular change across American higher education that we discussed previously can serve to inform this appraisal and reformulation process. The themes and learning objectives currently being promoted by the Association of American Colleges and Universities (AAC&U), for example, reflect a liberal and practical emphasis and a focus on integrated learning, and provide the foundation for a formative educational experience. These learning objectives are sufficiently varied and rich to serve as a framework for institutions to consider in articulating their own learning objectives to be addressed through required and elective courses and experiences. Furthermore, there are various ways of structuring the curriculum ranging from a common core to an emphasis on choice. More specifically, decisions about the curriculum must address the balance of student engagement not only with regard to breadth and depth across different knowledge and subject domains, but also with regard to the issues of interdisciplinarity and globalization. Student time and effort are finite. How should these precious resources be allocated? The point is that with regard to both learning objectives and the structure of the curriculum, there are many options and the choices need to be made in relation to the intellectual agenda of the institution.

In many ways, colleges and universities are being asked to do both more and better with fewer resources. While some are arguing that economic necessities require restructuring the baccalaureate degree from a four- to a three-year experience and providing more courses online, it is not a compelling argument to decrease the time and interpersonal interactions devoted to the development of the array of intellectual and personal skills necessary to confront the challenges of the twenty-first century. In fact, as we will discuss below, the evidence indicates that high-impact educational practices are those that involve high levels of student engagement. It is also clear, however, that room must be made in the current curriculum to accommodate new learning objectives and engagements. We are past the point, from both a student and faculty perspective, of just adding experiences. More importantly, there needs to be a reformulation of the entire undergraduate experience to integrate engagements inside and outside of the classroom into a meaningful whole.

Beyond the Credit Hour System

It is time to go beyond conceptualizing the undergraduate degree only in terms of the course credit model that has been in effect for over a hundred years. This model apportions the four-year undergraduate experience typically into eight semesters with a total of 120 to 130 credit hours needed for graduation, of which approximately half are required and half are elective. Typically, 30 to 40 credit hours are required for a major and 15 to 20 credit hours for a minor. Within these credit hours, there is a mix of courses with general education and disciplinary learning objectives to which interdisciplinary learning objectives must now be added.

In addition to traditional courses, immersion experiences, research experiences, and capstone projects all require considerable time and need to be enabled by, and integrated with, the curricular structure. It is important to recognize that the undergraduate student only spends about 13% of her or his time during the week in the classroom—so there is time for experiential components that are intentionally linked to the curriculum. Also, it is increasingly the case that students use summers in educationally purposive endeavors. In addition to courses taken in summer school and through study abroad, students often engage in other practical experiences including internships and research projects that are translated into course credits through the mechanism of independent study. Some of these are scholarly engagements that warrant academic course credit, but sometimes the engagements are valuable but do not warrant academic credit. These experiential engagements need to be integrated into an overall course of study rather than being just valuable extracurricular experiences. One could, for example, envision that an undergraduate degree in the future might no longer reflect a combination of college and major course requirements totaling 120 credit hours, but rather some combination of academic courses plus community service and study abroad as part of the college level requirements and undergraduate research or a capstone project as part of the requirements for the major.

It is not only possible to envision a different approach to formulating degree requirements; initiatives in Europe, known as the Bologna process and the Tuning process, are providing a model that is based on establishing specific learning expectations or objectives against which to assess students learning and development of competencies across their undergraduate years.

The Bologna process began in 1999 to create a European Higher Education Area (EHEA) in order to strengthen the competitiveness and attractiveness of European higher education.[1] The aim was to establish a system of undergraduate and postgraduate studies with easily readable programs and degrees. The objectives included enhancing quality assurance and fostering student mobility and employability through promoting greater comparability and compatibility across the various higher educational systems and institutions in Europe.

To accomplish these objectives various groups and commissions worked to establish a degree qualifications framework, which describes student learning outcomes such as what learners should know, understand, and be able to do on the basis of a given qualification; it also describes how students can move from one qualification to another within a system. The Bologna process has identified competences for lifelong learning in terms of key abilities and knowledge needed to achieve employment, personal fulfillment, social inclusion, and active citizenship in a rapidly changing world. The framework includes competences in native language literacy, numeracy, knowledge of foreign languages, and science and IT skills, as well as other skills such as learning to learn, social and civic competence, initiative-taking, entrepreneurship, cultural awareness, and self-expression.[2]

A three-cycle degree qualifications system has evolved (bachelor, master, and doctoral). The first cycle (bachelor) lasts a minimum of three years and typically includes 180 to 240 ECTS (European Credit Transfer and Accumulation System) credits. Access to the second cycle (master) is dependent on successful completion of the first cycle. Qualifications for the first cycle are awarded to students who have demonstrated knowledge and understanding in a field of study that builds upon their general secondary education, and is typically at a level that, while supported by advanced textbooks, includes some aspects that will be informed by knowledge of the forefront of their field of study; can apply their knowledge and understanding in a manner that indicates a professional approach to their work or vocation, and have competences typically demonstrated through devising and sustaining arguments and solving problems within their field of study; have the ability to gather and interpret

---

1 See www.ond.vlaanderen.be/hogeronderwijs/bologna/.
2 See http://ec.europa.eu/education/lifelong-learning-policy/key_en.htm.

relevant data (usually within their field of study) to inform judgments that include reflection on relevant social, scientific, or ethical issues; can communicate information, ideas, problems, and solutions to both specialist and nonspecialist audiences; and have developed those learning skills that are necessary for them to continue to undertake further study with a high degree of autonomy.[3]

Closely related to the Bologna process has been another initiative, referred to as the Tuning process.[4] This is a university-led initiative to develop professional profiles and learning outcomes in main subject areas (mathematics, geology, business, history, educational sciences, physics, and chemistry) by defining commonly accepted professional and learning outcomes. The initiative also specifies the most suitable location for these outcomes in the first or second cycle of the degree qualifications framework.

The level of specificity with regard to learning outcomes provided through the degree qualifications framework enables a finer level of representation of the student's qualifications than a traditional degree or diploma conveys. Course descriptions across institutions specify learning outcomes (i.e., what students are expected to know, understand, and be able to do) and workload (i.e., the time students typically need to achieve these outcomes). Each learning outcomes is expressed in terms of credits, with one credit generally corresponding to 25 to 30 hours of work, and a student workload typically ranges from 1,500 to 1,800 hours for an academic year. Correspondingly, the diploma supplement has been established to accompany a higher education diploma and provides a standardized description of the nature, level, context, content, and status of the studies completed by its holder.[5]

The Degree Qualifications Profile

Similar initiatives are currently underway in the United States. Beyond whatever an institution requires in terms of credits, grades, and specific course completions, the degree qualifications profile, developed through the Lumina Foundation, defines the associate, bachelor, and masters degrees in terms of specific learning outcomes with regard to what students are expected to know and do with their knowledge.[6] The profile describes five basic areas of learning: broad integrative knowledge, specialized knowledge, intellectual skills, applied learning, and civic learning. While the learning outcomes are specified, these can be accomplished in many ways. Students can demonstrated

---

3 See www.ond.vlaanderen.be/hogeronderwijs/bologna/documents/050218_QF_EHEA.pdf
4 See www.relent.deusto.es/TuningProject/background.asp#1.
5 See http://ec.europa.eu/education/lifelong-learning-policy/ds_en.htm.
6 See www.luminafoundation.org.

their growth in knowledge and skills through courses; specific projects, such as a capstone project or honors thesis; art, music, and dance performances; videos, films, and documentaries; and educational experiences such as study abroad, internships, and community service. The profile captures student learning whenever and wherever it occurs, and informs the student of learning objectives remaining to be accomplished.

The degree profile can now be supported through electronic information systems that track individual student's accomplishment of expected learning outcomes with the same degree of precision that the traditional registrar system tracks course enrollments, grades, and GPA (Shupe, 2007). Implementing the degree qualifications profile not only enables an institution to specify a distinctive set of learning outcomes consistent with the institutions values and mission, but also enables a representation of the unique profile for each student within the institutional framework. The current student transcript provides very little information: courses taken, grades obtained, and cumulative GPA. In contrast, the degree qualifications profile provides a visible pattern of each student's achievement.

Align General, Disciplinary, and Interdisciplinary Learning Objectives

One approach to reshaping the curriculum structure is to better align and integrate general, disciplinary, and interdisciplinary learning objectives. As we have seen, general education aims to develop a set of skills that are general in the sense of being essential to all fields and able to be applied across situations and contexts. These general education skills typically include writing, critical thinking, quantitative reasoning, ethics, and citizenship. General education also aims for students to have a breadth of intellectual experiences in order to understand modes of thought and integrate knowledge from different fields. General education is not the domain of any specific discipline, but is transdisciplinary. Higher education has been through a period of expansion in emphasis on general education learning experiences such that these now constitute 38% of the baccalaureate degree (AAC&U, 2001). This segmentation of the curriculum into general education and disciplinary components is misplaced. The aim of studying a discipline in liberal education is not just to develop disciplinary expertise, but to understand the form of knowledge represented by that discipline. Both objectives, specialized knowledge and general understanding, can be pursued together:

> A liberal education approached directly in terms of the disciplines will thus be composed of the study of at least paradigm examples of all of the various forms of knowledge. This study will be sufficiently detailed and sustained to give

genuine insight so that pupils come to think in these terms, using concepts, logic and criteria accurately in the different domains (Hirst, 1974, p. 48).

With the increasing evidence that learning is in large part domain-specific and mediated by the disciplines, the admonition that "if we improve learning in the disciplines, we will have improved general education" (Beyer et al., 2007, p. 363) is particularly salient. Academic departments construct knowledge differently and the processes of writing, critical thinking, problem-solving, and quantitative reasoning vary from one discipline to another and thus are context bound. Students learn to think and act in accordance with the disciplinary framework of intellectual values and practices of specific communities of discourse. Thus, the dichotomy between general education courses and courses in the major should become increasingly blurred as courses in the major are intentionally structured to achieve general education as well as disciplinary learning objectives.

Another approach to reshaping the curriculum structure is to consider the institutional policies with regard to major, minor, and interdisciplinary certificates. It is relatively common for students to double major, and also to have one or more minors or complete an interdisciplinary certificate program. It is also common for students to double major and minor in disciplines within the same domain, such as psychology and sociology in the social sciences or biology and chemistry in natural sciences. While this may be the appropriate choice for an individual student, if one of the objectives for undergraduate education is for students to understand different ways of thinking that underlie the disciplines, then perhaps a better strategy would be to encourage students to formulate their academic plan to include a combination of majors, minors, and certificates that span several domains of disciplinary and interdisciplinary knowledge.

Interdisciplinary Certificate Programs

Clusters of courses around a theme or topic began to emerge in the 1980s as a way to address new fields, such as neuroscience, women's studies, or Latino/a studies, and salient issues such as social justice, form and function in nature, and humanities through the arts that were not the domain of one academic department or discipline. These interdisciplinary certificate programs offered students a way to complement their major and minor and engage topics and issues of particular interest. As important as the topic or content areas, these certificate programs engaged students in the dynamic interface of disciplinary perspectives from which different ways of knowing emerge. Increasingly, interdisciplinary certificate programs include among its learning objectives helping students develop fluency across the boundaries of knowledge and learn how to integrate knowledge across the natural and social sciences and the humanities.

Typically, the sequence of courses in a certificate program begins with an introductory gateway course, followed by three to four courses from several participating departments, and a culminating capstone course or experience. Community-based research and service-learning experiences are frequently a component of the certificate program. The capstone course in particular is intentionally designed to be an integrative experience and involves completing a major research paper or project. Completion of the sequence of these course clusters frequently is recognized on the student's transcript and by the awarding of a certificate. Increasingly, interdisciplinary programs engage themes of compelling societal issues and address the intersection of scholarship and public policy. Thus, interdisciplinary certificate programs provide a curricular structure to enable students to engage in an integrative experience with interdisciplinary scholarship around salient societal issues, and can serve as coherent curricular pathways through the curriculum. These certificate programs can provide the sustained engagement with social issues and the process of applying knowledge to address societal problems that can be transformative with regard to students' identity formation and commitment to social responsibility and civic engagement.

My own university is an example of the development of interdisciplinary programs as a way to address learning objectives and realize the benefits of a research university with many prominent interdisciplinary research centers and programs. Certificate programs first became available at Duke University in 1983. By 1997 there were 15 certificate programs, and the committee on curriculum formally defined a certificate program as "a course of study that affords a distinctive, usually interdisciplinary, approach to a subject matter that is not available within any single academic unit," with no fewer than six required courses across two or more departments. In 2001, the curriculum committee established the requirement for an introductory experience and a culminating capstone experience. In 2002, it was decided that certificate programs could have a home outside traditional departments, and could also be offered through research centers, institutes, and programs which were the infrastructures that emerged to support, encourage, and sustain interdisciplinary education and research. By 2007, there were 23 certificate programs reflecting a range of topics, such as children in contemporary society, global health, study of ethics, arts management and cultural policy, Islamic studies, modeling biological systems, energy and the environment, genome science and policy, marine science and conservation leadership, Latino/a studies, and the study of sexualities. Of the graduating class of 2007, 21% completed a certificate program in addition to fulfilling college and department (major) requirements for the Bachelor of Arts or Bachelor of Science degrees.

Faculty typically view their instructional roles primarily in terms of their responsibility to foster the intellectual development of their students. However, faculty also have the opportunity to impact student development more broadly. To do so, faculty need to adopt the current understanding of learning as a process of knowledge transformation, which changes the focus of instruction from knowledge transmission to promoting the student's active engagement in the process of constructing knowledge. As we discussed in Chapter 3 on personal epistemology, the goal of a liberal education is to promote students' functioning at the evaluative level of thinking. Most faculty, however, do not include this goal among the learning objectives for their course and thus have not designed assignments and experiences specifically to foster this type of thinking. Similarly, faculty often lament the lack of student engagement, but typically do not consider what steps they could take to enhance student engagement. Consistent with advances in our understanding of learning, advances in the scholarship of teaching are providing a foundation for teaching practices that are effective in promoting student engagement and fostering evaluative thinking.

We have known for some time that intellectual and personal growth in college is strongly related to the extent of overall student engagement (Pascarella & Terenzini, 2005). Furthermore, there is increasing evidence that some educational practices have high impact *because* these practices foster student engagement. For example, some of the evidence stems from analyses of the association of student self-report data, provided by the National Survey of Student Engagement (NSSE), with an array of educational and personal outcomes (Kuh, 2008). The NSSE collects basic information about students' background and demographic characteristics and institutional requirements, and students' participation in educationally purposeful activities, perceptions of the college environment, and estimates of educational and personal growth since starting college. The set of effective, high-impact, educational practices that have been identified include first-year seminars, common intellectual experiences, learning communities, writing-intensive courses, collaborative assignments and projects, undergraduate research, diversity/global learning, community-based learning and service learning, internships, and capstone courses and projects (Kuh, 2008).

These educational practices foster active learning by requiring that students devote considerable time and effort to purposeful tasks, interact with faculty and peers over extended periods of time, and engage with people who are different from themselves (Kuh, 2008). In addition, these practices provide students with frequent feedback and opportunities to integrate and apply knowledge to real life problems. Beyond intellectual and personal growth, these high-impact practices are viewed as promoting students' understanding of themselves and others and "they acquire the intellectual tools and ethical grounding to act with confidence for the betterment of the human condition" (Kuh, 2008, p. 17).

There is an emerging research literature in support of the claims that these practices have high impact. For example, Brownell and Swaner (2010) report on five specific practices (first-year seminars, learning communities, undergraduate research, service learning, and capstone experiences), and report the most common outcomes as including higher grades, higher persistence rates, intellectual gains, greater civic engagement, increased tolerance for and engagement with diversity, and increased interaction with faculty and peers. It is also recognized that research on learning outcomes needs to become more rigorous and systematic. More specifically, attention must be directed to determining the interactions of student and setting characteristics that moderate these outcomes and the mediating process through which these effects are achieved. One area of focus is pedagogical approaches.

PEDAGOGIES OF ENGAGEMENT

High-impact practices employ "pedagogies of engagement." The concept was introduced by Russell Edgerton (1997) as "pedagogies for engaged learning" in an education white paper in which he articulated an agenda for higher education for the Pew Charitable Trust. Edgerton argued for movement away from didactic, lecture-based, pedagogies based on "teaching as telling; learning as recall" to pedagogies that elicit intense student engagement and direct experience with methods and processes of inquiry. In particular, he identified four examples of engaged pedagogies: problem-based learning, collaborative learning, service learning, and undergraduate research. Consistent with the increasing focus on active student learning, these pedagogies of engagement are widely employed and research is now focusing on delineating the essential components and mechanisms of effect and comparing the differential effectiveness of specific pedagogies for particular learning objectives as a function of the interaction of student and situational characteristics. For example, studies have undertaken a comparison of problem-based learning and collaborative learning strategies with science and engineering students (Eberlein et al., 2008; Smith et al., 2005).

Three of these high-impact educational practices in particular, undergraduate research, study abroad, and service learning/community service, have relevance for fostering the development of the capacities that are the primary focus of this book: personal epistemology, empathy, and an integrated identity that includes active agency for engaging differences. These three practices are a type of experiential learning that when done well incorporate pedagogies of engagement.

Although it has become customary to interchange the terms experiential learning and experiential education, Itin (1999) makes the case for the importance of distinguishing these different concepts. Learning is change in the individual, whereas education is a transactive process between an educator and student. In this context, experiential learning is understood to refer to a "change in the individual that results from reflection on a direct experience and results in new abstractions and applications" (p. 92).

Experiential education has its foundation in the work of John Dewey and the progressive education movement, which was characterized by a focus on linking of experience with reflection and understanding with doing, and emphasized the use of experience to develop the whole person to participate in a democratic society. It is a philosophy of education under which a number of specific strategies and approaches can be integrated. The teacher and the student cocreate the educational process. The teacher is responsible for presenting opportunities, facilitating learning, and guiding reflection, and the student is responsible for taking the initiative, making decision, posing questions, investigating, constructing meaning, integrating previous knowledge and being accountable for the results (Itin, 1999). Building on the recognition that students learn best when they make an emotional connection to the content, experiential learning seeks to connect the learning to the person's life (Lutterman-Aguilar & Gingerich, 2002). The goal of experiential learning is to empower students through enabling them to acquire an understanding of how they learn best, take responsibility for formulating their learning goals, and evaluate their attainment.

Undergraduate Research

Directly engaging in the inquiry and discovery processes that characterize the research and scholarship process is one of the most powerful learning experiences that colleges and university can provide. These opportunities not only serve to bring students into communities of practice, but provide students with first-hand experience with various disciplinary epistemologies, ways of thinking, paradigms of evidence, and writing conventions. Evidence is accumulating that participating in research experiences improves undergraduate science students' skills with regard to critical thinking, problem-solving, and applying knowledge; and engenders a more sophisticated understanding of the nature and construction of knowledge, confidence and empowerment to make a contribution, and a sense of responsibility for the process and the outcome (Seymour et al., 2004; Lopatto, 2004). Furthermore, the experiences of generating, integrating, evaluating, and applying knowledge prepares students for the challenges they will face after graduation in bringing knowledge to bear on societal problems.

As involving undergraduates in research has become a focal point of undergraduate education, it has become necessary to evolve infrastructures to support and coordinate these activities. Sometimes the research activity garners academic credit and is thus a part of the curriculum. Increasingly, however, the involvement in research constitutes an emersion, typically in the summer, and financial support is often provided to faculty and graduate student mentors as well as housing stipends for the undergraduate students. The funds typically are provided through grants for undergraduate education, for example through the Howard Hughes Medical Institute program for undergraduate education in the life sciences, and from institutional resources. As part of the infrastructure, many institutions have established an office of undergraduate research to coordinate the matching of students with research opportunities and the public presentation of student work. Many institutions also publish a journal of undergraduate research. At the national level, the Council on Undergraduate Research (CUR) was founded in 1978 to support and promote high-quality undergraduate student–faculty collaborative research and scholarship, and individual and institutional memberships in the CUR now includes over 600 colleges and universities.[7] The CUR's meetings and publications are a source of support for faculty development and are designed to share successful models and strategies for establishing and institutionalizing undergraduate research programs.

Study Abroad

Studying abroad has been a longstanding optional component of undergraduate education and is now well recognized as a high-impact educational experience (Kuh, 2008). Over time, thinking about the study abroad experience has evolved and has resulted in a paradigm shift from a "junior year abroad paradigm" to a "student learning paradigm" (Vande Berg, 2007). The junior year abroad paradigm, a descendant of the nineteenth century's European Grand Tour, was characterized by a focus on enhancing foreign language proficiency and learning about another culture. The participants were predominately white, female, and relatively wealthy students majoring in the humanities and social sciences. The student learning paradigm is characterized by a focus on developing intercultural competence; democratization of the experience in terms of encouraging participation across the broad demographic range of undergraduate students; inclusion of students majoring in science, business, and engineering as well as the humanities and social sciences; and program diversification with regard to destinations, types of experiences, and disciplinary specific goals (Vande Berg, 2007).

---

7 See www.cur.org/.

The two paradigms also differ with regard to pedagogical assumptions and practices. The junior year abroad paradigm was characterized by the assumption that student who performed well on the home campus would perform well abroad and would acquire increased language skills and enhanced understanding of another culture. These assumptions were not generally evaluated through any systematic appraisal of actual student learning. With regard to maters of pedagogy, Vande Berg (2007) remarks: "Study abroad professionals on the home campus made little effort to intervene in their students' experiences abroad, beyond suggesting or arranging for specific courses at the study abroad site" (p. 393). In contrast, the change associated with the student learning paradigm is striking: There is an increasing focus of evaluating student learning outcomes as a function of student and program characteristics, and consistent with advances in our understanding of teaching and learning, study abroad professionals "have become interventionists, convinced that if our students are to learn effectively, we need to intervene, before, during, and after their experiences abroad to shape and support their learning" (Vande Berg, 2007, p. 394).

Data from the Institute of International Education (2010) indicate that the number of US students studying abroad for academic credit has been steadily increasing from the early 1990 and has more than doubled over the past decade. In the 2008–2009 academic year 262,416 students studied abroad for academic credit. Of these, 55% studied for a short term (summer, January term, or less than eight weeks during the academic year), 41% for one or two quarters or a semester, and 4% for the academic or calendar year. Nontraditional destinations are becoming more popular, with 14 of the top 25 destinations being outside of Europe and 19 of the 25 are destinations where English is not a primary language. The percentage of students studying in Europe has dropped from 62% in 1999–2000 but remains high at 55%, with the United Kingdom, Italy, Spain, and France being the top four destinations and China now fifth. While large universities lead in terms of absolute numbers of their students going abroad, many smaller institutions send a higher proportion of their students abroad, and 29 institutions reported that more than 70% of their students studied abroad at some point during their undergraduate careers. Recently, study abroad experiences have been expanded to offer internship and service-learning opportunities.

While many undergraduate have a study abroad experience, not all of these experiences result in experiential learning. The motivations and goals that a student has for studying abroad and the structure of the experience have an influence on the outcomes. For example, a recent study found that students report multiple motivations for studying abroad including to increase their cross-cultural skills, to become more proficient in a specific subject matter, and to socialize (Kitsantas, 2004). While studying abroad was associated with increases in student reported global understanding and cross-cultural competence reflected in emotional resilience, flexibility/openness, and auton-omy, the greatest gains were found for students who had the goal of increased cross-cultural competence.

In addition to student goals and motivations, the nature and quality of the study abroad experience makes a difference. Sometimes the study abroad experience is merely a "time out" from academic engagement in which friends travel abroad together and interact minimally with local students and the larger community. Also, the extent to which study abroad programs intention-ally incorporate principles of experiential learning varies (Lutterman-Aguilar & Gingerich, 2002).

Advances have been made with regard to greater differentiation about the nature of the study abroad experience. A classification system (Engle & Engle, 2003) has been developed that defines programs with reference to seven characteristics: length of student sojourn, entry target-language competence, language used in course work, context of academic work, types of student housing, provisions for guided/structured cultural interaction and experi-ential learning, and guided reflection on cultural experience. Based on these seven characteristics, programs are classified into one of five levels: study tour, short-term study, cross-cultural contact program, cross-cultural encounter program, and cross-cultural immersion program. With this advance in defin-ing program characteristics, studies can now evaluate differential impacts along various student learning outcome dimensions as a function of the inter-action of student characteristics and level of program.

Evidence is beginning to accumulate about the impact of study abroad across a range of student learning outcomes. For example, studying abroad has been found to be associated with increases in students' intercultural awareness, cultural knowledge, empathy, tolerance and acceptance of oth-ers, and decreases in use of stereotypes (Pascarella & Terenzini, 2005). These effects are typically understood in terms of the contact hypothesis regarding the benefits of engaging with those different than oneself that we discussed in the previous chapter. Studies are also becoming more rigorous in design. For example, a study conducted through the Georgetown Consortium, with over 1,300 study abroad students (Vande Berg et al., 2004), reported that com-pared with students who studied at home, students who the studied abroad demonstrated more growth in intercultural development and greater facility in using a second-language (Pedersen, 2010).

Studies are not only addressing the extent of student learning, but also beginning to address the relationship between the pedagogy utilized in study abroad and student outcomes such as intercultural effectiveness. For exam-ple, students participating in a year-long study abroad program in England were compared with a control group of students (n = 13) who stayed home. This study was notable because it evaluated the impact of a specific interven-tion designed to foster intercultural effectiveness. The study abroad students included a subgroup (n = 16) who participated in a psychology of group dynamics course, which integrated intercultural effectiveness and diversity training pedagogy including cultural immersion, guided reflection, and intercultural coaching, and another subgroup (n = 16) in the same study abroad experience who were not in the intervention. The study employed the widely used Intercultural Developmental Inventory (IDI) (Hammer, 2007; Hammer et al., 2003) that measures ones' primary orientation toward cultural difference. The findings indicated more growth in intercultural competence in those students who were in the intervention group (Pedersen, 2010). Findings from this research lend empirical support for the assertion that if the goal is increased cultural competence and global citizenship, it is not enough just to send students to study abroad. Intentional pedagogies must be employed:

> We need to look at quality beyond the academic curriculum we are offering. We need to work with students during their experience using guided reflection and intercultural pedagogy to help them to grow interculturally from that experience. It is this intentional work that will ultimately facilitate global citizenship (Pedersen, 2010, p. 79).

Experiential education is a transactive process between educator and student that involves "carefully chosen experiences supported by reflection, critical analysis, and synthesis, structured to require the learner to take initiative, make decisions, and be accountable for the results" through "constructing meaning, and integrating previously developed knowledge" (Itin, 1999, p. 93). For study abroad to have a transformative impact with regard to one's worldview, understanding of others, and sense of identity, agency and efficacy, it must be structured as an educational experience that fosters experiential learning by processing the experiences through reflection and analysis.

Community Service and Service Learning

We have discussed in Chapter 6 the considerable evidence that community service and service-learning experiences influence how students view others and themselves, and fosters the development of empathy and integrated identity that includes a sense of personal responsibility and agency for civic engagement. Moreover, there is empirical evidence that involvement in community service is associated with a number of other positive educational outcomes, including a deeper understanding and ability to apply subject matter, a reduction in negative stereotypes, an increase in tolerance for diversity, and an appreciation of other cultures (Eyler & Giles, 1999). Thus for many students community service and service learning can be a transformative experience.

Many students became involved in community service while in high school and enter college with a desire to continue to be involved. Many colleges and universities have established community service centers to coordinate service activities by their undergraduates in the surrounding community. These centers typically are units within student affairs and have established relationships with community organizations including the school system and social service agencies. These centers provide the infrastructure to establish and maintain the relationships between the college or university and the community agencies that enable students, as individuals or as members of social or religious groups, to be of service in the community.

As might be expected, colleges and university with a religious affiliation emphasize preparing students to address the needs of others as a central component of their mission. Given such a commitment, it also is not surprising that networks are being established to enable universities to collaborate in establishing structures through which their students can engage in community service. For example, one common commitment of Jesuit institutions is "developing men and women for others." In 2008, the Jesuit Universities Humanitarian Action Network was launched as a joint collaboration of Georgetown, Fairfield, and Fordham universities to enable Jesuit institutions to work together to advance both undergraduate humanitarian education and the professional field of humanitarian action.[8] Activities include developing leadership teams, providing academic courses, conducting national skill building conferences, and service to the community.

Service learning is distinguished from volunteer service by the explicit focus on the educational value to be gained through engaging in service to the community. Typically the service learning experience is linked to a specific course or academic program. Adding a service component to an academic course increases the demands on the faculty teaching these courses and support mechanisms have evolved to assist faculty in establishing and maintaining the collaborative relationships with the community agencies through which the student services are provided. These essential support services are typically provided through the community service center within student affairs or service-learning offices established in academic affairs. Sometimes the support is provided at the department level through service-learning coordinator positions, particularly in language departments that may provide translation and interpretation services in schools, health departments, and social service agencies on an ongoing basis as part of the language course sequence or in education departments as part of their preschool or early childhood education programs. While support mechanisms are necessary to establish and maintain collaborative relationships, the quality of the on-site supervision and instruction, particularly with regard to providing students with interpretive

---

8 See www.juhanproject.org/.

frameworks for their experiences, is essential for gains in higher-order thinking and prosocial reasoning (Batchelder & Root, 1994).

The alignment of service learning with college and departmental learning objectives has led to new forms of engagements such as research service learning. As part of a course or certificate program, students undertake a research project or a capstone project to address some question or issue of importance to a community agency regarding program development or for guiding its policies or practices. Through this alignment of two powerful pedagogies of engagement, service learning and community-based research, students acquire direct, mentored experience in being responsive to societal issues through generating, evaluating, integrating, and applying knowledge to community needs.

Service learning is also being combined with study abroad to achieve synergies with regard to both cognitive and affective dimensions of experiential learning. For example, a report on a study abroad course that included service learning (Parker & Dautoff, 2007) found both components contributing to a gain in content learning regarding culture, business, and economic development, but the service-learning component made a particular contribution to learning involving feelings of personal connection to people outside of one's group and intentions to act on community problems.

Many examples of service-learning courses and programs are now available. For example, discipline-specific examples of service learning were published in the twenty-one volume American Association of Higher Education (AAHE) monograph series on service-learning in the academic disciplines edited by Edward Zlotkowski (1997–2006). In addition, through a Service Learning Collaborative at Clemson University, service-learning courses have been implemented in departments ranging from psychology and education, to business and marketing, to horticulture and public health. These courses have been described and the outcomes documented to facilitate adoption by others (Madden, 2000).

Service learning needs to be understood and evaluated within the overall context of the quarter-century-old efforts to reassert the civic mission of higher education. One benchmark of the progress of these efforts is the increase in membership of Campus Compact, a national coalition of college presidents committed to the civic mission of higher education, from three colleges in 1985 to over 1,100 campuses, a quarter of higher education institutions (Hollander, 2010).[9] The commitment of colleges and universities to community engagement as part of their mission has reached the point that in 2006 the Carnegie Foundation for the Advancement of Teaching and Learning established a new elective classification of "institutions of community engagement." The foundation designed a framework to engage the institution in a

---

9 See www.compact.org/.

process of inquiry, reflection, and self-assessment not only to document their engagement with their communities, but also to promote ongoing improvement of their programs (Driscoll, 2008). This framework provided a definition of community engagement as "the collaboration between institutions of higher education and their larger communities (local, regional/state, national, global) for the mutually beneficial exchange of knowledge resources in a context of partnership and reciprocity" (Driscoll, 2008, p. 39). Institutions were asked to provide examples of curricular engagement, outreach and partnerships, and commitment of budgetary, infrastructure, and faculty development support. In the initial 2006 classification, 76 institutions were recognized. By 2008, the number had increased to 175 institutions.

One step that colleges and universities can take to provide a formative educational experience is to ensure that participating in experiential learning is not optional. Undergraduate research, study abroad, and service learning can be fostered as normative undergraduate experiences of an intellectually and civically engaged campus that seeks to develop the whole person to participate in a democratic society.

ACADEMIC ADVISING

Academic advising is one of those support services that all colleges and universities provide. It is also typically the area of the undergraduate experiences around which there is the most student dissatisfaction. Academic advising needs to be viewed by both the college and the student as more than a system for the provision of information about courses and requirements and monitoring of student progress through the curriculum. These information and monitoring functions are important and necessary, but not sufficient. Academic advising needs to be reframed and aligned in support of the developmental and learning objectives of the institution for the undergraduate experience. In particular, academic advising has a crucial role to play in fostering student's self-authorship.

Framed through the perspective of a developmental model, academic advising is fundamentally a teaching process that is accomplished in the context of a caring, affirming relationship. The purpose of academic advising is to empower students to engage the resources of the college and university for intellectual and personal development. The goal is to contribute to the development of students as self-regulated, lifelong learners.

Academic advising is one mechanism by which universities can promote students' development through intentionally attending to the basic human needs for relatedness, competence, and autonomy. The need for relatedness, to feel connected and valued, is a powerful motivator. People perform behaviors that are modeled and valued by significant others and social groups.

Academic advisors can model and articulate the institution's values and communicate to the student that his or her goals, aspirations, and development as an individual do matter and are worthy of time and support, through careful planning of curricular and cocurricular experiences and identifying services as needed. Academic advising is a relationship that has as its purpose to foster the students' development and provides the opportunity for students to feel valued and connected to the institution.

In helping students formulate their course of study, academic advisors can also address the student's needs for competence and autonomy. We know that competence is fostered by the combination of optimal challenges, feedback that indicates that the person has the resources and capabilities to be successful, and freedom from demining evaluations. Autonomy is fostered by contexts that the person perceives as affording choices and freedom from excessive external pressure toward behaving or thinking in a certain way. Academic advisors can engage students in the process of planning their course of study with the aim of promoting competence and autonomy in the process.

In particular, academic advisors have the opportunity to promote students' strategic help-seeking. Unfortunately, students often view help-seeking as an indication of incompetence and dependency, and therefore strongly resist accessing academic support service such as tutoring, study skills/learning styles, time management, and stress management. Help-seeking, however, needs to be presented as an adaptive skill that is used by self-regulated learners who monitor their performance, are aware of their needs, and seek the skills they need. Self-regulating learners ascertain what tools are necessary to accomplish a task and then ensure that they have the necessary tools in their toolbox.

As a teaching process, there are specific learning objectives for the academic advising system aligned with those of the institution in terms of the development of knowledge, skills, and dispositions. Knowledge objectives include an understanding of the purposes and values of higher education in general and of the institution in particular, and knowledge about curriculum requirements, educational programs and opportunities, and resources. Skill objectives include information gathering, analysis, integration, and planning. Most importantly, the academic advising system can help students learn to make accurate self-appraisals of their strengths and weaknesses and develop time and stress management skills. Dispositional objectives include openness to intellectual and personal growth, community engagement, and active agency for learning and growth. Through the academic advising process expectations can be communicated to the students that they have the responsibility for their own education and must be active in generating and taking advantage of opportunities for their own development.

Academic advising as a relationship-based teaching process provides an important context through which to engage the student in the central developmental tasks of emerging adulthood, identity formation and self-authorship. This requires reframing for the student the role of academic advising from providing advice about course selection to promoting growth. More specifically, the advisor can encourage students to connect their decisions about courses, programs, and majors with personal values, competencies, and life goals. A relationship characterized by advisor respect for the student's developmental tasks promotes openness and self-reflection, accurate self-appraisals, and strategic help-seeking when necessary.

Requiring students, as part of the advising process, to formulate and write a coherent academic plan that is integrated and consonant with their life goals is a powerful tool for promoting identity development and integration and serves as a focal point for student-advisor engagement. This task incorporates the process of critical reflection and makes use of the power of narrative writing to engage students in the process of self-authorship as an integral part of academic life. Well-designed academic advising systems that are intentionally driven by a developmental model of education provide multiple opportunities for critical reflection, typically at transition points such as matriculation, declaring a major, and graduation. Such a system enables students not only to revise and refine their self-appraisals, theory of themselves, and plans, but also to track changes over time as a function of their various experiences inside and outside of the classroom.

ASSESSMENT

We began this book with the argument that higher education needed to transform its purposes and practices to be responsive to societal needs for civic-minded graduates who have the capacities and dispositions to engage difference and generate knowledge in the service of society. It is fitting that we conclude with the consideration of another transformation in practice that is needed to be responsive to recent societal calls for increased accountability, transparency, and evidence regarding student learning on the part of higher education. This transformation involves changing the approach of higher education to assessment of student learning and establishing a culture of experimentation and evidence with regard to the efficacy of educational practices.

Reframing Accountability: Assessment as a Process of Inquiry

Calls for increased accountability in higher education, prompted in large part by the report of the Spellings' Commission on the Future of Higher Education (US Department of Education, 2006), have conveyed the notion that that institutions of higher education are unwilling to attend to student learning and therefore must be "held accountable" by external forces, primarily the regional system of accreditation agencies. One consequence has been a misplaced emphasis on assessment for the purpose of external accountability. Rather than relying on external modes of accountability, colleges and universities must hold themselves accountable to improve student learning and engage in assessment as a process of inquiry about how well our students are learning.

The response to the call for increased accountability needs to be framed in terms of the social contract between institutions of higher education and society. Institutions of higher education in the United States have been afforded the privilege of self-governance in expectation of contributions to enhancing the public good. The unique contribution expected of colleges and universities is the generation of knowledge and the provision of an educational experience that prepares its graduates to meet societal needs. Therefore, institutions of higher education should be held accountable by society for effective self-governance in accomplishing their mission of education and research. With regard to education, therefore, evidence must be provided not only of student learning but also of effective self-governance in terms of systemic quality assurance processes for continuous improvement of education and student learning. Institutions of higher education hold themselves accountable to their multiple constituencies by continuously engaging in systematic, iterative processes to improve the quality of teaching and learning.

Undergraduate Culture of Experimentation and Evidence

As part of holding themselves accountable, colleges and universities must institute a culture of experimentation and evidence, and, in effect, become a learning organization (Bok, 2006) that engages in a continuous and systematic process of experimenting with innovative teaching and learning approaches, assessing learning outcomes, and revising approaches to improve learning. In this culture of experimentation and evidence, assessment is undertaken not to document student learning but rather to improve it (Schneider, 2007). Faculty undertake assessment as a process of inquiry about how well students are attaining the learning objectives of the course or program and commit to the self-evaluative and self-correcting process with regard to teaching and learning that characterize their approach to scholarship. Beyond providing evidence of student learning, colleges and universities must also provide evidence of how assessment findings are being used to inform educational decisions and practices and improve student learning.

Just as it is important to invest in the development of structures to support student engagement in community service, study abroad, and undergraduate research, it is also important to invests in structures that support faculty development. More specifically, universities typically have developed centers for teaching that serves as a resource for fostering promising pedagogical practices and uses of instructional technology in teaching and learning. There is also a need for assessment centers to assist with the design and implementation of studies of the learning effectiveness of various pedagogical approaches or specific programs, as well as with the development of measures and approaches to assessing student learning. These structures serve the important function of nurturing faculty dialogue about issues and ideas, and effective teaching, learning, and assessment practices.

Assessment Plan

Having formulated their overall agenda for the undergraduate experience, it is important that institutions concurrently formulate and implement a corresponding assessment plan. The purpose of assessment is to provide the information necessary to improve teaching, learning, and development. The purpose of the assessment plan is to design and conduct inquiries that will provide information about the extent to which the institution's learning objectives across the various pedagogical, curricular, and cocurricular components of the undergraduate experience are being achieved. Student learning objectives can be assessed at the level of the course, academic and cocurricular program or department, and institution.

The assessment plan at the level of the institution establishes benchmarks of academic performance with regard to specific learning objectives—for example, demonstration of writing or critical thinking skills, and the extent to which students are engaging in specific experiences such as study abroad, service learning, mentored research, and internships. The advent of sophisticated electronic record systems (Shupe, 2007) enables tracking of student performance across courses and experiences in relation to specific leaning objectives.

In addition to assessing student performance in relation to learning objectives, the assessment plan can also formulate strategies and studies to evaluate the efficacy of specific pedagogical, curricular, and cocurricular initiatives. Studies can be at the descriptive, analytic, and experimental levels of investigation. It is not possible to assess all aspects of the undergraduate experience at the same time. The assessment plan should set priorities and seek to generate an assessment portfolio that is selective and diversified and includes outcomes at the course, program, and institutional levels. The methodologies employed should also be diverse, including student self-reports as well as direct measures of learning outcome in the form of rubrics that specify progressive levels of accomplishment. In particular, AAC&U has developed an array of Valid Assessment of Learning in Undergraduate Education (VALUE) rubrics for many liberal learning objectives including critical thinking, written communication, quantitative literacy, problem solving, ethical reasoning, and intercultural knowledge and competence (Rhodes, 2010).

Finally, it is essential that the assessment plan include an action plan for using the findings to inform pedagogical, curricular, and cocurricular efforts to improve student learning and for dissemination of the findings to various stakeholders. Although a great amount of assessment data are gathered, across higher education there is limited use of assessment findings and "student assessment data has only a marginal influence on academic decision making" (Peterson & Augustine, 2000, p. 44). Therefore, it is necessary to establish processes through which intended users, both faculty and academic administrators, are involved in formulating the learning objectives, generating questions about student learning, interpreting the findings, and making recommendations for improving educational practices and policies:

> The best way that we know to date of encouraging use of evaluation is through involving potential users in defining the study and helping to interpret results, and through reporting results to them regularly while the study is in progress (Weiss, 1998, p. 30).

Just as the institution must engage the entire academic community in the adoption of a developmental model and the formulation of an agenda for a formative, holistic, undergraduate education, the institution must engage the faculty and students in the formulation and implementation of the assessment plan as integral to a culture of experimentation and evidence.

Assessing Development as Well as Leaning

The assessment plan must be driven by the developmental model underlying the overall agenda for providing a formative education. One of the characteristics of the developmental model of education is that it provides a basis for integration of academic and student life dimensions of the undergraduate experience around the common task of promoting development of the whole person. Therefore the assessment plan must also be holistic and integrated and go beyond an appraisal of student learning in terms of general education and disciplinary education objectives to include multiple dimensions of student development.

It is the premise of this book that to prepare students for the challenges of the twenty-first century colleges and universities must provide a formative liberal education that in particular seeks to foster students' development of personal epistemology, their capacity for empathy, and an integrated identity that includes commitment and agency for engaging differences and generating and applying knowledge in the service of society. How might an assessment plan be devised to appraise developmental growth along these dimensions and in turn guide efforts to improve student development as well as student learning?

Such an assessment plan must contain strategies and methods to gauge the impact of pedagogical, curricular, and student life initiatives that are aimed at these developmental objectives. The essential first step is to articulate developmental objectives at the level of individual courses, such as perspective taking or ethical/moral reasoning; at the level of the program, such as collective identity; and at the level of the institution, such as a commitment to civic engagement. Methods for assessing the extent to which these objectives have been achieved include specific items on student course evaluations, and other self-report surveys available in the literature, structured interviews, and rubrics through which to evaluate developmental objectives such as moral identity, epistemic thinking, and empathy. Once the information is gathered, it needs to be analyzed to identify opportunities for improvement and greater impact.

Electronic Portfolios

The assessment plan must also include strategies and mechanisms for acquiring outcome information at various points across the students' undergraduate career and maintaining a cumulative record of engagements and growth. Electronic portfolios are a convenient mechanism for the accrual of information about students' engagements, and examples of their work can provide a rich data base for assessment of student learning and development. Portfolios can also be a repository for student's critical reflection. The portfolios may be structured with public sections available for institutional purposes as well as private sections for the students' personal use. With such a mechanism, students can be asked to place in their portfolios critical reflections in response to specific prompts at various points in their undergraduate career, such as their goals and aspirations as they begin college, again when they declare a major, and at graduation.

Some academic and student affairs initiatives, such as service-learning courses or community service, have increasing empathy as an explicit objective and student self-report measures obtained in conjunction with these activities could also be placed in the portfolio for future analysis at the program or institutional level. Similarly, the impact of experiential learning experiences such as study abroad, summer research and internship, and service learning can be assessed along a number of dimensions and this information can also be placed in student portfolios. Establishing an electronic portfolio system empowers students with regard to taking responsibility for monitoring their own leaning and development. The portfolio is a place for students to display their work in all its various forms—papers, images, films, or musical productions—as well as a place for self-reflections, insights, and personal narratives about their beliefs, values, and commitments in their ongoing processes of self-authorship and identity formation.

THIS IS WHO WE ARE. THIS IS WHAT WE DO

The assessment process is the essential feedback loop that enables continuous enhancement of learning and development. Furthermore, a culture that is characterized by inquiry, innovation, and assessment provides a visible manifestation of the core academic values of the provisional nature of knowledge and understanding, the commitment to continual efforts to replace good ideas and methods with better ones, and the process through which higher education continuously adapts to societal needs.

REFERENCES

Adams, G. R., Abrahams, K., & Markstrom, C. (1987). Relations among identity development, self-consciousness and self-focusing during middle and late adolescence. *Developmental Psychology, 23,* 292–297.

Adams, G. R., & Marshall, S. K. (1996). A developmental social psychology of identity: Understanding the person in context. *Journal of Adolescence, 19,* 429–442.

Alligood, M. R. (1992). Empathy: The importance of recognizing two types. *Journal of Nursing and Mental Health Services, 30,* 14–17.

Allport, G. W. (1954). *The nature of prejudice.* Garden City, NY: Doubleday.

American Psychological Association (2011). *Answers to Your Questions About Transgender People, Gender Identity, and Gender Expression.* Washington, DC: [Retrieved from http://www.apa.org/topics/sexuality/transgendered.pdf]

Ames, D. R. (2004). Inside the mind reader's tool kit: Projection and stereotyping in mental state inference. *Journal of Personality and Social Psychology, 87,* 340–353.

Anderson, C. W. (1993). *Prescribing the life of the mind: An essay on the purpose of the university, the aims of liberal education, the competence of citizens, and the cultivation of practical reason.* Madison: University of Wisconsin Press.

Andre, T., & Windschitl, M. (2003). Interest, epistemological belief, and intentional conceptual change. In G. M. Sinatra & P. R. Pintrich (Eds.), *Intentional conceptual change* (pp. 173–197). Mahwah, NJ: Lawrence Erlbaum Associates.

Antonio, A. L. (2001). Diversity and the influence of friendship groups in college. *The Review of Higher Education, 25,* 63–89.

Aquino, K., & Reed, A., II. (2002). The self-importance of moral identity. *Journal of Personality and Social Psychology, 83,* 1423–1440.

Aquino, K., Freeman, D., Reed, A., II., & Lim, V. K. G. (2009). Testing a social-cognitive model of moral behavior: The interactive influence of situations and moral identity centrality. *Journal of Personality and Social Psychology, 97,* 123–141.

Arnett, J. J. (2000). Emerging adulthood: A theory of development from late teens through the twenties. *American Psychologist, 55,* 469–480.

Arnett, J. J. (2002). The psychology of globalization. *American Psychologist, 57,* 774–783.

Arnett, J. J. (2006). *Emerging adults in America: Coming of age in the 21st century.* Washington, DC: American Psychological Association.

Arnheim, R. (1985). The double-edged mind: Intuition and intellect. In E. Eisner (Ed.), *Learning and teaching the ways of knowing: Eighty-fourth yearbook of the National Society for the Study of Education* (pp. 77–96). Chicago: University of Chicago Press.

Arum, R., & Roksa, J. (2011). *Academically adrift: Limited learning on college campuses.* Chicago: University of Chicago Press.

Ashmore, R. D., Deaux, K., & McLaughlin-Volpe, T. (2004). An organizing framework for collective identity: Articulation and significance of multidimensionality. *Psychological Bulletin, 130*, 80–114.

Association of American Colleges and Universities. (2001). *The status of general education in the year 2000: Summary of a national survey.* Washington, DC.

Astin, A. W. (1963). *What matters in college?* San Francisco: Jossey-Bass.

Astin, A. W., Korn, W. S., Sax, L. J., & Mahoney, K. M. (1994). *The American freshman: National norms for fall 1994.* Los Angeles: Higher Education Research Institute.

Astin, A. W., Sax, L. J., & Avalos, J. (1999). Long-term effects of volunteerism during the undergraduate years. *The Review of Higher Education, 22*, 187–202.

Avolio, B. J., Walumbwa, F. O., & Weber, T. J. (2009). Leadership: Current theories, research and future directions. *The Annual Review of Psychology, 60*, 421–449.

Banks, S. J., Eddy, K. T., Angstadt, M., Nathan, P. J., & Phan, K. L. (2007). Amygdala-frontal connectivity during emotion regulation. *Social Cognitive and Affective Neuroscience, 2*, 303–312.

Batchelder, T. H., & Root, S. (1994). Effects of an undergraduate program to integrate academic learning and service: Cognitive, prosocial cognitive, and identity outcomes. *Journal of Adolescence, 17*, 341–355.

Batson, C. D. (2009). These things called empathy: Eight related but distinct phenomena. In J. Decety & W. Ickes (Eds.), *The social neuroscience of empathy* (pp. 3–15). Cambridge, MA: MIT Press.

Batson, C. D. (2010). Empathy-induced altruistic motivation. In M. Mikulincer & P. R. Shaver (Eds.), *Prosocial motives, emotions, and behavior: The better angels of our nature* (pp. 15–34). Washington, DC: American Psychological Association.

Batson, C. D., Early, S., & Salvarani, G. (1997). Perspective taking: Imagining how another feels versus imaging how you would feel. *Personality and Social Psychology Bulletin, 23*, 751–758.

Baumeister, R. F., & Muraven, M. (1996). Identity as adaptation to social, cultural and historical context. *Journal of Adolescence, 19*, 405–416.

Becher, T., & Trowler, P. R. (2001). *Academic tribes and territories* (2nd ed.). Buckingham, UK: The Society for Research into Higher Education & Open University Press.

Bendixen, L. D., & Rule, D. C. (2004). An integrated approach to personal epistemology: A guiding model. *Educational Psychologist, 39*, 69–80.

Bergman, R. (2002). Why be moral? A conceptual model from developmental psychology. *Human Development, 45*, 104–124.

Bergman, R. (2004). Identity as motivation: Toward a theory of the moral self. In D. K. Lapsley & D. Narvaez (Eds.), *Moral development, self, and identity* (pp. 21–46). Mahwah, NJ: Lawrence Erlbaum Associates.

Bering, J. M. (2006). The cognitive psychology of belief in the supernatural. *American Scientist, 94*, 142–149.

Betancourt, H. (1990a). An attribution-empathy model of helping behavior: Behavioral intentions and judgments of help-giving. *Personality and Social Psychology Bulletin, 16*, 573–591.

Betancourt, H. (1990b). An attributional approach to intergroup and international conflict. In S. Graham & V. S. Folkes (Eds.), *Attributional theory: Applications to achievement, mental health, and interpersonal conflict* (pp. 205–220). Hillsdale, NJ: Lawrence Erlbaum Associates.

Beyer, C. H., Gillmore, G., & Fisher, A. T. (2007). *Inside the undergraduate experience: The University of Washington's Study of Undergraduate Learning.* Bolton, MA: Anker Publishing.

Biglan, A. (1973). The characteristics of subject matter in different academic areas. *Journal of Applied Psychology, 58,* 195–203.

Blair, C. (2002), School Readiness: Integrating cognition and emotion in a neurobiological conceptualization of children's function at school entry. *American Psychologists, 57,* 111–127.

Blakemore, S. J., & Choudhury, S. (2006). Development of the adolescent brain: Implications for executive function and social cognition. *Journal of Child Psychology and Psychiatry, 47,* 296–312.

Blakemore, S. J., den Ouden, H., Choudhury, S., & Frith, C. (2007). Adolescent development of the neural circuitry for thinking about intentions. *Social Cognitive Affective Neuroscience, 2,* 130–139.

Blasi, A. (1980). Bridging moral cognition and moral action: A critical review of the literature. *Psychological Bulletin, 88,* 1–45.

Blasi, A. (1983). Moral cognition and moral action: A theoretical perspective. *Developmental Review, 3,* 178–210.

Blasi, A. (2004a). Neither personality nor cognition: An alternative approach to the nature of the self. In C. Lightfoot, C. LaLonde, & M. Chandler (Eds.), *Changing conceptions of psychological life* (pp. 3–25). Mahwah, NJ: Lawrence Erlbaum Associates.

Blasi, A. (2004b). Moral functioning: Moral understanding and personality. In D. K. Lapsley & D. Narvaez (Eds.), *Moral development, self, and identity* (pp. 335–347). Mahwah: NJ. Lawrence Erlbaum Associates.

Bluck, S., & Habermas, T. (2001). Extending the study of autobiographical memory: Thinking back about life across the life span. *Review of General Psychology, 5,* 135–147.

Bocian, M. (1997). Housing on college campuses: Segregation, integration and other alternatives: A communitarian report. www.eric.ed.gov/ERICWebPortal/record Detail?accno=ED446596.

Bok, D. (2003). *Universities in the marketplace: The commercialization of higher education.* Princeton, NJ: Princeton University Press.

Bok, D. (2006). *Our underachieving colleges: A candid look at how much students learn and why they should be learning more.* Princeton, NJ: Princeton University Press.

Bosma, H. A., & Kunnen, E. S. (2001). Determinants and mechanisms of ego identity development: A review and synthesis. *Developmental Review, 21,* 39–66.

Boyes, M., & Chandler, M. J. (1992). Cognitive development, epistemic doubt, and identity formation in adolescence. *Journal of Youth and Adolescence, 21,* 277–304.

Boyer Commission on Educating Undergraduates in the Research University. (1998). *Reinventing undergraduate education: A blueprint for America's research universities.* New York: Carnegie Foundation for the Advancement of Teaching.

Boyle-Baise, M., & Efion, P. (2000). The construction of meaning: Learning from service learning. In C. R. O'Grady (Ed.), *Integrating service learning and multicultural education in colleges and universities* (pp. 209–226). Mahwah, NJ. Lawrence Erlbaum Associates.

Bowman, N. A., & Brandenberger, J. W. (2012). Experiencing the unexpected: Toward a model of college diversity experiences and attitude change. *Review of Higher Education, 35*(2), 179–205.

Bowman, N. A., Brandenberger, J. W., Hill, P. L., & Lapsley, D. K. (2011). The long-term impact of college diversity experiences: Well-being and social concerns 13 years after graduation. *Journal of College Student Development, 52*(6), 729–739.

Brandenberger, J. W. (2005). College, character, and social responsibility: Moral learning through experience. In D. Lapsley & F. C. Power (Eds.), *Character psychology and character education* (pp. 305–334). Notre Dame, IN: University of Notre Dame Press.

Bransford, J. D., Brown, A. I., & Cocking, R. R. (2000). *How people learn: Brain, mind, experience, and school.* Washington, DC: National Academy Press.

Bromme, R., Kienhues, D., & Porsch, T. (2010a). Who knows what and who can we believe? Epistemological beliefs are beliefs about knowledge (mostly) to be attained from others. In L. D. Bendixen & F. C. Feucht (Eds.), *Personal epistemology in the classroom: Theory, research, and implications for practice* (pp. 163–193). Cambridge: Cambridge University Press.

Bromme, R., Pieschl, S., & Stahl, E. (2010b). Epistemological beliefs are standards for adaptive learning: A functional theory about epistemological beliefs and metacognition. *Metacognition Learning, 5,* 7–26.

Brown, J. S., Collins, A., & Duguid, P. (1989). *Educational Researcher.* January–February, 32–42.

Brownell, J. E., & Swaner, L. E. (2010). *Five high impact practices: Research on learning outcomes, completion, and quality.* Washington, DC: Association of American Colleges and Universities.

Brownlee, J., & Berthelsen, D. (2008). Developing relational epistemology through relational pedagogy: New ways of thinking about personal epistemology in teacher education. In M. S. Khine (Ed.), *Knowing, knowledge and beliefs: Epistemological studies across diverse cultures* (pp. 405–422). New York: Springer.

Bruer, J. T. (2008). Building bridges in neuroeducation. In A, M. Battro, K. W. Fischer, & P. J. Lena (Eds.), *The educated brain: Essays in neuroeducation* (pp. 43–58). New York: Cambridge University Press.

Butin, D. W. (2010). *Service-Learning in theory and practice: The future of community engagement in higher education.* New York: Palgrave Macmillan.

Byrnes, J. P. (2001). *Minds, brains, and learning: Understanding the psychological and educational relevance of neurosceintific research.* New York: Guilford Press.

Carkhuff, R. R. (1969). *Helping and human relations: A primer for lay and professional helpers. (Vol. 1): Selection and training; (Vol. 2): Practice and research.* New York: Holt, Rinehart, & Winston.

Carroll, J. (2003). Why religion still matters. *Daedalus,* Summer, *132,* 9–13.

Chandler, M. J. (1988). Doubt and developing theories of mind. In J. W. Astington, P. L. Harris, & D. R. Olson (Eds.), *Developing theories of mind* (pp. 387–413). New York: Cambridge University Press.

Chandler, M. J., Hallett, D., & Sokol, B. W. (2002). Competing claims about competing claims. In B. K. Hofer & P. R. Pintrich (Eds.), *Personal epistemology: The psychology of beliefs about knowledge and knowing* (pp. 145–168). Mahwah, NJ: Lawrence Erlbaum Associates.

Chandler, M. J., & Proulx, T. (2010). Stalking young person's changing beliefs about belief. In L. D. Bendixen & F. C. Feucht (Eds.), *Personal epistemology in the classroom: Theory, research, and implications for practice* (pp. 197–219). Cambridge: Cambridge University Press.

Chang, M., Astin, A., Kim, D. (2004). Cross-racial interaction among undergraduates: Some consequences, causes, and patterns. *Research in Higher Education, 45,* 529–553.

Chickering, A. W. (1969). *Education and identity.* San Francisco. Jossey-Bass.

Colarusso, C. A. (1995). Adulthood. In H. I. Kaplan & B. J. Sadock (Eds.), *Comprehensive textbook of psychiatry, (VI,* pp. 2495–2506). Baltimore: Williams and Wilkins.

Colby, A. (2008). Fostering the moral and civic development of college students. In L. P. Nucci & D. Narvaez (Eds.), *Handbook of moral education* (pp. 391–413). New York: Routledge.

Colby. A., Ehrlich, T., Beaumont, E., & Stephens, J. (2003). *Educating citizens: Preparing America's undergraduates for lives of moral and civic responsibility.* San Francisco: Jossey-Bass.

Collins, A., Brown. J. S., & Newman, S. E. (1989). Cognitive Apprenticeship: Teaching the crafts of reading, writing and mathematics. In L. B. Resnick (Ed.), *Knowing, learning, and instruction: Essays in honor of Robert Glaser* (pp. 453–494). Hillsdale, NJ: Lawrence Erlbaum Associates.

Collins, W. A., & Sroufe, L. A. (1999). Capacity for intimate relationships: A developmental construction. In W. Furman, B. B. Brown, & C. Furman (Eds.), *The development of romantic relationships in adolescence* (pp. 125–147). New York: Cambridge University Press.

Collins, A., & Steinberg, L. (2006). Adolescent development in interpersonal context. In W. Damon, & R. M. Lerner (Eds.) & N. Eisenberg (Vol. Ed.), *Handbook of child psychology* (6th ed.). *Social, emotional, and personality development (Vol. 3,* pp. 1003–1067). New York: Wiley.

Choudhury, S., Blakemore, S. J, & Charman, T. (2006). Social cognitive development during adolescence. *Social Cognitive Affective Neuroscience, 1,* 165–174.

Côté, J. E. (1996). Sociological perspectives on identity formation: The culture-identity link and identity capital. *Journal of Adolescence, 19,* 417–428.

Côté, J. E. (1997). An empirical test of the identity capital model. *Journal of Adolescence, 20,* 577–597.

Côté, S., Lopes P. N., Salovey, P., & Miners, C. T. H. (2010). Emotional intelligence and leadership emergence in small groups. *The Leadership Quarterly, 21,* 496–508.

Crisp, R. J., & Hewstone, M. (2007). Multiple social categorization. *Advances in Experimental Social Psychology, 39,* 163–254.

Crisp, R. J., & Turner, R. N. (2009). Can imagined interactions produce positive perceptions? *American Psychologist, 64,* 231–240.

Cronon, W. (1998). "Only Connect . . ." The Goals of a Liberal Education. *The American Scholar,* Autumn, *67,* 73–80.

Damon, W. (1977). *The social world of the child.* San Francisco: Jossey-Bass.

Damon, W. (1988). *The moral child.* New York: Free Press.

Darden, M. L. (with Duderstadt, J. J.). (2009). In M. L. Darden (Ed.), *Beyond 2020: Envisioning the future of universities in America: American Council on Education Series on Higher Education.* Lanham, MD. Rowman & Littlefield.

Davidson, M. (2005). Harness the sun, channel the wind: The art and science of effective character education. In D. K. Lapsley & F. Clark Power (Eds.), *Character psychology and character education* (pp. 218–244). Notre Dame: IN. University of Notre Dame Press.

Davis, M. H. (1994). *Empathy: A social psychological approach.* Dubuque, IA: Brown & Benchmark.

Davis-Manigaulte, J., Yorks, L., & Kasal, E. (Spring, 2006). Expressive ways of knowing and transformative learning. *New Directions for Adult and Continuing Education*, no *109*, 27–35.

Deaux, K. (1996). Social identification. In E. T. Higgins & A. W. Kruglanski (Eds.) *Social psychology: Handbook of basic principles* (pp. 777–798). New York: Guilford Press.

Decety, J. (2005). Perspective taking as the royal avenue to empathy. In B. F. Malle & S. D. Hodges (Eds.), *Other minds: How humans bridge the divide between self and others* (pp. 143–157). New York: Guilford Press.

Decety, J., & Jackson, P. L. (2004). The functional architecture of human empathy. *Behavioral and Cognitive Neuroscience Reviews*, *3*, 71–100.

Delbanco, A. (2012) *College: What it was, is, and should be*. Princeton, NJ: Princeton University Press.

Díaz, A., Middendorf, J., Pace, D., & Shopkow, L. (2008). The history learning project: A department "decodes" its students. *Journal of American History*, *94*, 1211–1224.

Dillon, F. R., Worthington, R. L., & Moradi, B. (2011). Sexual identity as a universal process. In S. J. Schwartz, K. Luyckx, & V. L. Vignoles (Eds.), *Handbook of identity theory and research* (pp. 649–670). New York: Springer.

Dimaggio, G., Lysaker, P. H., Carcione, A., Nicolò. G., & Semerari, A. (2008) Know yourself and you shall know the other...to a certain extent: Multiple paths of influence of self-reflection on mindreading. *Consciousness and Cognition*, *17*, 778–789.

Dixon, J., Durrheim, K., & Tredoux, C. (2005). Beyond the optimal contact strategy: A reality check for the contact hypothesis. *American Psychologist*, *60*(7), 697–711.

Dovidio, J. F., Johnson, J., Gaertner, S. L., Pearson, A. R., Saguy, T., & Ashburn-Nardo, L. (2010). Empathy and intergroup relations. In M. Mikulincer & P. R. Shaver (Eds.), *Prosocial motives, emotions, and behavior: The better angels of our nature* (pp. 393–408). Washington, DC: American Psychological Association.

Downey, G., Bonica, C., & Rincón, C. (1999). Rejection sensitivity and adolescent romantic relationships. In W. Furman, B. B. Brown, & C. Furman (Eds.), *The development of romantic relationships in adolescence* (pp. 148–174). New York: Cambridge University Press.

Driscoll, A. (2008). Carnegie's community engagement classification: Intentions and insights. *Change*, January/February, 39–41.

Duderstadt, J. J. (2002). *A university for the twenty-first century*. Ann Arbor: University of Michigan Press.

Duderstadt, J. J. (2012). Creating the future: The promise of public research universities for America. In D. M. Fogel and E. Malson-Huddle (Eds.), *Precipice or crossroads? Where America's great public universities stand and where they are going midway through their second century* (pp. 221–240). Albany: State University of New York Press.

Duderstadt, J. J., Atkins, D. E., & Van Houweling, D. (2002). *Higher education in the digital age: Technology issues and strategies for American colleges and universities*. Westport, CT. American Council on Education/Prager Series on Higher Education.

Dweck, C. S., & Leggett, E. L. (1988). A social-cognitive approach to motivation and personality. *Psychological Review*, *95*, 256–273.

Eberlein, T., Kampmeier, J., Minderhout, V., Moog, R. S., Platt, T., Varma-Nelson, P., & White, H. B. (2008). Pedagogies of engagement in science. *Biochemistry and Molecular Biology Education*, *36*, 262–273.

Edgerton, R. (1997). Education White Paper. Unpublished report for the Pew Charitable Trust.

Eidelson, R. J., & Eidelson. J. I. (2003). Dangerous ideas: Five beliefs that propel groups toward conflict. *American Psychologist, 58*, 182–192.

Eisenberg, N. (2005). The development of empathy-related responding. In G. Carlo & C. Pope Edwards (Eds.), *Moral motivation through the life-span. Nebraska Symposium on Motivation*, (Vol. *51*, pp. 73–117). Lincoln: University of Nebraska Press.

Eisenberg, N. (2010). Empathy-related responding: Links with self-regulation, moral judgment, and moral behavior. In M. Mikulincer & P. R. Shaver (Eds.), *Prosocial motives, emotions, and behavior: The better angels of our nature* (pp. 129–148). Washington, DC: American Psychological Association.

Eisenberg, N., & Miller, P. A. (1987). Empathy and prosocial behavior. *Psychological Bulletin, 101*, 459–470.

Eisenberg, N., Shea, C. L., Carlo, G., & Knight, G. (1991). Empathy-related responding and cognition: A "chicken and the egg" dilemma. In W. Kurtines & J. Gewirtz (Eds.), *Handbook of moral behavior and development: Vol. 2. Research* (pp. 63–88). Hillsdale, NJ: Lawrence Erlbaum Associates.

Eisenberg, N., Fabes, R. A., & Spinrad, T. L. (2006). Prosocial development. In W. Diamon & R. M. Lerner (Series Eds.) & N. Eisenberg (Vol. ed.) *Handbook of child psychology. Vol.3, Social, emotional, and personality development* (6th ed., pp. 646–718). New York: Wiley.

Eisner, E. (1985). Aesthetic modes of knowing. In E. Eisner (Ed.). *Learning and teaching the ways of knowing. Eighty-fourth yearbook of the National Society for the Study of Education* (pp. 23–36). Chicago: University of Chicago Press.

Elby, A., & Hammer, D. (2001). On the substance of a sophisticated epistemology. *Science Education, 85*, 554–567.

Elfers, T., Martin, J., & Sokol, B. (2008). Perspective taking: A review of research and theory extending Selman's developmental model of perspective taking. *Advances in Psychology Research, 54*, 229–262.

Emmons, R. A., & Paloutzian, R. F. (2003). The psychology of religion. *Annual Review of Psychology, 54*, 377–402.

Engberg, M. E. (2004). Improving intergroup relations in higher education: a critical examination of the influence of educational interventions on racial bias. *Review of Educational Research, 74*, 473–524.

Engle, L., & Engle, J. (2003). Study abroad levels: Toward a classification of program types. *Frontiers: The Interdisciplinary Journal of Study Abroad, IX*, 1–20.

Erikson, E. H. (1963). *Childhood and society* (2nd Ed.). New York: Wiley.

Erikson, E. H. (1968). *Identity, youth and crisis*. New York: Norton.

Erickson, J. A., & O'Connor, S. E. (2000). Service-learning: Does it promote or reduce prejudice? In C. R. O'Grady (Ed.), *Integrating service learning and multicultural education in colleges and universities* (pp. 59–70). Mahwah, NJ: Lawrence Erlbaum Associates.

Eyler, J., & Giles, D. E., Jr. (1999). *Where's the learning in service-learning*. San Francisco: Jossey-Bass.

Fadjukoff, P., Pulkkinen, L., & Kokko, K. (2005). Identity processes in adulthood: Diverging domains. *Identity: An International Journal of Theory and Research, 5*, 1–20.

Fallis, G. (2007). *Multiversities, ideas, and democracy*. Toronto: University of Toronto Press.

Fausto-Sterling, A. (2012). *Sex/gender: Biology in a social world*. New York: Routledge.

Ferdman, B. M. (2000). "Why am I Who I am?" Constructing the cultural self in multi-cultural perspective. *Human Development, 43*, 19–23.

Finlay, K. A., & Stephan, W. G. (2000). Reducing prejudice: The effects of empathy on intergroup attitudes. *Journal of Applied Social Psychology, 30*, 1720–1737.

Fish, S. (2003) Aim low. *Chronicle of Higher Education*. http://chronicle.com/article/Aim-Low/45210.

Fisher, K. W. (2008). Dynamic cycles of cognitive and brain development: Measuring growth in mind, brain, and education. In A. M. Battro, K. W. Fischer, & P. J. Léna (Eds.). *The educated brain: Essays in neuroeducation* (pp. 127–150). New York: Cambridge University Press.

Fiske, S. T. (2010). Envy up, scorn down: How comparison divides us. *American Psychologist, 65*, 698–706.

Fletcher, J. H. (2008). Religious pluralism in an era of globalization: The making of modern religious identity. *Theological Studies, 69*, 394–411.

Frith, C. D., & Frith, U. (2006). The neural basis of mentalizing. *Neuron, 50*, 531–534.

Gibson, J. L. (2006). Do strong group identities fuel intolerance? Evidence from the South African case. *Political Psychology, 27*, 665–705.

Giles, D. E., & Eyler, J. (1994). The theoretical roots of service-learning in John Dewey: Toward a theory of service learning. *Michigan Journal of Community Service Learning, 1*, 77–85.

Gill, A. (2001). Religion and comparative politics. *Annual Review of Political Science, 4*, 117–138.

Gaertner, S. L., Dovidio, J. F., Banker, B. S., Houlette, M., Johnson, K. M., & McGlynn, E. A. (2000). Reducing intergroup conflict: From superordinate goals to decategorization, recategorization, and mutual differentiation. *Group Dynamics: Theory, Research, and Practice, 4*, 98–114.

Gaertner, S. L., & Dovidio, J. F. (2008). Addressing contemporary racism: The Common Ingroup Identity Model. In C. Willis-Esqueda (Ed.), *Motivational aspects of prejudice and racism: The Nebraska Symposium on Motivation*, Vol.53 (pp. 111–133). Lincoln: University of Nebraska Press.

Gardner, J. (1963). *Self-renewal: The individual and the innovative society*. New York: Harper & Row.

Gilbert, D. T., & Malone, P. S. (1995). The correspondence bias. *Psychological Bulletin, 117*, 21–38.

Goel, V., & Dolan, R. J. (2003) Explaining modulation of reasoning by belief. *Cognition, 87*, B11–B22.

Goldman, A. I. (2006). *Simulating minds: The philosophy, psychology, and neuroscience of mind reading*. New York: Oxford University Press.

Goldstein, A. P., & Michaels, G. Y. (1985). *Empathy: Development, training, and consequences*. Hillsdale, NJ. Lawrence Erlbaum Associates.

Gordon, M. (2009). *Roots of empathy: Changing the world child by child*. New York: The Experiment.

Grotevant, H. D. (1987). Toward a process model of identity formation. *Journal of Adolescent Research, 2*, 203–222.

Gurin, P., Dey, E., Hurtado, S., & Gurin, G. (2002). Diversity and higher education: Theory and impact on educational outcomes. *Harvard Educational Review, 72*(3), 330–366.

Hammack, P. L. (2008). Narrative and the cultural psychology of identity. *Personality and Social Psychology Review, 12*, 222–247.

Hammer, M. R. (2007). *The intercultural development inventory (IDI) manual (v.3)*. Ocean Pines, MD.

Hammer, M. R., Bennett, M. J., & Wiseman, R. (2003). Measuring intercultural sensitivity: The intercultural development inventory. *International Journal of Intercultural Relations, 27(4)*, 421–443.

Hardy, S. A., & Carlo, G. (2005). Identity as a source of moral motivation. *Human Development, 48*, 232–256.

Hardy, S. A., & Carlo, G. (2011). Moral identity. In S. J. Schwartz, K. Luyckx, & V. L. Vignoles (Eds.), *Handbook of identity theory and research*. Vo. 1 (pp. 495–513). New York: Springer.

Harward, D. W. (2012). The theoretical arguments and themes. In D. W. Harward (Ed), *Transforming undergraduate education: Theory that compels and practices that succeed* (pp. 3–33). Lanham, MD: Roman & Littlefield.

Hatcher, S. L., & Nadeau, M. S. (1994). The teaching of empathy for high school and college students: Testing Rogerian methods with the Interpersonal Reactivity Index. *Adolescence, 29*, 961–975.

Hatton, N., & Smith, D. (1995). Reflections in teacher education: Towards definition and implementation. *Teaching & Teacher Education, 11*, 33–49.

Havighurst, R. J. (1972). *Developmental tasks and education*. New York: David McKay Co.

Hill, T. L., Brandenberger, J. W., & Howard, G. S. (2005). Lasting effects? A longitudinal study of the impact of service learning. Center for Social Concerns, University of Notre Dame, Research Report 8. http://centerforsocialconcerns.nd.edu/faculty/research.

Hirst, P. H. (1974). *Knowledge and the curriculum: A collection of philosophical papers*. London: Routledge & Kegan Paul.

Hoare, C. (2006). Work as the catalyst of reciprocal adult development and learning: Identity and personality. In C. Hoare (Ed.), *Handbook of adult development and learning* (pp. 344–380). New York: Oxford University Press.

Hofer, B. K. (2004). Epistemological understanding as a metacognitive process: Thinking aloud during online searching. *Educational Psychologist, 39*, 43–55.

Hofer, B. K. (2006). Beliefs about knowledge and knowing: Integrating domain specificity and domain generality: A response to Muis, Bendixen, and Haerle (2006). *Educational Psychology Review, 18*, 67–76.

Hofer, B. K., & Pintrich, P. R. (1997). The development of epistemological theories: Beliefs about knowledge and knowing and their relation to learning. *Review of Educational Research, 67*, 88–140.

Hofer, B. K, & Sinatra, G. M. (2010). Epistemology, metacognition, and self-regulation: Musings on an emerging field. *Metacognition Learning, 5*, 113–120.

Hofer, B. H., & Bendixen, L. D. (2012). Personal epistemology: Theory, research, and future directions. In K. R. Harris, S. Graham, and T. Urdan (Editors-in-Chief), *APA educational psychology handbook: Vol.1. Theories, constructs, and critical issues* (pp. 227–256). Washington, DC: American Psychological Association.

Hoffman, M. L. (1978). Psychological and biological perspectives on altruism. *International Journal of Behavioral Development, 1*, 323–339.

Hoffman, M. L. (2000). *Empathy and moral development: Implications for caring and justice*. Cambridge, UK: Cambridge University Press.

Hollander, E. (2010). Forward. In D. W. Butin *Service-Learning in theory and practice: The future of community engagement in higher education* (pp. vii–xii). New York: Palgrave Macmillan.

Honnet, E., & Poulsen, S. (1989). *Principles of good practice for combining service and learning: Wingspread Special Report*. Racine, WI: Johnson Foundation, Inc.

Hooker, C. I., Verosky, S. C., Germine, L. T., Knight, R. T., & D'Esposito. M. (2008). Mentalizing about emotion and its relationship to empathy. *Social Cognitive and Affective Neuroscience, 3*, 204–217.

Hurtado, S. (2003). Preparing college students for a diverse democracy. *Final report to the U.S. Department of Education, Office of Educational Research and Improvement, Field Initiated Studies Program*. Ann Arbor: University of Michigan.

Hurtado, S., Dey, E. L., Gurin, P. Y., & Gurin, G. (2003). College environments, diversity and student learning. In J. C. Smart (Ed.), *Higher education: Handbook of theory and research, Vol. 1* (pp. 145–190). London: Kluwer Academic.

Itin, C. M. (Fall, 1999). Reasserting the philosophy of experiential education as a vehicle for change in the 21st century. *The Journal of Experiential Education, 22*, 91–98.

Institute of International Education (2010). Open Doors 2010 U.S. Study Abroad. www.iie.org.

Jacobsen, J. D., & Jacobsen, R. H. (2008a). Postsecular America: A new context for higher education. In J. D. Jacobsen & R. H. Jacobsen (Eds.), *The American university in a postsecular age* (pp. 3–15). New York: Oxford University Press.

Jacobsen, J. D., & Jacobsen, R. H. (2008b). Talking about religion. In J. D. Jacobsen & R. H. Jacobsen (Eds.), *The American university in a postsecular age* (pp. 222–231). New York: Oxford University Press.

Kardash, C. M., & Scholes, TR. J. (1996). Effects of preexisting beliefs, epistemological beliefs, and need for cognition on interpretation of controversial issues. *Journal of Educational Psychology, 88*, 260–271.

Keddie, N. R. (2003). Secularism and its discontents. *Daedalus*, Summer, *132*(3), 14–30.

Kegan, R. (1994). *In over our heads: The mental demands of modern life*. Cambridge: MA: Harvard University Press.

Keller, G. (2008). *Higher education and the new society*. Baltimore: Johns Hopkins University Press.

Kellett, J. B., Humphrey, R. H., & Sleeth, R. G. (2002). Empathy and complex task performance: two routes to leadership. *The Leadership Quarterly, 13*, 523–544.

Kimball, B. A. (Ed.) (1995). *Orators and philosphers: A history of the idea of liberal education*. New York: College Board.

King, P. M., & Kitchener, K. S. (2004). Reflective judgment: Theory and research on the development of epistemic assumptions through adulthood. *Educational Psychologist, 39*, 5–18.

Kitsantas, A. (2004). Studying abroad: The roles of college students' goals on the development of cross-cultural skills and global understanding. *College Student Journal, 38*, 441–452.

Koehler, G., & Skvoretz, J. (2010). Residential segregation in university housing: The mathematics of preferences. *Social Science Research, 39*, 14–24.

Kolb, D. (1984). *Experiential learning: Experience as the source of learning and development*. Upper Saddle River, NJ: Prentice Hall.

Korostelina, K. (2008). History education and social identity. *Identity: An International Journal of Theory and Research, 8*, 25–45.

Krettenauer, T. (2005). The Role of epistemic cognition in adolescent identity formation: Further evidence. *Journal of Youth and Adolescence, 34*(3), 185–198.

Kroger, J. (1993). Ego identity: An overview. In J. Kroger (Ed.), *Discussions on ego identity* (pp. 1–20). Hillsdale, NJ: Lawrence Erlbaum Associates.

Kroger, J. (2004). *Identity in adolescence: The balance between self and other.* New York: Routledge.

Kuh, G. (2008). *High impact educational practices.* Washington, DC: Association of American Colleges and Universities.

Kuhn, D. (2001). How do people know? *Psychological Science, 12,* 1–8.

Kuhn, D. (2003). Understanding and valuing knowing. *Liberal Education, 89,* 16–21.

Kuhn, D. (2005). *Education for thinking.* Cambridge, MA. Harvard University Press.

Kuhn, D., & Udell, W. (2001). The path to wisdom. *Educational Psychologist, 36,* 261–264.

Kuhn, D., Cheney, R., & Weinstock, M. (2000). The development of epistemological understanding. *Cognitive Development, 15,* 309–328.

Kuhn, D., & Weinstock, M. (2002). What is epistemological thinking and why does it matter? In B. K. Hofer & P. R. Pintrich (Eds.), *Personal epistemology: The psychology of beliefs about knowledge and knowing* (pp. 121–144). Mahwah, NJ: Lawrence Erlbaum Associates.

Kunda, Z., & Spencer, S. J. (2003). When do stereotypes come to mind and when do they color judgment? A goal-based theoretical framework for stereotype activation and application. *Psychological Bulletin, 129,* 522–544.

Lapsley, D. K., & Power, F. C. (Eds.). (2005). *Character psychology and character education.* Notre Dame, IN: University of Notre Dame Press.

László, J. (2008). *The science of stories: An Introduction to narrative psychology.* New York: Routledge.

Lazarus, A. (2004). *Personal and collective self-esteem and multiple identities as predictors of undergraduates' beliefs and behaviors after a four-day human relations program.* Durham, NC: Duke University.

Lerner, R. M. (2006). Developmental science, developmental systems, and contemporary theories of human development. In R. Lerner (Ed.), *Handbook of child psychology* (6th ed.). *Theoretical models of human development* (Vol. 1, pp. 1–17). New York: Wiley.

Levin, S., Sinclair, S., Sidanius, J., & Van Laar, C. (2009). Ethnic and university identities across the college years: A common in-group identity perspective. *Journal of Social Issues, 65,* 287–306.

Levin, S., Matthews, M., Guimond, S., Sidanius, J., Pratto, F., Kteily, N., Pitpitan, E. V., & Dover, T. (2012). *Journal of Experimental Social Psychology, 48,* 207–212.

Lieberman, M. D. (2007). Social cognitive neuroscience: A review of core processes. *Annual Review of Psychology, 58,* 259–289.

Lopatto, D. (2004). Survey of undergraduate research experiences (SURE): First findings. *Cell Biology Education, 3,* 270–277.

Lucas, C. (1998). *Crisis in the academy: Rethinking higher education in America.* New York: St. Martin's Press.

Lutterman-Aguilar, A., & Gingerich, O. (Winter, 2002). Experiential pedagogy for study abroad: educating for global citizenship. *Frontiers: Interdisciplinary Journal of Study Abroad, VIII,* 41–82.

Luyckx, K., Goossens, L., Soenens, B., & Beyers, W. (2006). Unpacking commitment and exploration: Validation of an integrative model of adolescent identity formation. *Journal of Adolescence, 29,* 361–378.

Luyckx, K., Goossens, L., Soenens, B., Beyers, W., & Vansteenkiste, M. (2005). Identity statuses based on 4 rather than 2 identity dimensions: Extending and refining Marcia's paradigm. *Journal of Youth and Adolescence, 34*(6), 605–618.

Luyckx, K., Schwartz, S. J., Goossens, L., & Pollock S. (2008). Employment, sense of coherence, and identity formation: Contextual and psychological processes on the pathway to adulthood. *Journal of Adolescent Research, 23,* 566–591.

Madden, S. J. (Ed.) (2000). *Service learning across the curriculum: Case applications in higher education.* University Press of America: Lanham, Maryland.

Magolda, M. B. (2004). Evolution of a constructivist conceptualization of epistemological reflection. *Educational Psychologist, 39,* 31–42.

Magolda, M. B. (2008). Three elements of self-authorship. *Journal of College Student Development, 49*(4), 269–284.

Marcia, J. (1966). Development and validation of ego-identity status. *Journal of Personality and Social Psychology, 3,* 551–558.

Marsden, G. M. (1992). The soul of the American university: A historical overview. In G. M. Marsden & B. J. Longfield (Eds.), *The secularization of the academy* (pp. 9–45). New York: Oxford University Press.

Mason, M. F., & Macrae, C. N. (2008). Perspective taking from a social neuroscience standpoint. *Group Processes & Intergroup Relations, 11,* 215–232.

Masten, A. S., & Coatsworth, J. D. (1998). The development of competence in favorable and unfavorable environments. *American Psychologist, 53,* 205–220.

Mayer, J. D., Salovey, P., & Caruso, D. R. (2008). Emotional intelligence: New ability or eclectic traits? *American Psychologist, 63,* 503–517.

Mayer, R. E. (1992). Cognition and instruction: Their historic meeting within educational psychology. *Journal of Educational Psychology, 84,* 405–412.

McAdams, D. P. (2001). The psychology of life stories. *Review of General Psychology, 5,* 100–122.

McIntosh, H., Metz, E., & Youniss, J. (2005). Community service and identity formation in adolescents. In J. L. Mahoney, R. W. Larson, & J. S. Eccles (Eds.),*Organized activities as contexts of development: Extracurricular activities, after-school and community programs* (pp. 331–351). Mahwah, NJ: Lawrence Erlbaum Associates.

Mckinnon, C. (2005). Character possession and human flourishing. In D. K. Lapsley & F. Clark Power (Eds.), *Character psychology and character education* (pp. 36–66). Notre Dame, IN: University of Notre Dame Press.

McLean, K. C., & Pratt, M. W. (2006). Life's little (and big) lessons: Identity statuses and meaning-making in the turning point narratives of emerging adults. *Developmental Psychology, 42,* 714–722.

Menand, L. (2010). *The marketplace of ideas.* New York: Norton.

Meeus, W., Iedema, J., & Maassen, G. H. (2002). Commitment and exploration as mechanisms of identity formation. *Psychological Reports, 90,* 771–785.

Meeus, W., van de Schoot, R., Keijsers, L., Schwartz, S. J., & Branje, S. (2010). On the progression and stability of adolescent identity formation: A five-wave longitudinal study in early-to-middle and middle-to-late adolescence. *Child Development, 81,* 1565–1581.

Meeus, W. (2011). The study of adolescent identity formation 2000–2010: A review of longitudinal research. *Journal of Research on Adolescence, 21*(1), 75–94.

Meyer, J. H. F., & Land, R. (2003). Threshold concepts and troublesome knowledge: Linkages to ways of thinking and practicing within the disciplines. In Rust, C. (Ed.), *Improving student learning: Improving student learning theory and practice—ten years on.* Oxford: Oxford Centre for Staff and Learning Development.

Meyer, J. H. F., & Land, R. (2005). Threshold concepts and troublesome knowledge (2): Epistemological considerations and a conceptual framework for teaching and learning. *Higher Education, 49,* 373–388.

Molden, D. C., & Dweck, C. S. (2006). Finding meaning in psychology: A lay theories approach to self-regulation, social perception, and social development. *American Psychologist, 61,* 192–203.

Montgomery, M. J. (2005). Psychosocial intimacy and identity: From early adolescence to emerging adulthood. *Journal of Adolescent Research, 20,* 346–374.

Morrill, R. L. (2007). *Strategic leadership: Integrating strategy and leadership in colleges and universities.* Westport, CT: American Council on Education/Praeger.

Moshman, D. (1999). *Adolescent psychological development: Rationality, morality, and identity.* Mahwah, NJ: Lawrence Erlbaum Associates.

Muis, K. R. (2007). The role of epistemic beliefs in self-regulated learning. *Educational Psychologist, 42,* 173–190.

Muis, K. R., Bendixen, L. D., & Haerle, F. C. (2006). Domain-generality and domain-specificity in personal epistemology research: Philosophical and empirical reflections in the development of a theoretical framework. *Educational Psychology Review, 18,* 3–54.

Murphy, P. K., Alexander, P. A., & Muis, K. R. (2012). Knowledge and knowing: The journey from philosophy and psychology to human learning. In K. R. Harris, S. Graham, & T. Urdan (Editors-in-Chief), *APA educational psychology handbook: Vol.1. Theories, constructs, and critical issues* (pp. 189–226). Washington, DC: American Psychological Association.

Nelson, C. A., Bloom, F. E., Cameron, J. L., Amaral, D., Dahl, R. E., & Pine, D. (2002). An integrative, multidisciplinary approach to the study of brain-behavior relations in the context of typical and atypical development. *Development and Psychopathology, 14,* 499–520.

Newman, J. H. (1976). *The idea of a university* (Edited by I. T. Ker). Oxford: Clarendon Press.

Nicole, D., Aumann, C., Santos, N. S., Bewernick, B. H., Eickhoff, S. B., Newen, A., Shah, N. J., Fink, G. R., & Vogeley, K. (2008). Differential involvement of the posterior temporal cortex in mentalizing but not perspective taking. *Social Cognitive and Affective Neuroscience, 3,* 279–289.

Nixon, J. (2011). *Higher education and the public good: Imagining the university.* London: Continuum International .

Nucci, L. (2001). *Education in the moral domain.* Cambridge, UK: Cambridge University Press.

Nucci, L. (2006). Education for moral development. In M. Killen & J. Smetana (Eds.), *Handbook of moral development* (pp. 657–681). Mahwah, NJ: Lawrence Erlbaum Associates.

Ochsner, K., Zaki, J., Hanelin, J., Ludlow, D. H., Knierim, K., Ramachandran, T., Glover, G. H.,& Mackey, S. C. (2008). Your pain of mine? Common and distinct neural systems supporting the perception of pain in self and other. *Social Cognitive and Affective Neuroscience, 3,* 144–160.

Omdahl, B. L. (1995). *Cognitive appraisal, emotion, and empathy.* Mahwah, NJ: Lawrence Erlbaum Associates.

Pace, D., & Middendorf, J. (Summer, 2004). Decoding the disciplines: Helping students learn disciplinary ways of thinking. In *New Directions for Teaching and Learning.* M. D. Svinicki (Editor-in-Chief), R. E. Rice (Consulting Ed.). Number 98. San Francisco: Jossey-Bass.

Pajares, M. F. (1992). Teachers' beliefs and educational research: Cleaning up a messy construct. *Review of Educational Research, 62,* 307–332.

Palmer, B & Mara, R. M. (2008). Individual domain-specific epistemologies: Implications for educational practice. In M. S. Khine (Ed.), *Knowing, knowledge and beliefs: Epistemological studies across diverse cultures* (pp. 325–350). New York: Springer.

Pals, J. L. (2006). Constructing the "springboard effect": Causal connections, self-making, and growth within the life story. In D. P. McAdams, R. Josselson, & A. Lieblich (Eds.), *Identity and story: Creating self in narrative* (pp. 175–199). Washington, DC: American Psychological Association.

Paluck, E. L., & Green, D. P. (2009). Prejudice reduction: What works? A review and assessment of research and practice. *Annual Review of Psychology, 60,* 339–367.

Parker, B., & Dautoff, D. A. (Spring, 2007). Service-learning and study abroad: Synergistic leaning opportunities. *Michigan Journal of Community Service, 13,* 40–53.

Pascarella, E. T., & Terenzini, P. T. (2005). *How college affects students: A third decade of research (Vol. 2).* San Francisco: Jossey-Bass.

Patel, E. (2006). Building an interfaith student movement. Remarks made at Duke University. November. Durham, NC.

Paul, E. L., Poole, A., & Jakubowyc, N. (January/February, 1998). Intimacy development and romantic status: Implications for adjustment to the college transition. *Journal of College Student Development, 39,* 75–86.

Paulsen, M. B., & Feldman, K. A. (2005). The conditional and interaction effects of epistemological beliefs on the self-regulated learning of college students: Motivational strategies. *Research in Higher Education, 46,* 731–768.

Paulsen, M. B., & Feldman, K. A. (2007). The conditional and interaction effects of epistemological beliefs on the self-regulated learning of college students: Cognitive and behavioral strategies. *Research in Higher Education, 48,* 353–401.

Pedersen, P. J. (2010). Assessing intercultural effectiveness outcomes in a year-long study abroad program. *International Journal of Intercultural Relations, 34,* 70–80.

Pedersen, P., & Pope, M. (2010). Inclusive cultural empathy for successful global leadership. *American Psychologist, 65,* 841–854.

Perkins, D. (1999). The many faces of constructivism. *Educational leadership, 57,* 6–11.

Perry, W. G. (1970). *Forms of intellectual and ethical development in the college years: A scheme.* New York: Holt, Rinehart & Winston.

Perry, W. G. (1981). Cognitive and ethical growth: The making of meaning. In A. Chickering (Ed.), *The modern American college* (pp. 76–116). San Francisco: Jossey-Bass.

Peterson, M. W., & Augustine, C. H. (2000). Organizational practices enhancing the influence of student assessment information in academic decisions. *Research in Higher Education, 41,* 21–52.

Pettigrew, T. F. (2008). Future directions for intergroup contact theory and research. *International Journal of Intercultural Relations, 32,* 187–199.

Pettigrew, T. F., Christ, O., Wagner, U., & Stellmacher, J. (2007). Direct and indirect intergroup contact effects on prejudice: A normative interpretation. *International Journal of Intercultural Relations, 31*(4), 41–425.

Pettigrew, T. F., & Tropp, L. R. (2006). A meta-analytic test of intergroup contact theory. *Journal of Personality and Social Psychology, 90,* 751–783.

Phillips, D. C., & Burbules, N. C. (2000). *Postpositivism and educational research.* Lanham, Maryland: Rowman & Littlefield.

Phinney, J. S. (1993). Multiple group identities: Differentiation, conflict, and integration. In J. Kroger (Ed.), *Discussions on ego identity* (pp. 47–73). Hillsdale, NJ: Lawrence Erlbaum Associates.

Phinney, J. S. (1989). Stages of ethnic identity development in minority group adolescents. *Journal of Early Adolescence, 9,* 34–49.

Phinney, J. S. (2006). Ethnic identity exploration in emerging adulthood. In J. Arnett and J. L. Tanner (Eds.), *Emerging adults in America: Coming to age in the 21st century* (pp. 117–134). Washington, DC: American Psychological Association.

Plowman, D., Baker, L. T., Beck, T., Kulkarni, M., Solansky, S., & Travis, D. (2007). The role of leadership in emergent, self-organization. *The Leadership Quarterly, 18*, 341–356.

Ratcliff, J. L., Johnson, D. K., La Nasa, S. M., & Gaff, J. G. (2001). *The status of general education in the year 2000: Summary of a national survey*. Washington, DC: American Association of Colleges and Universities.

Reed, A., & Aquino, K. F. (2003). Moral identity and the expanding circle of moral regard toward out-groups. *Journal of Personality and Social Psychology, 83*, 1270–1285.

Rescher, N. (2003). *Epistemology: An introduction to the theory of knowledge*. Albany: State University of New York Press.

Reuben, J. A. (1996). *The making of the modern university*. Chicago: University of Chicago Press.

Reuben, J. A. (2010). The changing contours of moral education in American colleges and universities. In E. Kiss & J. P. Euben (Eds.), *Debating moral education: Rethinking the role of the modern university* (pp. 27–54). Durham, NC: Duke University Press.

Rhodes, T. L. (2010). *Assessing outcomes and improving achievement: Tips and tools for using rubrics*. Washington, DC: Association of American Colleges and Universities.

Rhodewalt, F., & Tragakis, M. W. (2002). Self-handicapping and school: Academic self-concept and self-protective behavior. In J. Aronson (Ed.), *Improving academic achievement: Impact of psychological factors on education* (pp. 107–134). New York: Academic Press.

Rifkin, J. (2009). *The empathic civilization: The race to global consciousness in a world in crisis*. New York: Penguin.

Roberts, J. H., & Turner, J. (2000). *The sacred and the secular university*. Princeton, NJ: Princeton University Press.

Roehlkepartain, E. C., Benson, P. L., & Scales, P. C. (2011). Spiritual identity: Contextual perspectives. In S. J. Schwartz, K. Luyckx, & V. L. Vignoles (Eds.), *Handbook of identity theory and research* (pp. 545–562). New York: Springer.

Rogers, C. (1975). Empathic- An unappreciated way of being. *The Counseling Psychologist, 5*, 2–10.

Royce, J. R. (1978). Three ways of knowing and the scientific world view. *Methodology and Science, 11*, 146–164.

Royce, J. R. (1983). Psychological epistemology. *Methodology and Science, 16*, 164–180.

Ruby, P., & Decety, J. (2004). How would you feel versus how do you think she would feel? Neuroimaging study of perspective-taking with social emotions. *Journal of Cognitive Neuroscience, 16*, 988–999.

Ryan, R. M., & Deci, E. L. (2000). Self-determination theory and the facilitation of intrinsic motivation, social development, and well-being. *American Psychologist, 55*, 68–78.

Ryan, R. M., & Deci, E. L. (2003). On assimilating identities to the self: A Self-Determination Theory perspective on internalization and integrity within cultures. In M. R. Leary & J. P. Tangney (Eds.), *Handbook of self and identity* (pp. 253–272). New York: Guilford Press.

Salovey, P., & Mayer, J. D. (1990). Emotional intelligence. *Imagination, Cognition, and Personality, 9*, 185–211.

Saenz, Victor B. (2010). Breaking the segregation cycle: Examining students' precollege racial environments and college diversity experiences. *Review of Higher Education 34*, 1–37.

Saenz, V. B., Hoi N. N., & Hurtado, S. (2007). Factors influencing positive interactions across race for African American, Asian American, Latino, and White college students. *Research in Higher Education, 48*, 1–38.

Schneider, C. G. (2000). Educational missions and civic responsibility: Toward the engaged academy. In T. Ehrlich (Ed.), *Civic responsibility and higher education* (pp. 98–123). Phoenix, AZ: Oryx Press.

Schneider, C. G. (2007). From the President. *Peer Review, 9*, 3.

Schneider, C. G. (2009). *Practicing liberal education: Formative themes in the re-invention of liberal learning.* Washington, DC: Association of American Colleges and Universities.

Schommer, M. (1990). Effects of beliefs about the nature of knowledge on comprehension. *Journal of Educational Psychology, 82*, 498–504.

Schommer, M. (1993). Epistemological development and academic performance among secondary students. *Journal of Educational Psychology, 85*, 406–411.

Schommer, M., Crouse, A., & Rhodes, N. (1992). Epistemological beliefs and comprehension: Believing it is simple does not make it so. *Journal of Educational Psychology, 84*, 435–443.

Schommer, M., & Walker, K. (1997). Epistemological beliefs and valuing school: Considerations for college admissions and retention. *Research in Higher Education, 38*, 173–186.

Schommer-Aikins, M. (2004). Explaining the epistemological belief system: Introducing the embedded systemic model and coordinated research approach. *Educational Psychologist, 39*, 19–29.

Schwandt, T. A. (2000). Three epistemological stances for qualitative inquiry: Interpretivism, hermeneutics, and social constructionism. In Denzin & Lincoln (Eds.), *Handbook of qualitative research* (2nd Edition, pp. 189–214). Thousand Oaks, CA: Sage Publications.

Schwartz, S. J. (2001). The evolution of Eriksonian and neo-Eriksonian identity theory and research: A review and integration. *Identity: An International Journal of Theory and Research, 1*, 7–58.

Schwartz, S. J. (2002). In search of mechanisms of change in identity development: Integrating the constructivist and discovery perspectives on identity. *Identity: An International journal of Theory and Research, 2*, 317–339.

Selman, R. L. (1980). *The growth of interpersonal understanding: Developmental and clinical analyses.* New York: Academic Press.

Selman, R. L. (2003). *The promotion of social awareness: Powerful lessons from the partnership of developmental theory and classroom practice.* New York: Russell Sage Foundation.

Seymour, E., Hunter, A.-B., Laursen, S. L., & Deantoni, T. (2004). Establishing the benefits of research experiences for undergraduates in the sciences: First findings from a three-year study. *Science Education, 88*, 493–534.

Shapiro, H. T. (1997). Cognition, character, and culture in undergraduate education: Rhetoric and reality. In R. G. Ehrenberg (Ed.), *The American University: National treasure or endangered species?* (pp. 58–99). Ithaca, NY: Cornell University Press.

Shopkow, L. with Diaz, A., Middendorf, J., and Pace, D. (2013). From bottlenecks to epistemology in history: Changing the conversation about the teaching of history in colleges and universities. In R. J. Thompson, Jr. (Ed.), *Changing the conversation about higher education* (pp. 15–37). Lanham, MD: Rowman and Littlefield.

Shupe, D. (2007). Significantly better: The benefits for an academic institution focused on student learning outcomes. *On The Horizon, 15*, 48–57.

Sidanius, J., Van Laar, C., Levin, S., & Sinclair, S. (2004). Ethnic enclaves and the dynamics of social identity on the college campus: The good, the bad, and the ugly. *Journal of Personality and Social Psychology, 87*, 96–110.

Siegel, D. J. (2009). Foreword (p. xiii–xvi), In M. Gordon, *Roots of empathy: Changing the world child by child.* New York: The Experiment.

Simon, B. (2004). *Identity in modern society: A social psychological perspective.* Oxford: Blackwell.

Simon, B., & Klandermans, B. (2001). Politicized collective identity: A social psychological analysis. *American Psychologist, 56*, 319–331.

Singer, T. (2006). The neuronal basis and ontogeny of empathy and mind reading: Review of literature and implications for future research. *Neuroscience and Biobehavioral Reviews, 30*, 855–863.

Singer, J. A., & Bluck, S. (2001). New perspectives on autobiographical memory: The integration of narrative processing and autobiographical reasoning. *Review of General Psychology, 5*, 91–99.

Smith, K. A., Sheppard, S. D., Johnson, D. W., & Johnson, R. T. (2005). Pedagogies of engagement: Classroom-based practices. *Journal of Engineering Education, 94*, 87–101.

Sommerville, C. J. (2006). *The decline of the secular university.* New York: Oxford University Press.

Southerland, S. A., & Sinatra, G. M. (2003). Learning about biological evolution: A special case of intentional conceptual change. In G. M. Sinatra & P. R. Pintrich (Eds.), *Intentional conceptual change* (pp. 315–342). Mahwah, NJ: Lawrence Erlbaum Associates.

Southerland, S. A., Sinatra, G. M., & Matthews, M. R. (2001). Belief, knowledge, and science education. *Educational Psychology Review, 13*, 325–351.

Spong, J. S. (2009). *Eternal life: A new vision: Beyond religion, beyond theism, beyond heaven and hell.* New York: Harper Collins.

Staudinger, U. M. (2001). Life reflection: A social-cognitive analysis of life review. *Review of General Psychology, 5*, 148–160.

Steinberg, L. (2008). A social neuroscience perspective on adolescent risk-taking. *Developmental Review, 28*, 78–106.

Steinberg, L., Dahl, R., Keating, D., Kupfer, D., Masten, A., & Pine, D. (2006). Psychopathology in adolescence: Integrating affective neuroscience with the study of context. In D. Cicchetti & D. Cohen (Eds.), *Developmental psychopathology: Vol. 2: Developmental neuroscience* (pp. 710–741). New York: Wiley.

Stepien, K. A., & Baernstein, A. (2006). Educating for empathy: A review. *Journal of General Internal Medicine, 21*, 524–530.

Stephen, W. G., & Finlay, K. (1999). The role of empathy in improving intergroup relations. *Journal of Social Issues, 55*, 729–743.

Sullivan, W. M. (2000). Institutional identity and social responsibility in higher education. In T. Ehrlich (Ed.), *Civic responsibility and higher education* (pp. 19–36). Phoenix, AZ: Oryx Press.

Sullivan, W. M., & Rosin, M. S. (2008). *A new agenda for higher education: Shaping a life of the mind for practice*. San Francisco: Jossey-Bass.

The Overstatement of Black Student Self-Segregation on College Campuses (Winter, 1997–1998), *Journal of Blacks in Higher Education, 18*, 48–49.

Traux, C. B., & Carkhuff, R. R. (1967). *Toward effective counseling and psychotherapy*. Chicago: Aldine.

Turiel, E (2006). The development of morality. In W. Diamon & R. M. Lerner (Series Eds.) & N. Eisenberg (Vol. Ed.), *Handbook of child psychology. Vol. 3. Social, emotional, and personality development* (6th ed. pp. 789–857). New York: Wiley.

Turner, J. (1992). Secularization and sacralization: Speculations on some religious origins of the secular humanities curriculum, 1850–1900. In G. W. Marsden & B. J. Longfield (Eds.), *The Secularization of the academy* (pp. 74–106). New York: Oxford University Press.

Turner, J. C., & Reynolds, K. J. (2001). The social identity perspective in intergroup relations: Theories, themes, and controversies. In R. Brown & S. L. Gaertner (Eds.), *Blackwell handbook of social psychology: Intergroup processes* (pp. 133–153). Malden, MA: Blackwell.

Turner, R. N., Hewstone, M., & Voci, A. (2007). Reducing explicit and implicit prejudice via direct and extended contact: The mediating role of self-disclosure and intergroup anxiety. *Journal of Personality and Social Psychology, 93*, 369–388.

Tyler, T. R., & Smith, H. J. (1999). Justice, social identity and group process. In T. R. Tyler & R. M. Kramer (Eds.), *The psychology of the social self* (pp. 223–264). Mahwah, NJ: Lawrence Erlbaum Associates.

Uhl-Bien, M., Marion, R., & McKelve, B. (2007). Complexity leadership theory: shifting leadership from the industrial age to the knowledge era. *The Leadership Quarterly, 18*, 298–318.

Underwood, B., & Moore, B. (1982). Perspective-taking and altruism. *Psychological Bulletin, 91*, 143–173.

U.S. Department of Education (2006). *A Test of Leadership: Charting the Future of U.S. Higher Education*. Washington, DC, xxx.

Vallacher, R. R., Coleman, P. T., Nowak, A., & Bui-Wrzosinska, L. (2010). Rethinking intractable conflict: The perspective of dynamical systems. *American Psychologist, 65*, 262–278.

Vande Berg, M. (2007). Intervening in the learning of U.S. students abroad. *Journal of Studies in International Education, 11*, 392–399.

Vande Berg, M., Balkcum, A., Scheid, M., & Whalen, B. J. (Fall, 2004). The Georgetown University consortium project: A report from the halfway mark. *Frontiers: The Interdisciplinary Journal of Study Abroad, X*, 101–116.

Vasques, M. J. T. (2012). Psychology and social justice: Why we do what we do. *American Psychologist, 67*, 337–346.

Vignoles, V. L., Regalia, C., Manzi. C., Golledge, J., & Scabini, E. (2006). Beyond self-esteem: Influence of multiple motives on identity construction. *Journal of Personality and Social Psychology, 90*, 308–333.

Vignoles, V. L., Schwartz, S. J., & Luycky, K. (2011). Introduction: Toward an integrative model of identity. In S. J. Schwartz, K. Luyckx, & V. L. Vignoles (Eds.), *Handbook of identity theory and research* (pp. 1–27). New York: Springer.

Walker, L. (2004). Gus in the gap: Bridging the judgment-action gap in moral functioning. In D. K. Lapsley & D. Narvaez (Eds.), *Moral development, self, and identity* (pp. 1–20). Mahwah, NJ: Lawrence Erlbaum Associates.

Waterman, A. S. (1984). *The psychology of individualism*. New York: Praeger.

Waterman, A. S. (1990). Personal expressiveness: Philosophical and psychological foundations. *Journal of Mind and Behavior, 11*, 47–74.

Waterman, A. S. (1993). Finding something to do or someone to be: A eudaimonist perspective on identity formation. In J. Kroger (Ed.), *Discussion on ego identity* (pp. 147–167). Hillsdale, NJ: Lawrence Erlbaum Associates.

Waterman, A. S. (1997). An overview of service-learning and the role of research and evaluation in service-learning programs. In A. S. Waterman (Ed.), *Service-learning applications from the research* (pp. 1–11). Mahwah, NJ: Lawrence Erlbaum Associates.

Waterman, A. S. (2004). Finding someone to be: Studies of the role of intrinsic motivation in identity formation. *Identity: An International Journal of Theory and Research, 4*, 209–228.

Weiss, C. H. (1998). Have we learned anything new about the use of evaluation? *American Journal of Evaluation, 19*, 21–33.

White, J. B. (2004). "Meaning what you say" in A. Sarat (Ed.), *Law in the liberal arts*, (pp. 109–139). Ithaca, NY: Cornell University Press.

Wilson, J. (2000). Introduction. In J. Roberts & J. Turner, *The sacred and the secular university* (pp. 3–16). Princeton, NJ: Princeton University Press.

Wimmer, H., & Perner, J. (1983). Beliefs about beliefs: Representation and constraining function of wrong beliefs in young children's understanding of deception. *Cognition, 13*, 103–183.

Wolfe, A. (March/April, 2006). The evangelical mind revisited. *Change, 38*, 9–13.

Wolff, S. B., Pescosolido, A. T., & Druskat, V. U. (2002). Emotional intelligence as the basis of leadership emergence in self-managing teams. *The Leadership Quarterly, 13*, 505–522.

Yorks, L., & Kasal, E. (2002). Toward a theory and practice for whole-person learning: Reconceptualizing experience and the role of affect. *Adult Education Quarterly*, Vol. 52 (3), 176–192.

Youniss, J., & Yates, M. (1997). *Community service and social responsibility in youth*. Chicago: University of Chicago Press.

Zlotkowski, E. (1997–2005). (Series Ed.). *Service-Learning in the academic disciplines*, Washington, DC: American Association for Higher Education.

INDEX

aborization, brain development and, 27–28

academic advising, in undergraduate education, 165–167

Academically Adrift: Limited Learning on College Campuses, 15–17

academic community: civic engagement pedagogies and, 125–126; as developmental context, 32

academic disciplines: epistemology of, 50–52; personal epistemology and, 52; social context for, 60–61

academic integrity, 32

acceptance, evaluative thinking and, 56–57

accommodation, identity formation and, 100–101

accountability: in academic community, 32; assessment and, 167–168; for student learning, 3

achievement status, identity formation and, 92

action, moral identity and moral action, 114–116

adaptation, continuity and change in identity and, 108

adolescence: developmental and neurocognitive changes during, xi–xii; identity formation and, 93–94, 99–101

aesthetics, knowledge and, 40

affective response: collective identity and, 95–96; emotional regulation and, 71–72; empathy and, 68–70; neurocognitive development and, 25–26

African American students, self-segregation among, 134–136

agency, identity formation and, 100–101

American arts and sciences university, emergence of, 7–8

American Association of Higher Education (AAHE), 164

American Protestantism: influence in higher education of, 7; secularization and, 9–10

Anderson, C. W., 147

anxiety: contact hypothesis and reduction of, 138–139; religious identity as coping device for, 116–118

argumentation, intellectual engagement and, 56–57

artes liberalis ideology, 12

Arum, Richard, 15

assessment: developmental assessment, 170–171; electronic portfolios, 171–172; plan, 169; in undergraduate education, 167–172

assimilation: hierarchical enhancement and, 142–143; identity formation and, 100–101

Association of American Colleges and Universities (AAC&U), 14, 16–17, 169–170; curriculum reform initiatives, 149

attributions, empathy and, 72–78

autobiographical memory, inferences and attributions and, 74–75

autobiographical reasoning, self-authorship and, 104–105

autonomy: in emerging adulthood, 29; identity formation, 98

baby boom, U.S. mass education movement and, 8–9

balkanization, campus diversity and, 131–132

Baxter Magolda, Marcia, 104

behavioral patterns: moral identity and, 113–116; neurocognitive development and, 24–26

behaviorism, theories of, 39

belief-bias, empathy and, 72–75

beliefs: core beliefs, identity formation and, 106–107; epistemic beliefs, 52–55; evaluative thinking and, 55–57; knowledge and, 41–42; normative beliefs, 142–143; personal epistemology and, 43–45; service learning and challenges to, 122–123

benchmarks, academic assessment, 169–170

Betancourt, H., 77

Beyer, C. H., 127, 154

biases: inferences and attributions and, 72–75; intergroup bias, reduction of, 136–137; service learning and risk of, 122–123

bicultural identities, globalization and, 102

"big bang" period of American higher education, 7–8

Blasi, Augusto, 114–116

Bok, Derek, 1–2, 14, 20–21, 36, xi

Bologna process for degree qualification, 151–152

Bowman, N. A., 123

Boyer Commission, 15

brain function: cognitive functioning and experience and, 26–28; emotional regulation and, 71–72; empathy and, 65–66; neurocognitive development and, 24–26

brain imaging: empathy and, 65–66; shared representation and, 68–70

Brandenberger, J. W., 123

Butin, D. W., 123

Campus Compact, 164

Campus Compact, 11–12

campus culture: balkanization and self-segregation in, 131–132; collective identity and, 140–143; contact hypothesis and, 137–139; cross-racial interactions and, 130–131;

educational interventions and, 143–145; engagement with difference in, 127–146; experimentation and evidence in, 168–169; impact of diversity on, 127–129, xii; intergroup bias, reduction of, 136–137; intergroup dialogue and, 145–146; normative beliefs and, 142–143; procedural fairness and, 143; promotion of intergroup relations on, 136–137; racial/ethnic/cultural impacts on, 132–134; residential life and, 134–136; university identity and, 142

career identity, 118–119

Carnegie Foundation for the Advancement of Teaching, 2–3, 164

Carroll, J., 18

causal attribution model, empathy and, 76–78

causation, personal epistemology and, 48

Center for Race Relations (Duke University), 145–146

Chang, M., 128–129

change mechanisms: identity formation and, 108; personal epistemology and, 47–48

charitable donations, moral identity and, 115–116

Christianity, secularization *vs.,* 9–10

"circle of moral regard," 114–116

citizenship, higher education as preparation for, 11–12

civic education, moral education *vs.,* 11–12

civic engagement: liberal education and commitment to, 34–35; in undergraduate education, 16–17

civilization, prominence in curriculum of, 10

Civil War, higher education development after, 7–10

cognitive apprenticeship model, academy as social context and, 59–60

cognitive function. *See also* neurocognitive development: in adolescence, xi–xiii; brain development and experience and, 26–28; collective identity

degree qualifications: profile changes for, 151–153; undergraduate framework for, 151–152

Delbanco, Andrew, 18, 22

democratic theory: mass education linked to, 8–9; in undergraduate education, 16–17

developmental model of education, 32–33

developmental science: academic advising and, 165–167; academic community in context of, 32; adolescent development and, xi–xiii; education model in, 32–33; emerging adulthood research and, 23–36; formative liberal education guidelines and, 147–172; higher education transformation and role of, x–xii; identity formation and, 93–94, 96–98; personal epistemology and, 45–47; psychosocial tasks, 28–29; sexual identity and, 109–111; social identity and, 111–113

developmental tasks, 28–32; psychosocial tasks, 28–29; higher order mental capacities, 29–32

Dewey, John, 121, 158

dialogical engagement, empathy and, 82–83

difference: campus culture and engagement of, 127–146; empathy and recognition of, 65–66, 77–78, 87–88; epistemology of academic disciplines and, 50–52; higher education and engagement in, 4–5

differential effects, educational interventions, 144–145

differentiated/subjective developmental stage, empathy and, 82–83

differentiation: brain development and, 26–28; identity formation and, 90–96

disciplinary curriculum, learning objectives including, 153–154

discrimination, 136

distrust, identity formation and, 106–107

diversity: campus culture and impact of, 127–129; marginalization of morality and, 11–12; in residential life on campus, 134–136; service

learning and exposure to, 122–123; in undergraduate student bodies, 15

diversity within unity model, in campus residential life, 135–136

dopaminergic system, neurocognitive development and, 26

Duderstadt, James, 21

Duke University, 145–146; interdisciplinary certificate program at, 154–155

economic growth, U.S. mass education movement and, 8–9

education: developmental model of, 32–33; empathy enhancement and, 84–88; value of diversity in, 128–129

educational interventions, campus culture and, 143–145

effect, epistemic beliefs and mechanisms of, 54–55

egocentric bias: empathy and, 70–71; inferences and attributions and, 73–75

egoistic hypothesis, 76

Einfühlung (Lipps), empathy as, 66–67

electronic portfolios, assessment using, 171–172

Eliot, Charles, 7, 9

embedded systems model, epistemic beliefs and, 53–55

The Embedded Systemic Model (Schommer-Aikns), 43–44, 53–55

emerging adulthood: characteristics of, 5; cognitive functioning and experience, 26–28; defined, 23–24; higher-order mental capacities, 29–32; integrated identity in, 119–120; moral identity and, 115–116; neurocognitive development, 24–26; psychosocial tasks, 28–29; scientific perspectives on, 23–36; sexual identity and, 109–111; work and career identity in, 118–119

emotional development: cognitive function and, 80–83; moral identity and, 113–116

emotional intelligence, empathy and, 78–79

emotional reactivity, empathy and, 80

emotional regulation, empathy and, 71–72

emotion contagion, shared representation and, 68–70

empathetic accuracy, development of, 84–85

empathetic communication, development of, 85

The Empathetic Civilization (Rifkin), 80

empathy: affective response and shared representation, 68–70; bias, 86; characteristics of, 66–67; contact hypothesis and reduction of, 138–139; development and enhancement of, 79–88; emotional reactivity and, 80; emotional regulation and, 71–72; enhancement and fostering of, 84–88; higher education and development of, 5, 63–88, xii; inferential bias and attributions and, 72–75; intergroup bias and, 136–137; leadership and, 78–79; mental states and, 63–66; moral identity and, 113–116; neurocortical mechanisms in, 65–66; prosocial behavior and, 75–78; self-awareness and other-awareness and, 70–71; socialization process and, 83–84

empathy-altruism hypothesis, 76

empathy model, cognitive process and, 76–78

empiricism: epistemology and, 38–42; knowledge and, 40

engagement, pedagogies of, 4–6. *See also* civic engagement; academy as social context and, 57–61; collective identity and, 95–96; community service and, 120–121, 162–165; diversity and, 127–129; empathy enhancement and, 86–88; inquiry and argumentation and, 56–57; intergroup dialogues and, 145–146; liberal education and, 34–35; service learning and, 121–125, 162–165; sexual identity and, 109–111; study abroad and, 159–162; in undergraduate education, 15–17; undergraduate education and, 157–165; undergraduate research and, 158–159

Engberg, M. E., 143

Enlightenment ideology, postmodern critiques of, 17–19

enrollment in higher education institutions, statistics on, 2–3

"envy-up" bias, 74–75

epistemic doubt, 47–48; identity and , 99–101

The Epistemological Reflection Model (Magolda), 43

epistemic development, 45

epistemology: of academic disciplines, 50–52; academy as social context and, 57–61; beliefs and, 52–55; epistemology of academic disciplines and, 51; evaluative thinking and, 55–57; higher education and development of, xii; identity formation and, 99–101, 104; knowledge *vs.* beliefs in, 41–42; liberal *vs.* general education and, 14; personal epistemology, 37–62; philosophical principles of, 38–42; religious beliefs and, 18–19; types and sources of knowledge in, 39

equality and social responsibility (ESR) survey, service learning and, 122–123

equilibration, change mechanisms and, 47–48

Erikson, E. H., 90–91

ethical principles, in undergraduate education, 16–17

ethnic identity, 111–113; balkanization and self-segregation and, 131–132; impact on campus culture of, 132–134; university identity and, 142

eudemonia, identity formation and, 100–101

European Credit Transfer and Accumulation System (ECTS), 151–152

European Higher Education Area (EHEA), 151–152

evaluative thinking: academic assessment, 169–170; intellectual engagement and, 57; personal epistemology and, 55–57; fostering, 55

evaluativist model, epistemological judgment, 49–50

evidence-based learning, culture of, 168–169

metacognition: empathy and, 67; personal epistemological models and, 44–45
metaphorism, knowledge and, 40
Michigan Mandate, 128
Michigan Student Survey, 128
migration, brain development and, 26–28
moral education: empathy development and, 81–83; marginalization of, 10–12; postsecular universities and, 18–19; religious identity and, 116–118
moral identity, characteristics of, 113–116
moral reasoning, empathy and, 76–78
Morrill Act of 1862, 7–8
motivation, identity formation and, 99–101
Muis, K. R., 54
multiculturalism: campus culture and, 132–134; campus diversity and, 128–129; in campus residential life, 135–136; hierarchical attenuation and, 142–143; religious identity and, 117–118; social identity and, 112–113
Murphy, P. K., 39
mutuality, in service learning, 124–125
myelination, brain development and, 27–28

narrative processing, identity formation and, 104–105
National Aeronautics and Space Administration, 9
National Defense Education Act of 1958, 8–9
national identity: formation of, 105, 112–113; globalization and, 102
National Institutes of Health, 9
National Science Foundation, 9
national security, mass education and concerns about, 9
National Survey of Student Engagement (NSSE), 156–157
naturalism, secularization in higher education and, 10
neural networks, emotional regulation and, 72
neural plasticity, 27; experience-dependent, 27; experience-expectant, 27

neurocognitive development: in adolescence, xi–xiii; affective response and shared representation in, 68–70; emerging adulthood and, 24–26; emotional regulation and, 71–72; empathy and, 65–66; inferences and attributions and, 72–75; mass education movement and belief in, 9; psychosocial tasks, 28–29; self-awareness and other-awareness and, 70–71
Newman, John Cardinal, 12
nontraditional institutions, study abroad and, 160
normative beliefs, collective identity and, 142–143

objective self, identity formation and, 89–96
objectivity: knowledge vs. beliefs and, 41–42; marginalization of morality and, 11–12
operational thinking: cognitive and emotional development and, 46, 81–83; identity formation and, 99–101
oratorical tradition, liberal education and, 13–14
other-awareness, empathy and, 70–71
Our Underachieving Colleges (Bok), 1–2, xi
out-group identification: contact hypothesis and, 137–139; moral identity and, 114–116

pain perception, shared representation and, 69–70
Paluck, E. L., 144
paradigms, epistemology of academic disciplines and, 50–51
Patel, Eboo, 117, 146
pedagogical innovation. See also engagement, pedagogies of: community and service learning and, 162–165; culture of experimentation and evidence and, 168–169; "decoding the disciplines" model, 60–61; scholarship on, 19–20; social context in academy and, 57–61; study abroad and, 159–162; threshold concepts and, 61; undergraduate education and, 157–165; undergraduate research, 158–159

theory of mind (TOM), empathy and, 63–66
theory-theory approaches, empathy and, 64–65
thinking, personal epistemology and methods of, 37–62
third person/mutual stage, empathy and, 82–83
threshold concepts, personal epistemology and, 61
threshold problem in higher education, 1–2
tolerance: evaluative thinking and, 56–57; personal epistemology beyond, 62; religious identity and, 117–118
transformation of higher education, 6–14; from colleges to universities, 7–8
transformative experience, service learning as, 122–123
Tropp, L. R., 138–139
truth criteria, epistemology of academic disciplines and, 50–52
Tuning process for degree qualification, 151–152

undergraduate education: academic advising and, 165–167; academic disciplines and, 52; academy as social context and, 57–61; accountability and quality demands facing, 3–4; agenda for, 148–149; assessment in, 167–172; community and service learning and, 162–165; culture of experimentation and evidence in, 168–169; developmental model for, 6; empathy enhancement in, 88; guidelines for formative liberal education, 147–172; high-impact educational practices and, 156–157; liberal-general education transition in, 13–14; liberal principles in, 7–8, 34–35; personal epistemology in, 37–62; quality and purpose in, 15–17; reform of, 15; study abroad programs, 159–162; transformation of, ix–xiii; twenty-first century reform of, 15–22
Undergraduate Journal of Service Learning & Community-Based Research, 125
undergraduate research, guidelines for, 158–159

undifferentiated/egocentric developmental stage, empathy and, 82–83
United States: "big bang" period of higher education in, 7–8; twenty-first century higher education in, 1–22
universities: colleges' transformation to, 7–8; postsecular university, evolution of, 17–19
university identity, 142

Valid Assessment of Learning in Undergraduate Education (VALUE), 169–170
value-free scholarship: marginalization of morality and, 11–12; secular university and ideology of, 17–19
values, moral identity and, 114–116
volition, personal epistemology model, 48
volunteer service, service learning *vs.,* 163–165
vulnerability, identity formation and, 106–107

Waterman, A. S., 101
Weinstock, M., 46–47, 49–50
Weiss, C. H., 170
Western civilization: identity formation in, 101–102; inferences and attributions based on, 73–75; prominence in curriculum of, 10
White, James, 34
white matter (brain), neurocognitive development and, 24–26
Wingspread principles of service learning, 121
Wolfe, A., 117
work identity, 118–119
World War II, higher education development after, 9
writing assignments, service learning and, 125

Yates, M., 120–121
Youniss, J., 120–121

zero-sum conflict, core beliefs and identity formation and, 107
Zlotkowski, Edward, 164